SOCIAL CHANGE
AND THE LABOURING POOR

SOCIAL CHANGE
AND THE LABOURING POOR

Antwerp, 1770–1860

CATHARINA LIS

YALE UNIVERSITY PRESS

NEW HAVEN AND LONDON

Translated from the Dutch by James Coonan.

Set in Bembo by Boldface Typesetters, and
printed in Great Britain by the Bath Press, Avon.

Library of Congress Cataloging in Publication Data

Lis, Catharina.
    Social change and the labouring poor.

    Bibliography: p.
    Includes index.
    1. Antwerp (Belgium) – Social conditions.
2. Antwerp (Belgium) – Economic conditions. 3. Labor
and laboring classes – Belgium – Antwerp – History – 18th
century. 4. Labor and laboring classes – Belgium –
Antwerp – History – 19th century. I. Title.
HN510.A67L57 1986   306'.09493'2   85–52070
ISBN 0–300–03610–8

For Hugo Soly

Contents

Contents

Acknowledgements

This book was long in the making, and it would be impossible to enumerate the many people who contributed to its completion. I would, however, particularly like to express my debt to Jan Craeybeckx of the Free University of Brussels, under whose supervision I prepared the doctoral thesis on which this work is partly based. It was Craeybeckx who first introduced me to the problem of social change while I was still an undergraduate at Brussels. Later he encouraged me to study the forgotten people who paid the social costs of the Industrial Revolution; he facilitated my exploration and allowed me to develop my own interpretations. I would also like to record my gratitude to the late Jan Dhondt of the State University of Ghent, who offered financial support for my first year of research on this project, and to Etienne Scholliers with whom I had many stimulating discussions while his assistant at Brussels and later. I am greatly indebted also to Jos De Belder and Jules Hannes who generously gave me permission to use their unpublished dissertations on the social structure of Antwerp in the period under study here; without this vital information it would have been very difficult to develop some of my arguments.

I have been extremely fortunate, in addition, to receive help and guidance from the personnel of numerous archives and libraries in Antwerp, Brussels, The Hague, and Paris. I am particularly grateful to Jan Van Roey, director of the Antwerp Stadsarchief, who welcomed an awkward and ignorant student with kindness and good counsel, as did his assistants, especially Gilberte Degueldre and François Verbist; to Eva Païs-Minne and her assistant Arthur Van Herck who introduced me to the uncatalogued archives of the Openbaar Centrum voor Maatschappelijk Welzijn at Antwerp and allowed me to consult them in the stacks; and to Renold Huwel of the Antwerp Stadsbibliotheek who was helpful far beyond usual library practice.

The painful phase of the project came after the dissertation had been completed and submitted to Brussels University in 1975. No Belgian publishing firm was prepared to bring out a scholarly work of 1,000 pages. Fortunately, two years later, the Camille Huysmans Foundation awarded me its Triennial Socio-Economic Prize. I express my warmest thanks to the members of the committee for encouraging me to draft a shortened version of the thesis and for providing the means to cover the cost of translating the manuscript into English. In this connection I would like to thank Jim Coonan who took on the difficult task of setting my obscure Dutch phrases into English prose and Beth Damon Coonan who typed version after version of a continually revised manuscript with remarkable speed and accuracy. Their perfectionism has been of the greatest help to me.

I am especially grateful to Charles Tilly, who took time to read the entire manuscript thoroughly, offered valuable criticisms and suggested changes in organization and content. His frankness and shrewd judgement, freely given, compelled me to see weaknesses that I would otherwise not have seen, and saved me from many misstatements and obscurities. Any errors which remain are of course my own.

The preparation of the final book draft took much longer than I had originally planned, because new professional obligations made greater demands on my time. Without the constant enthusiasm and willing aid of my dearest friend and sharpest critic, Hugo Soly, this work could not have come to completion. For the last ten years we have collaborated so closely and interchanged so many views that I cannot any longer tell which historical arguments are his and which are mine. Hence this book is dedicated to him.

List of Figures and Maps

Note on Spelling, Currency and Metrology

Where there is a recognized English version of a foreign place-name (Antwerp, Brussels, Ghent, and so on) I have adopted it. Otherwise I have preferred the style used in the place itself (Kempen, not Campine; Mechelen, not Malines).

The official money of account used in the Austrian Netherlands was the guilder (often called the Brabant or current guilder) of twenty stivers. Shortly after the annexation by France, the franc was introduced. Between 1816 and 1832, the Dutch guilder of 100 cents was used. Finally, in 1832, the Belgian franc was created as the official money of account.

<pre>
1 Brabant (current) guilder = 20 stivers
                             = 0·85765 Dutch guilder
                             – 1·81406 French or Belgian francs

1 Dutch guilder   = 100 cents
                  = 1·1660 Brabant guilders
                  = 2·1164 French or Belgian francs

1 French or Belgian franc = 100 centimes
                           = 0·55125 Brabant guilder
                           = 0·47250 Dutch guilder
</pre>

All weights and measures have been converted into metric units.

	British standard
1 metre	1·09 yards
1 hectare (10,000 square metres)	2·47 acres
1 kilometre	0·62 miles
1 square kilometre	0·39 square miles
1 litre	1·75 pints
1 hectolitre	21·9 gallons
1 kilogram	2·2 lb
1 metric quintal (100 kilograms)	220 lb
1 metric ton (1,000 kilograms)	0·98 tons

Preface: The Dialogue between Yesterday and Today

In the 1950s and early 1960s, poverty in the western world was rarely seen as a major social problem. No batteries of statistics measured the phenomenon; no academics studied it; politicians and journalists failed to discuss it. Everyone accepted that destitution had been largely eliminated and that the 'pockets of poverty' which remained were nothing but remnants of underdevelopment, temporary and localized backwardness, or the results of various kinds of individual disability. The prevailing model of socio-economic development was based on the premise that all countries and regions would gradually be dragged along in a general and continuing process of economic growth. After all, did not W.W. Rostow postulate that 'the tricks of growth are not all that difficult'?

This euphoric belief propelled many historians upon a quest for the mechanism of the 'take-off', for the magic formula of the Industrial Revolution. Those who flatly declared that the task of the economic historian was to analyze successive stages of that process rather than to 'quibble about the defects in the social system that supported it'[1] earned a reputation for their seriousness and discernment. The debate on living standards in the period 1750–1850 was reduced to the calculation of real wages, the study of patterns of consumption, and the measurement of changes in the extent and distribution of national income. In the end, the only point at issue was the year after which the purchasing power of the working class as a whole began to improve.[2] The debate, moreover, lost much of its relevance because most participants seemed to agree that the transition should be evaluated in the light of the end result: the Industrial Revolution paved the way for the welfare state.

Scarcely any attention was directed to the poor themselves. They were either identified with a lumpenproletariat of marginal individuals or classed with the artisans who in their short-sightedness had struggled against the machine. Their mere existence provoked irritation, since they biased median wage levels downwards and disguised gains made by the growing sectors of the economy.[3] Besides, why worry about groups which would in the long run participate in the prosperity of industrialization and modernization? This same line of thought kept most researchers from studying regions or towns in which the factory system arose late, if at all: economic backwardness and poverty went hand in hand, 'naturally'.[4]

In short, the Industrial Revolution was deemed a fundamental divide: there lay, on one side, a 'world of scarcity', and on the other, an 'affluent society'. According to one eminent historian, 'with industrialization, the age-old problem of poverty was solved, so that in the developed industrial societies it poses merely an exceptional problem, impinging on small groups or individuals'.[5] From such a point of view, modern day poverty could only be labelled a marginal phenomenon: 'There will always be at the fringe of society, individuals who cannot come to terms with its demands, and who will need institutional or semi-institutional care'.[6] Hence, the genesis of the welfare state and the formation of diverse systems of social security were very much under scrutiny. To all of which the historian contributed materials for a theory of development – a theory which in the eyes of some dissidents, however, verged on propaganda.[7]

Great indeed was the initial disbelief, followed in turn by petulant hostility, when in the 1960s Michael Harrington and others revealed that one in four Americans lacked the socio-vital minimum and that the living conditions of this group had barely improved since the Second World War.[8] Further studies showed that the situation was no better in western Europe. In whatever way the (often incomplete) data were collected and interpreted, the conclusion was everywhere the same: a fifth to a fourth of the population lived beneath the officially-established poverty line.[9] Even so it was thought that the war on poverty would be short and painless. Basic needs were defined; the needy were counted and organized into sub-groups, their characteristics analyzed and described in detailed reports. Subsequently large-scale programmes were established, all of them intended to meet specific needs: pension schemes, child-benefit or family-allowance schemes, programmes to build decent dwellings for low-income groups or to provide rent subsidies, medical care, job-training, and so on. An army of social workers and technocrats was mustered to patch up gaps in the welfare state. Poverty became the grist of the specialist. The underlying assumption, however, was that the needy themselves were part of the problem: they had their distinct 'culture of poverty', *i.e.* specific norms and values which hindered their integration into society at large and which continued from generation to generation. Poverty, so it went, had generally to be considered as a form of deviant behaviour, the sole remedy for which was a change in attitudes.[10] From the technocrats' point of view, one of the benefits of such an attitude was that the fundamental credos of the 'Great Society' did not have to be called into question.

In the course of the 1970s, a realization grew that the social problem cannot be solved in this way, that poverty cannot be analytically reduced to the subculture of ghetto residents or the misery of those who fell through the safety net of social security, the so-called 'Fourth World'. Abundant evidence demonstrates that great numbers still live at or beneath the official poverty line, that social insecurity is growing rather than diminishing.[11] Hence gradually more attention has been paid to phenomena endemic to broad strata of the working population, particularly low wages and underemployment.

Two processes accelerated this tendency towards a radical reassessment of the social problem. In the first place, it appeared from the continued worsening of living conditions in the Third World — where more and more suffered from malnutrition or starvation — that the western model of development was failing. In the second place, it became steadily clearer that the future of the capitalist world itself was far from certain. Increasing signs point towards a fundamental redivision of economic activity — not only between the North and South, but also within the developed countries themselves. This reshaping of the international division of labour threatens more serious consequences for low income groups, because many governing regimes seek their salvation in anti-social policies: they drive women out of the labour market, cut off social services, prune assistance programmes, and blame it all on the unemployed.[12]

The growing problems confronting present-day society indicate that earlier assertions regarding the causes of poverty and impoverishment must be scrapped. The historian's contribution to this reassessment is indispensable. Past experience provides an unparallelled touchstone for putting actual processes in their proper perspective. In an earlier book, I attempted in collaboration with Hugo Soly to show that destitution in pre-industrial Europe was not a 'natural' phenomenon, inherent to a 'society of scarcity' but rather that it can be fully understood only as the outcome of specific structures of surplus-extraction relations.[13] In this study, I shall investigate the period 1750–1850 in greater detail. At its heart is the question of whether poverty is to be explained from the perspective of the underdevelopment of the areas concerned — thus on the basis of a model of linear growth — or whether the century after 1750 must essentially be considered as a phase of acceleration in the development of capitalism, entailing on the one hand the restructuring and reallocation of economic activities and on the other social dislocation on a massive scale?

My first aim was to re-examine some traditional interpretations. Is it true that core cities were better off socially than others? Was poverty more acute in non-industrializing centres than in the new manufacturing towns? Did the growth of new businesses really compensate for the decline of the old? This consideration explains the choice of period and place: between 1770 and 1860 Antwerp turned from a textile centre into an international port, overtaking first Amsterdam and then almost Rotterdam too. We are thus confronted with a process of restructuring that did not result in economic decline. But did the rapid growth of port-associated activities preserve the population of Antwerp from impoverishment? Or did the expansion of shipping and commerce fail to compensate fully for the loss of jobs caused by the decay of the textile industry, so that Antwerp was worse off than a town like Ghent where cotton-manufacturing grew at an accelerated pace? Or does neither proposition apply and, hence, is it impossible to relate the number of paupers to the presence or absence of industrialization or modernization? To answer these questions, I have studied the changes in Antwerp's occupational structure which took place between the end of the *ancien régime* and the middle of the nineteenth century, the demographic composition of the city's population, the level of overcrowding, average *per capita* food consumption, and the numbers entitled to public assistance.

My second task was to analyse the poor themselves. Did the families on relief constitute a distinct social category – a 'lumpenproletariat' – or did they form an integral part of the working-class? Thanks to exceptionally rich archival sources it has been possible to study in some detail the demographic composition and occupational distribution of the regular dole-drawers, so that several characteristics of the supported population can be revealed. I have also tried to shed light on the various means of survival available to Antwerp's proletariat during the first half of the nineteenth century, paying special attention to the significance of family and kinship relationships as sources of aid.

It is clear that a monograph cannot answer every question relating to the extent, manifestations and causes of poverty during a period of transition. Although my findings were carefully compared with (mostly unpublished) research done on other Belgian towns, the available evidence is still too limited to draw far-reaching conclusions. Many detailed investigations will be required before an overall picture can be drawn; it is my hope that many more historians will have an opportunity to research this field. Comparative studies are as important as the diachronic approach.[14]

PART 1

Economic Transformation

CHAPTER 1

Antwerp as an Industrial Centre

During the century after 1750 the international division of labour was restructured, strongly influencing socio-economic relations within many of the cities of Europe. For some urban centres the breakthrough of the capitalist mode of production was an unmitigated loss, while others profitted from the powerful growth of the world economy. Antwerp was among the winners. Its expansion, however, did not go hand-in-hand with continuing industrialization; this is puzzling, because during the *ancien régime* this town had been a pre-eminent producer of textiles in the southern Netherlands. To understand this paradox, it is necessary to describe briefly the causes and consequences of Antwerp's industrial development between the late sixteenth and the late eighteenth centuries. Given that the focus of this study is the effect of the subsequent economic transformation upon the mass of the population, particular attention will be devoted to the importance of textile manufacturing for employment opportunities and the income of the lower classes.

The fall of the town to Parma in 1585, the subsequent blockade of the Scheldt by the Dutch, the emigration of nearly half of its population, and the dramatic flight of capital to the North put an end to Antwerp's 'Golden Age.' Nonetheless, the former metropolis continued to play during the first half of the seventeenth century a prominent role in the economy of the southern Netherlands and indeed of western Europe. The explanation for the relatively important function which Antwerp retained as a production and consumption centre is four-fold: the continuation of overland trade with Italy, Germany, and France, though on a lesser scale than previously; the foundation of a strong network of commercial relations between Antwerp's firms and dispersed family members and friends; the town's strategic position as a money market in the financing of the Eighty Years War; and, last but not least, its role as an industrial centre, especially for the manufacture of luxury fabrics.[1] For lack of data, the numbers engaged in textile production in the mid seventeenth century cannot be accurately determined. Conservative estimates suggest however that at least 8,000 lived off various kinds of linen, about the same number off silk, and some 2,000 off lace work. Since Antwerp's population was scarcely 57,000 in 1645, these three branches of industry provided a living for about 30 per cent of its inhabitants.[2]

From the 1650s, Antwerp's textile industry met increasing competition both inside and outside the Netherlands. As in other western European countries, manufacturing in the southern Netherlands shifted from the towns to the countryside, where wages were significantly lower. Antwerp's entrepreneurs tried to protect themselves by improving quality, by securing charters from the Crown which forbade all industrial activities in the surrounding villages, and by limitations on imports. But these measures proved ineffective. In 1734, the town's linen manufacturers complained that at most thirty or forty of them made a decent living. It was perhaps an exaggeration, but the census of 1738 showed that linen weaving employed only about 700 masters, journeymen, apprentices and children, while the production of linen ribbons had collapsed totally.[3] Weaving of galloons ('passementen') and silk ribbons, on the other hand, was severely affected by higher tariffs in the 1660s, the price of Italian silk rising sharply and the export of finished products becoming more difficult. Growing foreign competition posed an even greater threat. By 1660, the 'ribbon frame', an improved loom that allowed twelve to fourteen ribbons to be worked at a time, became widely accepted in many parts of Europe. Antwerp's galloon weavers refused to introduce the device because they feared the great entrepreneurs would use these technological innovations to dominate the industry, small masters, who made up the majority, not being able to afford the costs involved. With the support of their colleagues in Brussels and Ghent, they convinced the central government to forbid the use of ribbon frames and the import of such produce into the southern Netherlands. The policy resulted in the gradual but certain loss of foreign markets. In 1738, only 290 masters, journeymen, and apprentices remained in the manufacture of galloons and silk ribbons, compared to nearly 5,000 in 1650.[4]

The decline of these once flourishing industries was partially compensated for by the expansion of lace working – partially, because only women and children were employed in the trade and received extremely low wages (see page 14). In 1738, there were between 10,000 and 12,000 lace workers in Antwerp, five or six times more than a century earlier. Since the population of the town amounted to 43,810 in 1740, lace working employed not less than 25 per cent of the total population.[5] Silk weaving was the sole traditional sector to hold its own in the second half of the seventeenth century. Although Antwerp's manufacturers had to compete with the French silk industry, favoured by the protectionist measures of Colbert, and with growing English production, they were able to maintain their grip on the internal market.[6] From the early eighteenth century, however, imported Indian calicoes and other exotic cottons flooded the southern Netherlands. This influx revolutionized fashions and posed the severest threat to Antwerp's silk industry. In 1738 about 1,700 workers were involved in silk weaving. Ten years later, two thirds of them were unemployed.[7]

Lace work aside, Antwerp's textile industries were demolished during the 1740s. Yet in this same period the first signs of recovery manifested themselves. Though the decline of traditional branched continued irreversibly, two 'new' occupations expanded rapidly: the manufacture of mixed fabrics and cotton-printing. Antwerp's linen weavers had produced textiles of mixed linen and cotton, wool, or silk sporadically during the sixteenth and seventeenth centuries. From the second quarter of the eighteenth century, however, they began to rely increasingly on these trades. In the southern Netherlands production of 'siamoises' with linen warp and cotton weft was greatly stimulated by the central government's prohibition in 1744 of the importation of similar materials from France. In 1764, six of Antwerp's entrepreneurs, who together owned 350 looms, specialized in the manufacture of cotton linens.[8] The creation of at least seven new businesses in the course of the 1770s highlights the spectacular expansion of the new industry. In 1778, the Antwerp manufacturer F.P. de Meulder declared that thousands were involved in the production of mixed fabrics, with the bulk of the spinners consisting of women, children and the aged.[9]

From the early seventeenth century, there were textile printers in Antwerp with small shops and few workers, manufacturing a few pieces at a time. In the first half of the eighteenth century, however, these businesses collapsed in the face of competition from the Dutch Republic, where cotton printers employed the so-called 'Indian method' with its colourfast results. The new technique was introduced to Antwerp in 1751. Two years later Jan Beerenbroek, Adriaan Janssens, Johan van Eersel, and Johannes Carolus van Heurck received from Maria Theresa a charter which guaranteed them a twenty-five year monopoly on cotton printing in the Austrian Netherlands. These entrepreneurs established their business at Dambrugge, a hamlet near Antwerp. The 'factory' of Beerenbroek & Co. grew into one of the most important in Europe: by 1769, its annual output amounted to nearly 78,000 pieces; only the printing works of Oberkampf at Jouy (in the vicinity of Versailles) had a greater capacity. Immediately after the termination of the charter, similar businesses sprang up on all sides.[10]

The growth of these new industries significantly changed the occupational structure of Antwerp. The censuses of 1789 and 1800 show that by the end of the *ancien régime* the town had become predominantly an industrial centre and that textile manufacturing occupied the body of the labour force.[11] In both years about 58 per cent of the population over 6 years of age or 76 per cent of the total active population was engaged in the secondary sector. Textile manufacturing was of paramount importance, accounting for 36 to 38 per cent of all inhabitants or 48 to 50 per cent of those in employment. No other occupation could match it. Only the clothing trade, closely connected to the textile industry, employed a significant proportion of the labour force – roughly 10 to 11 per cent of the total population. Diamond polishing and tobacco processing gained importance only in the second half of the nineteenth century.

An analysis of the occupational distribution of textile workers shows that manufacture of mixed fabrics and cottons had become the foremost branch of the industry by 1800. Nearly half of all textile workers, or one fourth of the active population, tried to make a living in this sector. The growth in the

Occupational classification of textile workers at Antwerp in 1789 and 1800

Occupation	Numbers		Per cent	
	1789		1800	
Cottons and mixed fabrics	5,904	8,283	38·09	46·78
Lace	5,030	5,020	32·45	28·35
Linens	1,508	2,286	9·73	12·91
Silk	1,291	221	8·32	1·25
Ribbons	807	808	5·21	4·57
Woollens	746	885	4·81	5·00
Miscellaneous	215	202	1·39	1·14
Total	15,501	17,705	100·00	100·00

number of textile workers during the last decade of the eighteenth century must chiefly be ascribed to the increase in the numbers of cotton spinners. In 1789, there were 3,930 masters, journeymen, and apprentices dependent on this trade; ten years later they numbered 6,140, half as many again. The number engaged in linen production rose by 50 per cent too but, without doubt, most of them worked for manufacturers of mixed fabrics for the number of actual linen weavers dropped by one third between 1778 and 1800.[12] All other branches stagnated or declined. The lace industry provided a living for some 5,000 at the turn of the century, against 10,000 to 12,000 in 1738. Qualitative information too indicates that the trade in lace at Antwerp indeed had difficulties to face after 1750. It should however be noted that occupational data may give too sombre a picture of the recession, for many lace workers were children (see below) and, as a result, not registered by the census-takers. In any case, these considerations do not hold for the silk industry, which on the whole employed adult males; around the turn of the century, this occupation had lost all importance.

The restructuring of industry was accompanied by the reduction to proletarian status of large numbers of master craftsmen. Wage labour was nothing new, of course, but during the second half of the eighteenth century proletarianization in traditional sectors as well as in the newer trades reached unprecedented levels. This process was clearly visible in 1751, for example, when the richest silk weavers used the bankruptcy of the poor-box as a pretext to raise guild entry fees dramatically, sharply curtailing opportunities for journeymen to work their way up to the level of independent producers. Furthermore, in 1784 the central government withdrew the restriction on the numbers of employees. With all restraints out of the way, capitalist entrepreneurs recruited more and more workers. Small masters were no match for this competition and were driven out one by one. In consequence by 1789 fourteen master silk weavers together controlled 1,200 workers.[13]

A similar process was at work in linen weaving. The rising demand for mixed fabrics, the production of which lay outside guild regulation, accelerated the social degradation of small master linen weavers. As early as 1725 they complained that some 'guild-brothers' had 10 to 18 looms in operation, eliminating less fortunate artisans. The next year the town government determined that no one could own more than six looms. The prohibition however only affected actual linen weavers, not the entrepreneurs who processed cotton yarn and other raw materials. Hence Jan van der Smissen, dean of the guild, could produce mixed fabrics on a large scale. By 1731, he owned 57 looms. Thirty years later he employed in his workshop no fewer than 42 journeymen, with an extra 341 domestic labourers in service. His example found imitators: in 1764, the 3,000 or so who lived by the manufacture of cotton-linens depended on six entrepreneurs.[14] Cotton spinning itself was dominated from the very outset by capitalists. In 1789, the ratio of employers to workers was 1:48. Ten years later it had risen to 1:101. Two manufacturers, Bosman and Vandenbol, each then employed more than 300 workers.[15]

Nor did the other textile branches escape the grip of capital. Cloth dyeing and finishing provide a striking example. In 1781 the brothers Bernard and Renier Musschen asked the municipal government for approval to set up a 'factory' of fine cloth. The deans of the guild advised against it, arguing that 'great enterprises in general do nothing other than enrich the few' and that the small producers would be reduced to beggars. The authorities ignored their protests and agreed to the proposal of the brothers Musschen. Even worse, in 1783, the Council of Brabant stipulated that cloth dyeing henceforth could be done at will. The result was that in 1789 400 cloth-dressers worked for two of Antwerp's entrepreneurs. Three years earlier a similar offensive had been launched against the silk throwers. P. Beirens & Co. then asked the government for approval not only to weave mixed fabrics in their 'factory' at Antwerp, but also to process silk thread without submission to corporate regulations. Despite the forceful opposition of small masters, they received the required charter.[16]

Technological improvements increased the impact of capital on the organization of production. In 1785, the government withdrew its prohibition on ribbon frames. The measure put new life into the trade so that, between 1778 and 1789, the number of weavers of silk ribbon in Antwerp rose from 271 to 807. The fears of the smaller producers were realized: one after another they forfeited their independence. Most had insufficient means to acquire the expensive tools needed, so that they were no match for the intense competition. Soon they were themselves obliged to become wage labourers for the great entrepreneurs, who let them carry out the preparatory stages or tie the broken threads – tasks requiring no skills and, therefore, poorly paid. The guild had numbered more than 100 *masters* in 1778; in 1789, 800 *workers* were employed by seven capitalists.[17]

These any many other examples indicate that in the second half of the eighteenth century local and central authorities systematically encouraged large-scale entrepreneurs to break through corporative shackles. Without this support the industrial expansion of the Austrian Netherlands would most probably not have been so rapid. Encouragement of free enterprise, however, undermined the protective functions fulfilled by corporatism and consequently accelerated the social degradation of the small masters.[18] Among the 17,500 inhabitants of Antwerp who made a living from the textile industry at the end of the eighteenth century, there were scarcely 800 independent producers, and most of these purported entrepreneurs had few if any employees.[19] A very restricted number of capitalists, in other words, controlled this sector of the economy.

Who raised the money needed to transform industrial production? Antwerp was one of the richest towns in the Austrian Netherlands, and even western Europe. Around 1750, fifty families possessed more than 600,000 Brabant guilders each; another eighty families had between 300,000 and 600,000 each.[20] Since their assets vastly exceeded local demand for capital, these families continuously sought new investment opportunities. They bought shares in overseas trading companies and subscribed to loans in industrial undertakings, as evidenced by the many sugar refineries financed by Antwerp capital.[21] Until the middle of the eighteenth century, however, they invested little in textile manufacture, for obvious reasons: with the exception of lace, the production of luxury goods was in a steady decline. Elite attitudes shifted radically in the 1740s and 1750s when the introduction of new techniques, the more favourable customs policies of the Austrian government, and rising international demand for cheap fabrics combined to create the necessary preconditions for industrial reorientation and expansion.

It comes as no surprise then that most of the founders and shareholders of the large textile enterprises which arose in the second half of the eighteenth century emerged from commercial, financial and noble circles. The four owners of the 'factory' at Dambrugge were merchants, and the majority of their financial backers consisted of bankers, wholesalers, and nobles. The same holds true for the cotton-printing works established in the 1770s and 1780s. Christiaan de Visser may have been a foreman for Beerenbroek & Co., but his partner was a merchant and the initial capital was provided largely by noble families. In other branches of the Antwerp textile industry, commercial and financial capital played just as decisive a role. The thread-twister Johannes Hilarius van den Berghe, who directed an extensive workshop, was to the outside world an independent artisan; in reality he was wholly dependent upon the merchant Hermannes Josephus

Botermans. Pieter Beirens, one of the foremost manufacturers of mixed fabrics, was a merchant, as were his partners. Pieter de Heyder, Jan Daniël van Scherpenbergh, and Jan Baptist Beeckmans, who in 1757 founded a great weaving-shed of 'dimittes' and 'siamoises' at Lier, were Antwerp wholesalers. Bosman and Vandenbol, who employed hundreds of cotton spinners, were both merchants. These and many others invested in industrial enterprises for lack of profitable alternatives, given a three to four per cent *per annum* return on investments in Antwerp during the second half of the eighteenth century. Hence Beerenbroek & Co., for example, between 1753 and 1768 made loans totalling no less than 539,000 Brabant guilders, while investing a mere 74,000 in their own cotton printing works.[22]

Industrial expansion not only went hand in hand with a growing division between capital and labour, but also with the mobilization of a youthful work-force and the employment of the 'scum' of society. In the second half of the eighteenth century innumerable children spun cotton in Antwerp's basement rooms under the supervision of so-called *kelderboeren* ('cellarmen'); the rooms were deliberately chosen for their dampness, the threads benefiting from staying moist. 'To be an eyewitness,' wrote F.P. de Meulder, 'all it takes is to wander through a few wards of the city; you'll see one cellar after another crammed full of poor children from morning to late at night, spinning cotton, with sweat in their eyes.'[23] In the lace industry too, children formed a significant proportion of the labour force. In 1780, Antwerp counted no fewer than 149 schools where the pupils made lace. The 'education' was free, but in return parents bound their children to work unpaid for the schoolmaster for a certain number of years. A dozen ecclesiastical institutions had similar policies. In two convents of the Apostolines, for example, 110 nuns and 150 children made lace, as did 130 lay sisters and 100 children in the foundation of canon Terninck.[24] Without question, the enormous supply of cheap labour drastically lowered the wages of adult workers.

The growing need for industrial workers and the simultaneous rise in the number of impoverished artisans made fertile soil for a reform of traditional poor relief. In 1778, the almoners proposed a plan with a two-fold purpose: to diminish the expenses of charitable institutions and to encourage industrial growth. The administrators of poor relief testified that in the first instance it was necessary to forbid begging, for 'idleness leads to sin, and it is materially deleterious, too, since it makes scarce the hands which are needed for the factories and makes the price of labour dear'. Second, all relief funds had to be centralized in order to give more efficient financial and social control. Third, a poor tax had to be levied to ensure the continuity of the system. Fourth, it was necessary to abolish the relief funds of the guilds, so that the déclassé guild masters would be obliged to change quickly to other tasks. Fifth, the almoners argued that no more than minimal allowances should be given to the able-bodied poor, in order 'to move them to seek work'.[25]

It was not by chance that the administrators of poor relief came up with such a project in 1778. The production of mixed fabrics had come to employ more and more workers, with two new enterprises founded in 1775–1776. The manufacturers of cotton yarn complained in 1778 that they found too few women in Antwerp prepared to work for them – in other words, to accept low wages. Hence they were obliged to call upon cotton spinners from Bergen op Zoom, 's-Hertogenbosch, Tilburg, Dendermonde and even from far off Namur. The expiration of the exclusive charter granted to the cotton printers at Dambrugge also had an effect: many entrepreneurs were ready to create similar businesses in 1778.[26] The labour market, therefore, needed to be stimulated as quickly as possible. No wonder that mayor Jan Dewael accepted the proposal. One year later all the measures proposed by the almoners received the force of law, save for the poor tax. The *Nieuwe Bestiering van den Armen* (New Poor Law Administration) was entrusted with the supervision of all matters relevant to public assistance: administration of donations and subsidies destined for the needy, organization of support, and control of those on the dole. The town was divided into 32 quarters, each ruled by six overseers. Two of them, along with eight of the eldest almoners, had to conduct a tour of inspection twice a year, visiting the poor to investigate their material and moral situation and to decide whether or not they were to be considered for support. They noted on printed sheets the name, address, age, occupation, earnings, and even the illnesses and physical complaints of all those in receipt of poor relief; these lists were checked by the treasurer of the *Nieuwe Bestiering*.[27] Half of the overseers were ecclesiastics, whose co-operation was necessary for two reasons: no one was better informed of the conduct of the poor than the parish priest, and the lower classes had to be shown that labour was a religious obligation. Bishop J. Wellens stressed that point in a pastoral letter, read out in all of Antwerp's churches. Moreover, he established a *Catechismusfundatie* to propagate the Christian message in a simple, easily grasped way among the poor. By 1780, more than 2,500 wage labourers were receiving such instruction from their parish priests on Sundays.[28]

In subsequent years, the system was further refined. The shortage of youthful labour led the poor law administration to stipulate that the children of the supported needy, eight years old and over, should learn a trade on pain of their parents being struck from the poor lists. In 1782, the directors set up a spinning workshop in which the unemployed poor were compelled to work for their alms. Four years later there came a regulation commissioning the police to ensure that no poor children played in the street during working hours.[29]

The success of the new social policy was demonstrated when, barely two weeks after the creation of the *Nieuwe Bestiering*, eighteen entrepreneurs turned to the almoners requesting the labour of some 500 able-bodied poor. In 1783, the municipal government declared proudly that the reorganization of poor relief had enabled textile manufacturers to reduce wages substantially, 'for those on relief have been compelled to toil the whole week through without a break, whereas earlier they worked only a few days and then begged the rest of the time'.[30] Yet, the system did not fulfil every expectation of the manufacturers, who needed child labour above all. They stridently opposed the plan of the almoners to lodge orphans with farmers instead of placing them in the orphanage, the *Knechtjeshuis*. The almoners judged that it was excessive to demand that 'the community, which maintains the children, should facilitate the profits realized by the manufacturers who employ orphans in place of apprentices'. This consideration, dictated by a desire to cut down public expenditure, was not appreciated by the entrepreneurs, who contended that the closure of the orphanage would harm their interests; they demanded the immediate re-establishment of the 'training school of the factories'. The chaplain of the orphanage, who was controlled by the textile manufacturers, intervened in the dispute 'on behalf of the children' and instituted proceedings against the almoners. It needs hardly saying that the manufacturers won their suit. The *Knechtjeshuis* remained and in 1785 was even provided with its own cotton spinning workshop.[31]

The connection between the growing demand of manufacturers for an extensive, cheap, and docile labour force on one hand and the reform of poor relief on the other was not peculiar to Antwerp. Between 1772 and 1787, seven other towns in the Austrian Netherlands carried out similar reorganization with an eye towards the profitable employment of the indigent. These centres were all characterized by labour-intensive industries in a state of rapid expansion. Many other western European countries experienced comparable changes in their social policy. Nearly everywhere, entrepreneurs and public authorities tried to use public assistance as an instrument for the regulation of the labour market. Whether such measures were sustained or not depended on local or regional economic developments: so long as the trinity of charity, control, and labour regulation coincided with the real or imagined interests of employers, the system remained in vogue. The result was, one way or the other, everywhere the same: the systematic depression of adult male wages as a result of large-scale employment of poor women and children.[32]

With the exception of the printing works at Dambrugge, no wage records of eighteenth-century Antwerp textile businesses have been preserved. Some industrial 'censuses', taken by contemporaries, record the daily or weekly earnings of certain categories of workers. But these data are unfortunately useless: for every occupation, only a single wage is mentioned, so that it is impossible to determine whether the figures relate to typical or exceptional remuneration. The sole available sources of information are the poor lists of 1780, in which, *inter alia*, are to be found the earnings of the supported-needy. Considering solely the occupations of able-bodied men and women between the ages of 20 and 54 for which sufficient information is available, and expressing average wages in kilograms of rye bread,[33] it is clear that the largest groups of workers were the most poorly paid. The bulk of laceworkers, who represented 16 per cent of the active population, received two stivers or about 1·4 kg. of rye bread per day. On the presumption that they were employed 300 days a year – and even that is highly unlikely – their average daily income amounted to little more than 1 kg. of rye bread a day, *i.e.*, just enough to survive. Certainly, there were lace workers whose wages were three or four times higher, but they were

a tiny minority.[34] Cotton spinners, 11 per cent of the active population, were
not much better off: women earned on the average 2 kg. of rye bread, men 2·4 kg.
The low wage level of the latter must be ascribed to the negligible skills required
to practice this trade and to the large supply of female labour – in 1796, more
than half the adult cotton spinners were women.[35] For similar reasons, minimum and maximum wages differed little, the ratio being 1 to 2·5. Hence, comparatively more cotton spinners than lace workers were propertyless, 97 per
cent against 75 per cent, respectively.[36] Both groups were all the more vulnerable because the massive employment of children entailed permanent low-wage
competition. An analysis of the poor lists shows that nearly 70 per cent of
young girls over the age of six learned to make lace and that some 60 per cent
of boys spun cotton. Lace workers aged between 6 and 10 received less than
one stiver a day, and those between 11 and 15 one and a half stivers, or 75 per
cent of the average wage paid to adult women. The daily wage of 10-year old
cotton spinners amounted to at most one and a half stivers; when they were 15
years old, it varied between 2 and 2·5 stivers, *i.e.*, only 30 to 40 per cent below
the daily wage of adult men.

Silk workers and weavers of mixed fabrics generally earned twice as much
as cotton spinners, but these represented barely 7 per cent of the working
population. Their 'favourable' situation was, moreover, only relative. First,
the majority consisted of former masters or their descendants, who had been
both materially and socially degraded. Second, under- and unemployment
recurred in these trades. If a weaver worked only 200 days a year, his average
daily *income* fell to 4·5 stivers, or some 3 kg. of rye bread.

Cotton printing was the only branch of Antwerp's textile industry in
which high wages were paid. In 1779, the designers, engravers, and master
printers of Beerenbroek & Co. received 30 stivers a day, but these highly trained
workers, some recruited outside the country, were in the minority: around
1769, 'white collar workers' and the technicians together comprised a mere 20
per cent of the total personnel. The wages of the other 80 per cent were much
lower. Bleachers earned 14 stivers a day, polishers 10 to 18, printer's helpers 6
to 10, and the *schildermeiden*, women who painted the printed cottons, 2 to 16
stivers. The latter two categories, which made up nearly half the labour force,
worked on a piece-rate basis. Defects were to their cost: they paid for the spoiled
cottons, including the printer's wages. The system held other disadvantages,
too. When work slowed as a result of technical difficulties, the labourers suffered. Above all, the *schildermeiden* were hit by sharp fluctuations in their
income, for the introduction of more complex, timeconsuming designs was
never matched by higher piece-rates. Finally, no one was employed throughout
the whole year. Printer's helpers, for example, faced unemployment during the
winter months, so that their average daily incomes were at least 25 per cent
lower than their daily wages.[37] Nonetheless, workers engaged in this trade
were comparatively better off than other textile workers. None of them had to
be supported by poor relief in 1780, and in 1796 scarcely half of the printers
and their helpers were totally propertyless.

All things considered, the growth of the textile industry provided few benefits for the mass of the population. The lower classes enjoyed full employment,
but most artisans had been reduced to the level of wage labourers and were
generally underpaid as a result of large-scale mobilization of the needy, including children. In 1780, the poor relief administration admitted that 'the entrepreneurs provide their workers with only the barest necessities to stay alive,
but not enough to care for their families, so that nearly every wage labourer
must be supported if he has more than two children or if he is without work,
even if only for a few days.'[38] Shortly thereafter the almoners wondered: 'How
was it possible that in Antwerp industries were created in which the wages are
so low that workers with children or facing the least misfortune are not able to
survive?'[39] The thousands of men, women, and children who made a living
from textile manufacturing did indeed constitute a highly vulnerable proletariat.
Investigation of the distribution of wealth in 1795–1796 shows that scarcely 14
per cent of the town's inhabitants were comfortably off; adding to that figure
all those who had a small income from their own house or workshop brings it
to a total of 35 per cent. In other words, two-thirds of the population had next
to nothing, while among those engaged in textile manufacturing, this figure
rose to four-fifths; domestic service aside, no other occupational group was so
disproportionately bereft of property.[40]

CHAPTER 2

Textile Manufacturing: A Lost Chance

The spectacular revival of Antwerp's textile industry proved short-lived. By 1820, mixed fabric production and cotton printing had entirely lost their former importance. How is this sudden collapse to be explained? Hypothetically, three factors may have played a role: 1) economic difficulties sparked by international conflicts and successive changes of regime; 2) the technological backwardness of Antwerp's cotton industry, which at the end of the *ancien régime* remained completely based on hand work; and 3) the lack of capital resulting from the policies of industrial divestiture practiced by most important businessmen. Each of these potential causes will be examined in this chapter, beginning with the political events which impinged upon Antwerp's economy.

As long as the textile industry flourished, Antwerp's proletariat escaped utter destitution, but for most working families regular employment was the *sine qua non* of their meager existence. Until the mid-1780s, this condition was generally met; thereafter, things were different. Growing export difficulties and sharp rises in the prices of raw materials compelled manufacturers to lay off more and more workers. The economic crisis was further aggravated by political troubles and a severe scarcity of grain. In 1787, the almoners declared that Antwerp contained more than 10,000 needy, *i.e.*, nearly a fifth of the total population, and that their number grew from day to day 'due to the unemployment of all the artisans, whose last reserves are exhausted'.[1] Succeeding years brought no improvement. The Brabant Revolution, followed in turn by the restoration of Austrian authority, the first French occupation, the return of the Austrians, and the second invasion of the Republican armies completely dislocated economic life. The social consequences were all the more severe because the bourgeoisie turned a deaf ear to the entreaties of the almoners to grant greater subsidies to the *Nieuwe Bestiering*: the upper classes did not see why they should maintain an institution which no longer functioned as an instrument of labour regulation.[2]

Although the annexation of the southern Netherlands by France in 1795 revived hope, Antwerp's textile industry did not recover. In 1801, the cotton printers complained that their annual output had diminished by a third since 1790. They scarcely exaggerated, for the amount of cotton printed by Beerenbroek & Co. dropped by nearly 45 per cent between 1785–1789 and 1795–1799. The decline of cotton spinning was of the same order of magnitude. Bosman and Vandenbol, the two foremost manufacturers of cotton yarn, testified that their production was halved during the 1790s. Manufacturers of mixed fabrics said much the same thing. Lacemaking too was weak: according to the municipal authorities, few women and children engaged in the industry could meet their daily needs.[3]

Yet textile manufacturers did not cease their business activities during the 1790s. Most felt that the crisis would be of short duration and that the restoration of internal order and the coming of peace among the great powers would rejuvenate Antwerp's industry. When in 1801 the French administration asked the producers of cotton yarn, the manufacturers of mixed fabrics, and the cotton printers what prospects they foresaw, they answered that their sales would undoubtedly rise the moment the political situation was resolved.[4]

However when Charles Cochon, prefect of the *département des Deux-Nèthes*, reported on the situation of Antwerp's cotton industry to the central government in Paris in February 1806, the town counted only 3,000 cotton spinners, against 6,140 at the turn of the century. In succeeding years, employment diminished even more. Again the prefect reported that trade was evaporating and, by February 1816, the number of cotton spinners had fallen to 200. The manufacture of mixed fabrics fared no better. Between 1800 and 1806 the number of weavers fell from 1,037 to 576. In the latter year, the prefect estimated the value of total production at 2 million francs at most, against over 3 million around 1790. The decline was irreversible. Year after year manufacturers were forced to lay-off workers and by 1813 most had closed their doors. Cotton printing declined similarly. In 1806 Beerenbroek & Co. produced only 8,000 pieces, a third of the yearly average during the period 1795–1799. Cotton printers together employed at most 200 workers in 1806. Seven years later, this once so flourishing enterprise had disappeared. The printing of cottons was henceforth a business for small dyers, just as in the first half of the eighteenth century.[5]

The rapid decline of the Antwerp cotton industry under the French régime is puzzling, since quite the opposite happened at Ghent. In April 1816, there were there twenty printing works, 28 spinning mills, and a dozen weaving factories employing a total of nearly 12,000 men, women, and children, a fifth of the local population.[6] The cotton industry developed in other centres too. An inquiry in 1806 showed that, since 1790, no fewer than 323 cotton factories had been founded in the nine Belgian *départements*. Most of these were relatively small, but some concentrated a large number of workers under one roof, as in the hydraulic spinning mills founded by the Parisian banker, Pierre François Tiberghien, and his countryman G. Bardet at Saint-Denis near Mons; or the 'factory' for mixed fabrics founded by the same Tiberghien and his brothers Joseph and Emmanuel in the former abbey of Heylissem near Tienen; or the printing works of Petrus Schavye and his son Jean-François at Anderlecht near Brussels; or finally the textile business of de Heyder & Co. at Lier, near Antwerp itself.[7] In short, while the cotton industry declined at Antwerp, it expanded in Ghent and several other Belgian towns. How is this divergent development to be explained?

In the early 1800s, the pacesetting sector of the cotton industry was no longer printing, as it had been in the second half of the eighteenth century. The role played by this branch did remain important, since it kept high the demand for textiles and, accordingly, for yarn, but it was only the mechanization of spinning which enabled a cotton industry independent of England to be founded. This was precisely what happened at Ghent. The 'epic' story of Lieven Bauwens is well known. In 1798 he smuggled all the materials necessary for a spinning mill, including the steam engine, out of England and assembled the parts at Passy, near Paris. Two years later, Bauwens created a second spinning mill at Ghent and in 1804 a third in the neighbourhood of Drongen. This entrepreneur exploited to the full his *de facto* monopoly over construction of spinning-mules at Ghent by putting the new tools exclusively in the hands of relatives or business partners, thus founding a veritable empire of family and associated businesses. Although Bauwens himself ended in total bankruptcy, the rise of the Ghent cotton industry had begun. By the end of the French régime, the industry was vertically integrated: weavers made use of yarn spun locally, and the printers worked calicoes woven there.[8]

Antwerp's cotton industry, by contrast, remained technologically backward. Although local manufacturers of mixed fabrics were often obliged to import their cotton yarn from neighbouring centres, cotton spinning in the town on the Scheldt was not mechanized during the French régime.[9] Yet the correspondence of Charles d'Herbouville, the first prefect of the *département des Deux-Nèthes*, indicates at the turn of the century that English engineers repeatedly offered to construct spinning-mules and other machines at Antwerp. On 26 September 1800, d'Herbouville wrote to the Minister of the Interior that the Englishman John Mitchell, accompanied by several relatives and skilled workers, had come to Antwerp with the intention of founding a muslin factory. Since Mitchell lacked sufficient capital, the prefect asked the government whether it was prepared to provide him with a workshop and a loan to build machines and buy raw materials. However much d'Herbouville urged the matter, the Minister remained aloof. In December the prefect argued that the State had an obligation to support Mitchell, because the technical knowledge of the workers trained by him would then become public property, spurring other manufacturers towards adoption of similar initiatives. But it was fruitless. The

Bureau consultatif des Arts et des Manufactures at Paris judged that Mitchell should be satisfied with a resident permit and refused to provide a cent.[10]

The prefect did not give up. In July 1801, he wrote to the Mayor of Antwerp that it was time for local manufacturers to transcend their technological backwardness if they wished to compete with entrepreneurs from other towns. Given its favourable location, the town seemed destined once again to be an important port; nonetheless, according to the prefect, not all efforts should be directed exclusively to the restoration of commercial enterprises. Antwerp's commerce, as in the sixteenth century, had to be backed by a flourishing industrial base, balancing the inherent risks to overseas trade. More factories should be set up, especially for cotton which, as a result of growing demand for cheap fabrics, had a shining future. Modernization of this sector posed no problems, or so the prefect argued, for various English engineers were ready to provide the requisite machinery. Two of them were lodged at Antwerp at that moment and offered to build a spinning-mule, a carding-machine, and a twining-mill if the necessary materials were provided, along with a small reward and a long-term working contract. The plea brought no result. Neither the authorities nor local entrepreneurs followed up d'Herbouville's proposals.[11]

In 1802 the prefect tried another tack. He communicated to the Minister of the Interior that an Englishman, Henry Houlden, had offered to build a water-driven flax mill at Antwerp and advised the government to finance the project. Houlden had given sufficient proof of his technical knowledge, and with his help the production of canvas for the merchant and naval fleets could be increased. Since the English had only seven mechanized flax-mills, there was little to fear from their competition. Antwerp appeared to d'Herbouville to be the natural centre for the manufacture of canvas, because the town possessed harbour facilities, shipyards, and a textile industry. The government's answer was its customary negative.[12]

Clearly, lack of know-how does not explain the decline of the Antwerp textile industry. At least three opportunities for the introduction of labour saving devices presented themselves. One might suppose that the authorities and entrepreneurs had significant doubts about the value of these machines and therefore refused to approve d'Herbouville's proposals. This hypothesis must be rejected. Houlden could show that he had built a wool-spinning machine in Berlin in 1799, and two other Englishmen demonstrated to the prefect detailed plans for a spinning-mule. Did the central government shrink from making Antwerp both a maritime *and* an industrial centre? This is not improbable, for the French ports did all they could to hinder Antwerp's economic advance. In 1801 Bordeaux, Nantes, Rouen, and Marseille formulated a demand that the town on the Scheldt should be excluded from France's colonial trade.[13] Although the petition was rejected, the authorities may have decided not to trouble matters further by modernizing Antwerp's textile industry at public expense. Other factors too could have played a role. Ghent's Lieven Bauwens had close contacts with many influential men in Paris. When the soldiers of the Republic conquered the Austrian Netherlands, the brothers Bauwens immediately rallied to the new order and became provisioners of cloth and leather goods to the French army. In 1796, they obtained the concession of the leases and income of national lands in the Belgian *départements*. By the beginning of the Consulate, Lievens Bauwens was mayor of Ghent – a further compromising position. Finally, one ought to remember that this Ghent entrepreneur established his first spinning mill not in Belgium but at Passy near Paris.[14]

All these factors considered, it is not surprising that Antwerp's textile industry failed to receive state aid. But why did local commercial circles not take advantage of the many opportunities to mechanize cotton spinning? Although the available evidence does not allow a final answer to this question, the explanation must surely be sought in the alternative investment opportunities available after 1800.

The treaty of 17 May 1795, proclaiming freedom of navigation on the Scheldt remained a dead letter until 1800 because of the active opposition of the Hollanders in 1795–1796 and the decree of 18 January 1798, which determined that the nationality of a ship depended on its cargo. This law severely damaged Antwerp's commercial interests. Since French ships had the right to stop neutral vessels to investigate whether English goods were on board, and confiscate the goods if they were, most shippers sent their cargoes to Holland's harbours, whence they could be smuggled into Belgium.[15] Napoleon's *coup d'état* ushered in a new era for Antwerp. On 14 December 1799, the First Consul not only declared void the 'piracy article' of 1798, but also proclaimed measures for the protection of neutral shipping.[16] The results were swift: in 1800, 111 sea-going vessels put into the harbour at Antwerp; by 1805 that number had more than doubled. This commercial resurgence was mirrored too in the quick growth of overseas trade. In the year XI (1802–1803) three times as much coffee, five times as much sugar, eight times as much spice, and twelve times as much cotton were imported as in the year VIII (1799–1800).[17] No wonder then that the early 1800s witnessed the creation of a *Kamer van Koophandel* (Chamber of Commerce) and a pilotage, the foundation of shipyards, and the establishment of foreign (mainly German) trading houses. Ambitious plans were put forward to restore and expand the harbour facilities. Prefect d'Herbouville urged the central government, municipal authorities, and local 'capitalists' to build docks, recruit mariners and naval architects, and erect storehouses: in a word, to bring into being an efficient commercial infrastructure. Nor were private initiatives lacking. The merchant Michel Simons and the banker Jean Johannot, for example, bought the extensive lands of the abbey of Sint-Michiels along the the Scheldt to build a great entrepôt there.[18]

As long as the closure of the Scheldt had hindered overseas trade, the elites of Antwerp were prepared to invest money in manufacturing and even to carry out entrepreneurial experiments. This dependence on external sources of investment capital meant that the lifespan of the Antwerp textile industry was greatly determined by the profit margins offered to speculative money-lenders. Until about 1780, entrepreneurs such as Beerenbroek and Beirens realized an annual profit of at least 15 to 20 per cent. Thereafter profits gradually declined until by the early nineteenth century they amounted to scarcely 5 per cent. All available figures indicate that other textile manufacturers faced similarly declining profits.[19] Overseas trade, in contrast, expanded quickly after 1800. In these circumstances, Antwerp's capitalists naturally chose commercial and financial ventures which promised high returns rather than risky investments in new means of production for which the returns were uncertain.

Certainly the commercial revival was short-lived. Like other continental ports, Antwerp was seriously affected by the escalation of the economic struggle between France and England. The number of ships entering the port dropped from 265 in 1805 to 92 in 1807. The collapse of the American trade with western Europe provided the *coup-de-grâce*: in 1808 Antwerp's shipping was at a complete standstill. The stagnation lasted until the end of the French régime.[20] Yet capital was not transferred to the textile industry during this period. Three factors were responsible for this continued uninterest. First, the continental blockade did not totally end commercial activities at Antwerp: trade along internal waterways remained very important and many speculators were drawn to contraband trade in colonial wares.[21] Second, other towns' headstart in industrial activity was so great that Antwerp's merchants would have had to invest huge sums just to catch up. Even though only a few years had been lost, they were of decisive importance in a period of rapid industrialization. By 1 May 1808, Ghent (with the inclusion of the neighbouring communities of Drongen and Ledeberg) already had eight spinning mills and ten weaving factories; the spinning mills alone represented a capital investment of two million francs. Third, the Belgian cotton industry did not expand smoothly: from August 1808 to the end of 1809 and from the summer of 1810 to mid 1811, severe crises led to numerous bankruptcies.[22] It is easily understandable that in these circumstances no one was inclined to sink large amounts of money into Antwerp's outdated cotton industry.

Some of Antwerp's businessmen did lend large sums to the firm de Heyder of Lier, the sole textile enterprise in the *département des Deux-Nèthes* which concentrated various subsidiary processes – weaving of woollens and mixed fabrics, cotton printing, and bleaching; in 1807, the three production units together employed about 300 workers. Several factors made this undertaking still more attractive to capital investors. Since the confiscation of ecclesiastical property, a number of buildings at Lier had remained unoccupied, so that there was no shortage of cheap space; water power was available nearby from the Nete River; wages were much lower than at Antwerp because of the lower cost of living; and the labour force was more than adequate in view of the decline of all other industries. The separation of centre of production from centre of distribution was no severe handicap, for Lier was barely fifteen kilometres from Antwerp and manufactured goods could be transported by paved roads as well as by waterways. With the capital provided by Antwerp's financiers, de Heyder & Co. bought the former religious house of Sion on the Nete and there installed a completely mechanized cotton mill. At the same time the firm changed to the weaving of pure cotton fabrics, so that the concern was vertically integrated.

Success was not far away: in August 1808 the factory employed more than
twice as many workers as in 1807, and by September 1811 the number had
doubled yet again. By 1816, 1,200 spinners, weavers, printers, and bleachers
produced an average of 20,000 pieces of cotton per annum.[23]

If Antwerp's textile producers thought that the bottom of the recession
had been reached at the end of the French régime, they had miscalculated. The
loss of the French market, to which the Belgian *départements* had had access
while it was protected by high tariffs, was a heavy blow to the industries of the
southern Netherlands. Import duties established by the allies in June 1814 were
so low that the market was flooded with English manufactured goods. Although
the tariffs were raised in October the same year, Belgian industry remained
uncompetitively expensive. In 1815 and 1816, the entrepreneurs of the South
petitioned for more protective measures. Needless to say, Holland's commercial circles, with Amsterdam and Rotterdam at their head, had other intentions.[24] They were even supported by Antwerp's *Kamer van Koophandel*, which
in 1814 had already pleaded for low import duties on both raw materials and
finished products. Since they had received an assurance that, after the union of
Belgium and Holland, Antwerp would be treated on an equal footing with the
commercial ports of the North, the leading businessman of the town had no
objections to a policy which in large measure sacrificed industrial interests to
commercial expansion. The provincial Estates, in which the representatives of
Lier, Mechelen, Turnhout, and the countryside formed the majority, reacted
vehemently. They swore that thousands of wage labourers would be thrown
into the direst need if the import of cheap fabrics was not forbidden or at least
heavily taxed. William I nonetheless refused to adopt a protectionist policy and
on 3 October 1816 proclaimed a notably liberal tariff law.[25] To make matters
worse, a subsistence crisis struck in 1816–1817, sharply limiting the demand
for manufactured goods. The Belgian cotton industry entered the greatest
slump in its history. In July 1817, 12 of Ghent's 29 spinning mills closed their
doors; the others had work for only three days a week. Some manufacturers
moved to Roubaix-Tourcoing or to Lille to escape English competition and to
dispose of their products on the French market. The number of cotton printing
works at Ghent dropped from 20 to 15 between 1816 and 1819.[26] During the
same period the number of workers employed by de Heyder & Co. at Lier was
halved; the bankruptcy of the firm was averted only by virtue of two loans
each of 50,000 guilders from William I.[27]

By the early 1820s a general revival set in. The prices of essential foodstuffs such as potatoes and rye fell to a level so low that internal demand for
fabrics rose. Cotton manufacturers, moreover, found a new outlet for their
goods: the Dutch East Indies were opened to them by William I. Indeed the
King founded a company to encourage the export of manufactured articles to
the colonies, the *Nederlandsche Handel-Maatschappij*. Only centres making efforts
to modernize their industries, however, were in a position to take advantage of
the new opportunities. Ghent's cotton manufacturers immediately introduced
numerous technological improvements. The steam engine, which during the

French period had had only a modest success, now found general acceptance. From 1821, entrepreneurs mechanized the processes of cotton weaving, too. Power looms were initially smuggled out of England or made at Ghent by English engineers, but soon most were constructed in the town itself by Phoenix, a firm which was to become famous throughout Europe. In the late 1820s, the annual production of the Ghent spinning mills amounted to *c.* 4·5 million kg. and of the weaving factories *c.* 1·2 million pieces.[28]

Antwerp's textile industry had on the other hand lost its significance by 1820 – with the exception of lace work. According to a census begun in 1819 and completed the following year, textile workers numbered barely 8,300 or about 15 per cent of the population, compared to 17,705 or about 33 per cent at the turn of the century. This catastrophic decline was chiefly caused by the collapse of the cotton industry: from 8,238 workers in 1800 it employed only a thousand or so in 1820, and even that included some 150 prisoners working for private entrepreneurs. Linen production, which since the second half of the eighteenth century had largely relied upon supplying the manufacturers of 'dimittes' and 'siamoises', was dragged down with the cotton industry; the numbers employed diminished between 1800 and 1810 from 2,286 to 336.[29]

It was a structural crisis, as the producers of cotton yarn plainly stated. When the census takers inquired as to the causes of the decline the answer repeatedly given was that non-mechanized textile trades had no future. The Antwerp cotton industry had indeed missed its chance. The few spinning-jennies introduced in the second decade of the nineteenth century were relatively small machines, each with only 20 or 30 spindles. Since manufacturers could not raise the capital required for mechanization and the great trading houses in the 1820s continued with their policy of industrial disinvestment, the Antwerp cotton industry was doomed. In June 1827, the number of cotton spinners had dwindled to 206; two and a half years later, only 121 remained.[30]

Lacemaking was the only labour-intensive branch of the textile industry more or less to survive into the first quarter of the nineteenth century. The number of women and children engaged in this work even rose from 5,020 to 6,012 between 1800 and 1820. Occupational figures however can be misleading. From the correspondence of the poor relief authorities it is clear that things went badly for the lace workers. Their number increased only because it was the last refuge for innumerable women and children left unemployed through the decline of other textile industries. Since the supply of labour far exceeded the demand, merchant-entrepreneurs could systematically depress wages. In 1816–1817, the living standards of lace workers reached their nadir. They faced both outrageous food prices and diminished markets. Austria, Prussia, and Russia forbade the import of lace, while England and France significantly raised their tariffs. As a result exports from Antwerp dropped by some 40 per cent. Employers of course tried to make up their losses as much as possible from their employees, and wages were halved.[31]

Moreover, from about 1815, traditional lacemaking – where the thread was worked by hand around a number of needles fixed in a cushion – gradually gave way to embroidery on tulle. This transformation was brought by the spread of the 'bobbin-net' machine, patented by the Englishman John Heathcoat in 1808.[32] The new tool was so expensive that only factory production became practical. Yet this in no sense meant the end of outwork in the lace industry: although the basic nets were henceforth made in factories, the final processes of mending, drawing, scalloping, and especially embroidering the nets remained unmechanized and continued to involve hand needlework.[33] After the end of the continental blockade, English engineers and entrepreneurs introduced 'bobbin-nets' or 'tulle-bobbins' into French towns such as Calais, Saint-Quentin, Douai, and Cateau-Cambrésis.[34] In Antwerp bobbin-nets were imported on a large scale from 1815 by the Englishman William Wood, who had established himself in the town. The success of this new and cheap article was so overwhelming that Wood founded a large factory in 1824 at Borgerhout near Antwerp, the 'Phoenix Works', where raw cotton yarn and tulle were bleached and refined to such an extent that their quality rivalled that of fine flax. The concern, equipped with steam engines, a gas-works, and artesian wells, was the first true factory in the vicinity of Antwerp.[35] Hundreds of lace workers switched to embroidery on tulle, not only in Antwerp but also in Dendermonde, Diest, Geel, Herentals, Hoogstraten, Kessel, Leuven, Lier, Mechelen, Mol, Roosendaal, Tongeren, Lokeren, Sint-Niklaas, Ghent, Bruges and Liège. In 1827 the total number of women working for Wood amounted to some 15,000, of whom 1,200 were at Antwerp, where the entrepôts for the export to the North, to Germany, and to France were located.[36]

Before long however the tulle 'bubble' burst. In the late 1820s, production in western Europe had grown so much that the market was saturated and prices collapsed.[37] The blow was worsened when the government raised the import duty on bobbin-nets in May 1828, in order to protect home manufacturers. William Wood protested, testifying that the government would sacrifice thousands of embroiderers for a few small enterprises which offered little employment. But in vain: William I held to his decision and aggravated the results of the crisis for the innumerable women and girls who made a living from the bobbin-net lacework. In February 1829, 90 per cent of Antwerp's embroiderers were out of work.[38]

In short, the most vulnerable portion of Antwerp's textile proletariat was wasted in two phases. First, the bulk of the traditional lace workers were eliminated because of the introduction of the 'bobbin-net' machine, which greatly reduced the demand for manual labour. Then women who were engaged in embroidering and finishing the tulle were faced with growing international competition (which led to overproduction), and the unfavourable tariff law of 1828 (which drove up the price of the nets). The result was that, by 1830, only 1,573 lace workers and 561 embroiderers remained. When the Jacquard apparatus was applied, some years later, to the mechanical manufacture of 'figured' lace, the fate of the Antwerp embroiderers was sealed. Although demand for pillow-lace revived in the 1840s, the trade never again regained its previous importance in the town.[39] Antwerp's textile industry had wholly decayed. In

1846 scarcely 2,800 workers, or 3·15 per cent of the total population, were employed in this once so flourishing sector.[40]

Although at the present state of investigation general conclusions are risky, it is clear that spatial factors as well as entrepreneurial forces worked against the rise of large-scale factory production in European port towns during the Industrial Revolution. On one side, lack of cheap energy, space, and labour put most commercial ports at a disadvantage compared to the industrial centres of the interior. On the other, more profitable commercial and financial ventures attracted local businessmen away from those industries which in growing measure relied on capital-intensive means of production. The case of London illustrates this point. Although London has remained to this day Britain's largest concentration of manufacturing, it has never undergone the great concentration of productive units that Manchester, Leeds and other places experienced in the early nineteenth century. Instead of large-scale factory industry, a whole series of consumer-goods trades emerged in the commercial and financial capital of the British Empire; these trades were characterized by simple, relatively inexpensive, and hand-driven machinery and by the employment of a cheap, supernumerary, and unskilled pool of labour.[41] The few port cities which became major production sites for cotton cloth during the Industrial Revolution confronted either a long-lasting contraction of their total volume of trade or a reorientation of their harbour function from an international or a national to a regional scope.[42]

Certainly there were major harbour towns where factory production developed in this period, but in general this was confined to what might be called processing industries such as flour-mills, soap-works, sugar-refineries, tobacco-factories, and the like. Port cities were not only points at which goods changed conveyance. They were also 'break-in-bulk' points, where raw materials or semi-finished products were gathered for processing or finishing before shipment overseas or onward distribution in the hinterland. For some industries, port cities had (and indeed have) a decisively advantageous location: a certain level of processing substantially reduced the weight of raw and heavy staple items – grains, oils, sugar, etc. – and consequently lowered transport costs.[43] But such manufacturing activity offered little employment compared to textile production.

CHAPTER 3

Antwerp as a Port Town

So far it has been established that, under the French régime, commercial circles in Antwerp carried out a continuing policy of industrial disinvestment and thus brought about the collapse of the town's flourishing textile industry. It has also been suggested that the basic explanation for this must be sought in the choice made by most holders of capital in favour of high and quick profits from commerce and finance instead of significant investment in durable means of production which could only be written off after long periods of time. This chapter will show the transformation which the harbour traffic and its related activities underwent between 1815 and the mid nineteenth century; the effects which these developments had upon the level and structure of employment; and, finally, the way in which family incomes within the working population evolved during this period.

The union of Belgium and Holland after the defeat of Napoleon at last put Antwerp in a position to develop into a commercial port of international importance. On 21 June 1814, the Prince of Orange abolished tonnage dues on Belgian ships which had since 1809 been levied by the Hollanders on the Scheldt traffic. A month later, the 'Eight Articles of London', which would form the constitution of the United Kingdom of the Netherlands, guaranteed complete freedom of trade between North and South, including the right of Belgians to trade with the colonies on the same basis as the Hollanders.[1] Nonetheless it was several years before Antwerp could take full advantage of these favourable circumstances. The spectacular growth in shipping between 1814 and 1817 was the result of contingent factors. Until 1 December 1816, Antwerp profited from low transit duties in comparison to its rivals in Holland, with the result that most English exports to the Continent passed through the town. Although the European market was soon saturated with English manufactured goods, traffic on the Scheldt continued to grow until 1817. Nearly 40 per cent of the total tonnage, however, consisted of German or Russian grain imported after the failure of the harvest of 1816 and the consequent food shortages. After 1818, food prices gradually began to fall, dropping so low that the peasantry could scarcely hold their heads above water. The agrarian depression further aggravated the structural difficulties against which Belgian industry struggled after the separation from France. Sustained commercial expansion was, consequently, out of the question.[2] The tide turned during the 1820s. Grain prices rose anew, while industry redirected itself to meet the new marketing conditions and underwent a period of rapid growth. The real possibilities of Antwerp's harbour now became evident. As the French consul-general in Amsterdam wrote to his government in 1828:

> Whatever one may say or do, Amsterdam must bow to the force of circumstances. The habits of commerce and the need for credit shall always keep this town secure, but Antwerp is by nature destined, sooner or later, to become the commercial capital of the Netherlands.

He was not mistaken. In 1829 more than 1,000 ships, with a total capacity of *c*. 129,000 tons, entered the harbour – twice as much as around 1820. The annual growth of traffic on the Scheldt far exceeded that of Amsterdam and Rotterdam. These quantitative changes went in tandem with a qualitative transformation: between 1821 and 1829 Antwerp's share of the imports of colonial produce rose from 40 per cent to 55 per cent, at the expense of competitors in Holland.[3]

The rapidity with which Antwerp raised itself to a first-rank port are attributable to various causes. In contrast to Amsterdam and Rotterdam, the town offered not only an easy and safe connection to the sea, but also docks where ships could be moored for protection against wind and frost, and Antwerp was the preferred point of importation for the southern provinces, a market of 3·4 million people, while the North had only 2 million inhabitants. Moreover, all important industries were located in the South, so that the import of raw cotton, wool, and hides (for the leather industries of Liège) came to be routed through Antwerp. To these natural advantages were added lower wages and taxes, less complex sales regulations, and, last but not least, the absence of strict labour regulations relating to the carrying trade. Ships could be loaded and unloaded much more quickly and cheaply than in the harbours of Holland.[4] For all these reasons, during the 1820s the town on the Scheldt witnessed the establishment of numerous foreign traders (English, French, and above all Germans), the promotion of its colonial trade, ship-building, and maritime insurance by the *Nederlandsche Handel-Maatschappij*, and the foundation of the *Banque d'Anvers*, a branch of the *Société Générale* which gained extensive financial responsibilities.[5] These improvements in the commercial infrastructure in turn stimulated the expansion of the harbour, which by 1830 had become the axis of maritime commerce in the United Kingdom of the Netherlands.

The Belgian Revolution brought severe disruption to Antwerp's economic

Figure 1: Tonnage entering the harbour of Antwerp, 1800–1860

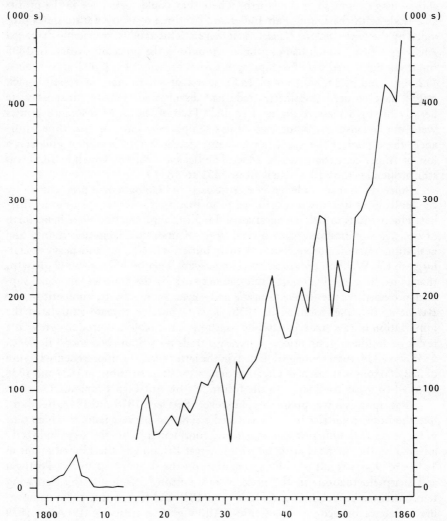

growth. The transfer of power was not only accompanied by acts of war such as military forays and bombardments and by price rises and social unrest, but it meant simultaneously the loss of colonial markets and of the transit trade to Germany.[6] The results were clearly and sharply felt. The number of ships entering

Antwerp's harbour dwindled from more than 1,000 in 1829 to scarcely 400 in 1831 and the total tonnage from *c*. 129,000 to *c*. 46,000. Many merchants and shipowners emigrated to the North, where they could participate in the profitable trade with the Dutch East Indies and continue to enjoy the subsidies provided by the *Nederlandsche Handel-Maatschappij*. This exodus irreparably damaged Antwerp's fleet, which had expanded strongly in the preceding years. In 1835 the town numbered only 54 ships with a total capacity of *c*. 8,000 tons, against 112 ships and *c*. 23,000 tons in 1830; worst of all, the largest vessels which might have ensured translantic trade had disappeared. Finally, finances were heavily hit by a massive flight of capital. Two of the eight insurance houses went out of business, while two others temporarily gave up maritime insurance; the capital of the other houses amounted to barely 3 million guilders, a loss of 70 per cent compared to 1830. The *Banque d'Anvers*, which in 1830 was still profitable, showed a deficit from 1831 to 1834.[7]

Since the transit trade between Antwerp and Cologne had been cut off by the Hollanders, the town was forced to incline itself towards the internal market. Fluctuations in Belgian agrarian and industrial production were henceforth of decisive significance. After several years of understandable uncertainty and hesitation, manufacturers resumed their initiatives. Mining and heavy metallurgy in the Walloon provinces even underwent a period of accelerated growth, thanks to the construction of a railroad network by the State and financial support provided by the *Société Générale* and – even more – by its competitor, the *Banque de Belgique*, founded in 1835. This favourable climate stimulated the importation of raw materials, while consumption of colonial produce grew as a result of declining grain prices. Antwerp's trade now flourished anew. Between 1833 and 1838, total tonnage doubled; in the latter year, the unprecedented figure of 222,000 tons was reached. Creation of new credit institutions in 1837 and 1838 testified to great confidence in the future felt by Antwerp's capitalists.[8]

The optimism was premature, however. Between 1838 and 1842, Belgium, like the other countries of Europe, faced a series of harvest failures which sent grain prices rocketing. At the same time, continental industries were indirectly affected by the financial crisis which hit Great Britain and the United States in 1836–1839 as a result of risky speculation on the debts of Spain and Portugal and sharp fluctuations in the price of raw cotton.[9] Alongside this, growing tensions between Belgium and Holland in 1838 and fear of war had a dampening influence on economic activities. Although the treaty of 19 April 1839 ended political difficulties, it meant for Belgium the loss of Limburg over the Maas, German Luxemburg, and the town of Maastricht, some 380,000 consumers. These factors considered, the decline of traffic on the Scheldt was hardly surprising. In 1840 and 1841, total tonnage was nearly 30 per cent below the level of 1838.[10]

From 1843 there were signs of recovery. Completion of the *ijzeren Rijn*, an 'Iron Rhine' of direct rail lines linking Antwerp and Cologne, gave an enormous impetus to the transit trade. Shipping gradually increased and, in 1846, surpassed all earlier peaks: *c*. 282,000 tons were moved on the Scheldt.[11]

The wave of expansion, however, soon broke. The potato blight of 1845 and the failure of the rye harvest in 1846 caused a terrifying dearth throughout western and central Europe, and, since workers had to devote all their wages to foodstuffs, demand fell for cheap fabrics. The implications for the cotton industry were all the more serious because entrepreneurs faced sharp rises in the prices of raw cotton as a result of poor American harvests. Rural linen-weaving, which had already long struggled against structural difficulties, was the most severely hit: it could no longer compete with the mechanized production of England. And all was compounded by financial crisis. Railroad companies were forced to seek new funds from their stockholders in order to complete construction begun during the preceding short-lived boom. External credit was lacking, since it had been mobilized for massive imports of grain from Russia, and the balance of trade was pushed even further into deficit. The climax came when grain prices collapsed after the good harvest of 1847, ruining countless farmers and bankrupting many speculators. Several banks stopped payments. In 1848 the economic crisis was further aggravated by social and political revolutions which broke out in many countries of Europe.[12]

Shipping at Antwerp clearly reflected the general depression: in 1848 only 176,000 tons entered the harbour, nearly 40 per cent less than in 1846.[13] This sharp decline, combined with the paralysis of all industrial activities, vastly increased the misery. According to the director of communal tax service, the economic crisis created social dislocation incomparably more severe than in the preceding years. Unemployment reached such high levels that the municipal authorities resolved to open large workshops and to carry out public works at their own cost.[14]

Fortunately this slump in the trade cycle did not last long. In 1852 there came a period of rapid expansion, lasting until 1873 and interrupted only by two short recessions. Never before had European international trade progressed with such gigantic strides as between 1850 and 1860: its volume increased by more than 87 per cent.[15] This unequalled growth stimulated Belgian industrial production, further encouraged by the strong growth of internal demand heightened by agrarian development, rapid extension of the railroad network, and the expansion of credit. Between 1850 and 1860 real industrial output increased by 63 per cent, the highest level in the nineteenth century.[16] Antwerp's trade thus received extremely powerful stimuli simultaneously. Shipping jumped to *c.* 500,000 tons in the early 1860s, twice as much as around 1850. The town on the Scheldt had bypassed Amsterdam and stood on the verge of overtaking Rotterdam.[17]

Did the growth of shipping and commerce compensate for the loss of jobs caused by the decay of the textile industry? The census of 1796 and the population registers of 1830, analyzed by Jos De Belder and Jules Hannes, respectively,[18] permit an estimate of the proportion of people over 12–13 years of age who were employed. Although these sources have their limitations,[19] they do suggest some general trends. Within thirty years, the level of employment had fallen by more than 14 per cent. For the female labour force in particular the economic transformation had disastrous results: the proportion of women employed

Proportion of men and women over 12–13 years of age in employment in Antwerp, 1796 and 1830

	Total over 12–13	Employed	Proportion (per cent)
1796			
Males	15,831	14,036	88·16
Females	21,231	12,410	58·45
Total	37,062	26,446	71·36
1830			
Males	22,980	18,803	81·82
Females	28,964	11,969	41·32
Total	51,944	30,625	58·96

fell from 58·5 per cent in 1796 to scarcely 41 per cent in 1830. The following two decades brought no improvement. In 1846 the proportion of all those over 13 in employment was less than 58 per cent; for men and women, the proportions were 80 per cent and 37 per cent respectively. In no other of the major towns of Belgium were such low levels to be found.[20] Ghent, the most industrialized town in

Employed men and women as percentages of total male and female population over 13 years of age in Antwerp, Liège, Brussels, and Ghent, 1846

	Males	Females	Total
Antwerp	79·93	37·10	57·58
Liège	86·95	43·01	64·15
Brussels	87·61	43·66	64·48
Ghent	93·30	53·91	72·47

mid-nineteenth century Belgium, included the greatest number of employed: some 93 per cent of men and nearly 54 per cent of the women over thirteen. The female labour force was predominantly concentrated in the cotton factories, flax mills, the lace industry, and the clothing trade. Brussels was in second place, although it had only a few factories; 'outwork industries' such as clothing, footwear manufacture, lacework and furniture, various luxury trades, construction, and the domestic sector provided a living for many wage labourers. The working population in the capital was nearly 7 per cent larger than in Antwerp. Brussels was followed closely by Liège, where heavy engineering and coal mining grew rapidly; in 1846 these two sectors employed 15 per cent of the total population over thirteen years of age. The discrepancy between Antwerp on one hand and Ghent, Liège, and

Brussels on the other was too pronounced to be ascribed simply to hypothetical differences in statistical procedures. That Antwerp and Ghent had respectively the lowest and highest rates of employment suggests rather than the explanation lies in the divergent economic development of the two cities: a commercial port offered far less employment than an industrial town.[21]

The economic transformation of Antwerp also brought drastic changes in occupational distribution.[22] The conversion from textile centre to port town signified that on one hand a large slice of the female population was eliminated from the labour market and that on the other the majority of those occupied had henceforth nothing more to supply than unskilled labour. Whereas in 1796 more than 30 per cent of all women or 51 per cent of those employed were engaged in lacework and textile manufacture, the proportions thirty years later were 8 per cent and 20 per cent respectively. Domestic service and casual labour now played predominant roles; together they accounted for 19 per cent of the total female population or 47 per cent of all women in active employment. The growth of casual labour was most spectacular: the number of women dependent on it for a living rose twenty-fold between 1796 and 1830. The other sectors of economic life made hardly any impact on female employment. The sole exceptions were the clothing and retail trades, which in 1830 occupied 10 per cent of all women or 23 per cent of those employed. It can be assumed that the proportions of those engaged in the latter trade were in reality much higher than the official figures indicate. It seems scarcely plausible that around 1830 not one woman collected rags, nor that only 36 made a living selling vegetables and another 22 as fishwives – the less so since the number of male costermongers was negligible.[23] The explanation for this must be that such activities were not conducted full time. Along with a host of odd jobs which met the demands of low-income groups for second-hand goods, repairs, and cheap services, they made up part of what Third World specialists today call the 'informal sector'. In any case, even supposing that many former cotton spinners, laceworkers, and embroiderers could take refuge in such forms of economic activity, the conclusion must stand that by 1830 few women in Antwerp had a more or less regular income.

The census of 1846 shows no fundamental changes following the Belgian Revolution.[24] The vast majority of employed women were still engaged in casual labour, domestic service, retailing, lacework, and the clothing trade at mid-century. The latter was the sole sector which both absolutely and proportionally employed more women than before. This trade now brought together *c.* 15 per cent of the total female population over thirteen, against *c.* 7 per cent in 1830. The growth took place at the expense of the male labour force: while in 1796 only 0·5 per cent and in 1830 around 13 per cent of all self-employed tailors were women, the proportion in 1846 had soared to 64 per cent – a clear sign of social degradation.

Two transformations took place in the occupational distribution of the male population between the end of the eighteenth century and the Belgian Revolution. In the first place, the proportion of men over 12–13 employed in the textile industry and clothing trades dropped from *c.* 29 per cent to *c.* 10 per cent. In the second place, the occupations which directly or indirectly depended on shipping grew significantly. In 1830 trade provided a living to some 11 per cent of all men, against 9 per cent in 1796, while the proportion of those engaged in transport more than doubled. The percentage of woodworkers also rose significantly: from *c.* 4 per cent in 1796 to *c.* 8 per cent in 1830. Although this growth derived partially from construction of public works, as shown by the expansion of employment in the building trades, it must above all be ascribed to the foundation of shipyards during the mid 1820s; between 1825 and 1829 at least 45 large ships were built at Antwerp.[25] For similar reasons, the number of smiths rose from 88 in 1796 to 395 in 1830, when they represented nearly 48 per cent of all metal workers.

No single occupation, however, could compare with casual labour, which in 1830 provided some 11 per cent of the total male population with a living, around 9 per cent more than thirty years earlier. If all casual labourers are considered as dockers and added to the percentages of those employed in trade, transport, wood-working, and the smiths, then around 38 per cent of the total male population over thirteen was engaged directly or indirectly in port-associated activities at the time of the Belgian Revolution. In any case, casual labour and transport remained predominant, even expanding, during the second quarter of the nineteenth century. Together they provided a living for 23 per cent of all men over thirteen in 1846, 6 per cent more than in 1830. Wood-working, on the other hand, used only 5 per cent, compared to around 8 per cent in 1830.[26] This decline must be ascribed to the collapse of ship-building at Antwerp. Although the government did all it could to favour this once flourishing industry, Antwerp's businessmen refused to provide the requisite capital. They were no longer interested in direct sales and transport but concentrated on the trade in goods already delivered. In the short term this was sensible: Belgium had no colonies with which to trade to the benefit of national shipping, and its industries were not yet sufficiently developed as a basis for a profitable export trade.[27] In the long term, however, the choice of the Antwerp merchants after 1830 of non-risky commission trading entailed a serious loss of industrial opportunities.[28]

Only two industries received any impetus at all from the expansion of trade. According to the licence fees, the number of workers employed in the tobacco factories rose from 122 in 1830 to 208 in 1842.[29] During the following years, this growth continued, but its tempo diminished as a result of protectionist policies which the Belgian government introduced from 1844 to encourage internal tobacco cultivation. Not until the last quarter of the nineteenth century did the Antwerp tobacco industry experience a real boom.[30] The second industry, sugar refining, had developed strongly during the union of Belgium and Holland. Antwerp not only became the greatest importer of raw sugar on the Continent but also concentrated on the processing of the raw material because of the fiscal advantages conceded to sugar refiners by William I in 1822. For every 55 kg. exported they received total reimbursement of the import duties levied on a quintal of raw sugar; given that the weight loss during refining amounted to as much as 25 per cent, the entrepreneurs in fact received an export premium.[31] Hence the number of Antwerp's refineries rose in 1831 to 31; the industry at that point provided a living for more than 500 workers.[32] The Belgian Revolution signified only a temporary halt to this growth, as is indicated by the foundation of new firms: at least 22 between 1831 and 1837, although most were small businesses.[33] From then on Antwerp's sugar refiners had to combat growing difficulties. The German customs union, the *Zollverein*, raised import duties to protect its own products, while the Belgian government heavily taxed foreign sugar to support internal sugarbeet cultivation. One firm after another collapsed. In 1842 the remaining businesses employed barely 280 workers. When the import duty was lowered four years later, the industry received a fresh impulse, but the recovery was not long-lasting. Antwerp soon lost to England its position as the leading European market for sugar.[34]

The dearth of new employment opportunities altered the social status of some men's occupations. After the decline of textile manufacturing only a limited number of 'honourable' trades remained open to skilled artisans. Since the supply of labour far exceeded the demand, more and more craftsmen had to make do with underpaid jobs. Among painters the proportion of journeymen in the total number employed rose from 3 per cent to 51 per cent between 1796 and 1830; in footwear manufacturing from 8 per cent to 39 per cent; in the clothing trade from 8 per cent to 45 per cent; in metallurgy from 8 per cent to 53 per cent; in carpentry from 21 per cent to 50 per cent; in masonry from 50 per cent to 76 per cent.[35] Men who because of their age, physical infirmities, or illnesses could not perform heavy labour had to find an alternative in the retail trade, which generally meant hawking fruit, vegetables, fish, matches, rags, etc.

In short, by the mid-nineteenth century, the socio-economic situation of the Antwerp working class differed radically from that of the *ancien régime*. From a textile centre in which men as well as women and children, young as well as old, strong as well as weak could win a meagre living, Antwerp turned into a port town in which one type of work, based on male physical strength predominated. This structural shift not only disqualified and degraded thousands of artisans but also brought chronic underemployment or unemployment to all workers whose physical condition did not permit heavy labour. When the Charity Bureau drew up a detailed report on poverty in 1860, it declared:

> Antwerp is no longer an industrial town. Nearly all of the needy are jacks-of-all-trades without permanent occupations. Those who mainly and increasingly depend on public support are, in order: day-labourers, longshoremen, ropemakers, tailors, painters, carpenters, and masons' labourers. The overwhelming majority are described as 'casual labourers'. Although it is impossible to be accurately informed about the poor in such a large town, they are mainly described as 'dockers', and that is generally correct. There are few men who wholly lack professional qualifications, but above a certain age they simply cannot find work.[36]

Growing dependence on shipping, moreover, meant heightened economic insecurity. Dock employment was not only dangerous and exhausting but also particularly vulnerable to cyclic depression and seasonality. The number of ships entering the harbour might fluctuate by up to 50 per cent from one year to the next and by a fifth from one month to another.[37] Nor was irregular work limited to dockers. For seamen, bargehands, carriers, porters, shipyard men, sawyers, carpenters, metalworkers, sailmakers, and ropemakers work was sporadic, though dockers were the worst off, because they were the most easily replaced. A minority of foremen and stowers excepted, work in the harbour required only physical strength and a certain amount of dexterity. Hundreds of men fulfilled the requirements, creating fierce competition amongst casual labour.[38]

What impact did these sharp and profound changes in the structure of employment have on the income of Antwerp's labouring classes during the first half of the nineteenth century? There is no single easy answer. No business archives so far identified allow wage patterns to be re-constructed; the daily or weekly wages of specific categories of workers included in the industrial censuses are useless for reasons already given (see p.14); and accounts of the municipal authorities and other public institutions contain data on the salaries of clerks and officials but very little on wages. To get some crude indication of the general trend, one must apply the same method as in Chapter I: to assemble the wages of all able-bodied men and women between 20 and 54 noted in the poor lists, and to express average earnings of the occupational groups for which sufficient information is available in kilograms of rye bread.[39]

From this investigation it appears that the higher money wages gained by workers in the textile, foot wear, and clothing industries merely sufficed to hold their purchasing power at more or less the same level. In 1855 the real wages of adult males engaged in these trades were on average 11 per cent lower than around 1780. The living standards of painters and masons' labourers, on the other hand, fell sharply: in 1855 they earned, in real terms, 32 per cent and 35 per cent less per day respectively than in 1780. Expansion of the building trades in the first quarter of the nineteenth century thus in no sense improved the welfare of the workers concerned; their growth in numbers testified to the lack of alternative employment opportunities rather than to the attractions of the industry itself.

The figures also show that in 1855 casual labourers earned much less than artisans and, more importantly, that their real income contrasted unfavourably with that received by skilled textile workers around 1780. While the daily wage of the latter had been equivalent to *c.* 5·5 kg. of ryebread, the former in the mid-nineteenth century had to make do with *c.* 4·2 kg., a decrease of nearly 24 per cent. It could be argued that the figures from 1855 give too sombre a picture and that male cotton spinners in 1780 had made only 3·5 stivers or *c.* 2·4 kg. of ryebread a day in 1780. These objections, however, are of limited validity. If the real wages of casual labourers are calculated for the entire period 1851–1860, then the average reached only 4·6 kg. of ryebread or 16 per cent less than the incomes of silk weavers and weavers of mixed fabrics seventy years earlier. As for cotton spinners, in 1780 they represented scarcely 12 per cent of all adult males noted in the poor lists, while textile workers who averaged 8 stivers or *c*. 5·5 kg. of ryebread a day, made up more than 37 per cent. Moreover it must be noted that the difference between the minimum and maximum wages was sharply reduced. In 1780, the ratio for silkworkers was 1:3 and for men employed in the cotton industry even 1:10. A half-century later, the best paid casual labourers received only half as much again as their colleagues; 90 per cent of them received the same daily wage. All in all, around 1780 *c*. 40 per cent of able-bodied men aged 20 to 54 earned less than 5 kg. of ryebread a day, in 1827 70 per cent, and by the middle of the century nearly 80 per cent.

The purchasing power of female workers was drastically affected. Despite the increase in prices of essential foodstuffs their nominal wage did not rise between 1780 and 1827, so that real incomes fell by 28 per cent. According to the poor lists, two thirds of all able-bodied women between 20 and 54 earned less than one kg. of ryebread a day. In other words, the wages of the vast majority failed to support a single adult, even ignoring short-term fluctuations. A single example: the famine of 1816–1817 reduced the purchasing power of knitters to *c*. 0·375 kg of ryebread a day. It seems incredible that women were prepared to work for such a pittance, but most had no choice. After the collapse of the cotton industry, Antwerp lacked industries which could absorb the supply of female labour, resulting in extremely low wagerates. There were women, it goes without saying, who earned more than the averages given in the table, but they were a small minority. As one high official wrote in 1833: 'Laceworkers who receive 0·50 francs [5·51 stivers] a day are considered well paid. Most, however, get 0·20 francs [2·20 stivers] a day with the greatest of difficulty, and for that pittance they must work very hard and toil for many hours.'[40]

Although working women received wage rises during the 1830s,[41] they did not manage to restore their earlier living standards. Between 1840 and 1860 the real daily wages of laceworkers equalled or surpassed the level of 1780 only in 6 out of 21 years. Knitters, embroiderers, laundresses, and seamstresses never again received the same equivalents of ryebread. In 1850, the year in which food-prices were at their lowest, their real wages were still 10 per cent lower than at the end of the eighteenth century. In contrast, the growing demand for casual labour had positive effects. Indeed, no other women were as well paid: around 2 kg. of ryebread a day in 1827 and an average of 2·4 kg. between 1840 and 1860. The relative affluence of this category however did not counterbalance either the socio-economic degradation of other female workers or the expulsion of numerous women from the labour market. While in 1780 barely 20 per cent of adult women registered in the poor lists were unemployed, by the middle of the nineteenth century the figure had risen to 45 per cent.

The glut of female labour depressed the wages of children.[42] Since the great majority of employed girls lived from lacemaking and more than half of the employed boys were engaged in textile manufacture (especially cotton spinning) and in the clothing trade, there is little sense in classifying them by occupation, nor, due to the small difference in wages, in making distinctions between sexes. If the average daily wage and the corresponding quantity of ryebread paid to children aged 6 to 10 and 11 to 15 are calculated for the years 1780 and 1827, it becomes clear that the fall in purchasing power was nothing short of catastrophic. In 1827, boys and girls from 6 to 10 had to work a whole day for the equivalent of about one-third of a kg. of ryebread, or 28 per cent less than in 1780. Those aged 11 to 15 were even worse off: despite inflation, their average daily wage declined from 2 to 1·75 stivers – a reduction of 37 per cent in real terms. Since more and more adults were forced to take odd jobs and many others were permanently unemployed, it no longer made sense for entrepreneurs to hire the labour of children during the second half of the nineteenth century. The proportion of boys and girls employed fell from 45 per cent in 1827 to 11·5 per cent in 1855.

The transition from textile centre to port town thus had disastrous consequences for Antwerp's working class. Although the nominal wages of adult men rose between 1780 and 1855, they could scarcely keep pace with inflation. Growing dependence on shipping, moreover, meant that a wide spectrum of occupations became prey to more casual hiring practices and that the irregularity of employment was accentuated. The same process entailed underemployment or even unemployment for a majority of women and children, while real wages of those who could find a job were drastically reduced. The combination of these factors brought a sharp decline in family incomes. As the Charity Bureau in 1860 plainly stated:

> Even a skilled and steady worker whose family is not too numerous and whose wife is strong and active nowadays has difficulty in making ends meet with the daily wages paid in most occupations; he does not enjoy the same welfare as in former times. The explanation for this is that wages have risen too little while rent and food have steadily grown more expensive, and although the cost of clothing has fallen, the quality has deteriorated.[43]

PART II

A Market for Casual Labour

CHAPTER 4

The Uprooted

Antwerp would never have become a harbour of international importance in such a short time without the availability of an extensive and cheap proletariat. Indeed, keeping labour costs low was one of Antwerp's most important advantages in the face of its Dutch rivals. It is doubtful, however, that workers engaged in port-associated activities came primarily from the ranks of textile workers, most of whom were neither able nor eager to get a job in the harbour; casual labour not only required great physical strength but also meant loss of perceived status. As long as there was still the chance of employment in 'honourable trades', even if increasingly poorly paid, skilled artisans did not offer themselves for employment on the docks. How, then, is the spectacular rise in the number of casual labourers to be explained? The only reasonable answer is that the local reserve force was supplemented by outsiders. Therefore it is necessary to discover whether immigration patterns changed during this period. Did the growth of shipping and commerce parallel demographic expansion, and, if so, was there a causal connection between the two processes? In other words, did new employment opportunities in the port attract workers from the countryside, or did migrants leave home because all their other options had been exhausted? The question requires a survey of the relative overpopulation in the regions from which most immigrants came.

During the second half of the eighteenth century, Antwerp's population expanded slowly; in 1755, the town had between 42,000 and 43,000 inhabitants;[1] By 1780, the number had climbed to c. 50,000[2] at an average annual growth rate of 0·65 per cent. Although we lack reliable data, the net gains between 1780 and 1800 were unquestionably modest: at the turn of the century, the number of inhabitants amounted to 55,000 at the most.[3] During the first decade of the nineteenth century, there were some signs of an upsurge. By 1812 the population had risen to c. 60,000[4], some 11 per cent more than around

Figure 2: Population of Antwerp, 1801–1860

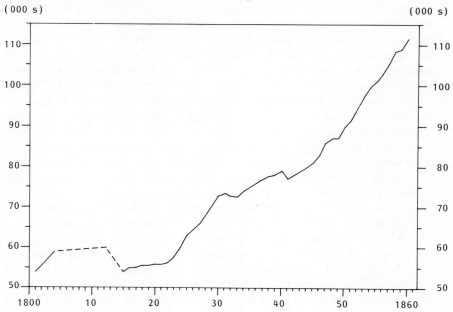

(000 s)   (000 s)

1800, or an annual average increase of 0·7 per cent. This expansion however was of short duration. Political, military, and – above all – economic difficulties combined with changes in regime to induce massive emigration, returning the population to the level of 1800. Despite a minor recovery in 1816, the number of inhabitants remained almost constant until about 1820, when a century of sustained growth, interrupted only by short, temporary declines, began. Between 1821 and 1830, the average increase amounted to no less than 3·1 per cent *per annum*, a figure exceeded only during the period 1881–1890. The general dislocation caused by the Belgian Revolution checked this expansion, but after several years the population began to grow anew and from 1846 rose at an accelerated tempo (Figure 2). To be precise: the annual average growth-rate leapt from 0·7 per cent in 1831–1845 to 1·8 per cent in 1846–1860. By 1860, Antwerp had nearly 112,000 inhabitants or twice as many as 40 years earlier. Never before had the town been so densely populated.[5]

Demographic expansion resulted mainly from immigration. Between 1841 and 1850, migration accounted for 58 per cent of the town's population growth, and during the following decade the proportion jumped to 71 per cent.[6] Although no continuous series of data is available on either the numbers of migrants or births and deaths during the previous century, it can be presumed with some degree of certainty that the town's net gains were primarily due to immigration in that period as well. From 1750, complaints came with increasing frequency from the poor relief authorities about the growing proportion of outsiders among the total population eligible for public support. In the early 1760s, immigrants deemed unable to provide for themselves were forbidden to reside in the town. This ordinance was apparently not enforced, for in 1779 it was declared that all transgressors should leave Antwerp, and one year later it was further specified that those who had lived in the town for fewer than three years should provide information concerning their incomes.[7] Despite these and other measures, migrants continued to stream in. After the turn of the century, the number grew even faster, as evident from the percentages of immigrants in the total population: 27 per cent in 1796; 32 per cent in 1830; and nearly 36 per cent in 1846.[8] This last figure was on the same scale as those estimated for Rotterdam and London around 1850: 33 per cent and 39 per cent, respectively.[9]

Why did so many come to Antwerp? Were they drawn to the town by the prospect of improved living conditions, or were they driven from their birthplace by lack of means of subsistence? In the third quarter of the eighteenth century, both factors may have played a role: Antwerp's textile industry was in full expansion, giving the town drawing power, and the accelerated growth of the rural population probably aggravated social dislocation in the countryside.[10] Can the same be said of the first half of the nineteenth century? Undoubtedly, the massive public works carried out by Napoleon, who planned to turn the town on the Scheldt into a naval harbour, stimulated immigration between 1804 and 1814, though this primarily involved movement from France and the Walloon provinces. Construction of the docks proceeded slowly, so Napoleon brought hundreds of galley-slaves from Bicêtre and Brest to Antwerp in 1804 and put them to work. Apart from these extraordinary labour forces, there were no fewer than 2,000 foreigners, mostly French, engaged in the construction of the docks around 1807. The fortifications begun a few years later quickened immigration. In 1811, the prefect, Charles Cochon, declared that 800 to 900 labourers came to Antwerp annually: some 100 carpenters, joiners, locksmiths, and the like, all natives of French ports such as Brest, Cherbourg, Dunkirk, Le Havre, and Rochefort; 250 to 300 *terrassiers* (navvies) from the Walloon provinces recruited by the military engineers; and at least 300 to 400 masons, mostly Walloons, engaged in the construction of roads and bridges. Cochon believed that only a few of the labourers would remain in Antwerp. He was right: in 1816, the provincial governor wrote that the vast majority of foreign construction workers had left the town.[11]

The period 1820–1860 poses more problems. During these forty years, the population doubled, mainly as a result of immigration, even though employment possibilities had receded sharply. The demographic growth of Antwerp was exceeded by that of Brussels, Ghent, and Liège. Each also experienced considerable immigration[12] but, unlike Antwerp, the three other centres had labour-intensive industries, so that pull factors applied. The harbour town, in contrast, had little to offer: by 1820, textile manufacturing had lost its importance and the growth of shipping benefited only a portion of the male population. Local authorities themselves were thoroughly conscious that immigration worsened the structural imbalance between population and employment opportunities. From the end of the eighteenth century, impoverished newcomers who listed as their occupation cottonspinner, silk-thrower, laceworker, knitter, or seamstress were forbidden to settle in the town.[13] In order to staunch the flow of countrydwellers, the minimum residence period before which claims for public relief could be made was sytematically lengthened. In the early nineteenth century, one year sufficed, but the crisis of 1816–1817 changed that. On 1 May, 1817, the director of the Charity Bureau wrote to the mayor: 'The number of those drawing support is reaching enormous proportions because of the admission of immigrants, who are robbing our native poor of a growing part of their patrimony, although it is all too insufficient to cover the slimmest needs.'[14] Since the municipal authorities were not prepared to increase the support funds, it was resolved to increase the residence period to four years. A quarter-century later, new measures were introduced. Immigration during the preceding decades had been so continuous and extensive that the authorities pessimistically argued that

> within a few years we shall have to spend the greatest part of our income on the maintenance of a mass of immigrants who lack the means of subsistence; they come to Antwerp and vegetate for four years, either of their own free will or at the advice of others, after which they live at the expense of our native poor or enlarge the already significant number of beggars who remain at our cost in the provincial *dépôt de mendicité*.[15]

Other large towns faced the same problem. Everywhere the disparity between social needs and relief funds reached unprecedented levels. Hence, the central government legislated in 1845 that in the future paupers could request aid from the poor relief only if they had lived in the community longer than eight years.[16]

One might suppose that most migrants left their birthplace primarily to better their position; in other words, that they came to the town on the Scheldt because they were attracted by the vigorous expansion of shipping and commerce. At first sight, this hypothesis seems to be supported by the strong connection between the increase in tonnage entering the harbour and the growth in population: for the period 1818–1860, the correlation between the two variables is 0·93 or, expressed otherwise, 86 per cent of the variation in population is explicable in terms of variations in shipping. That both variables had rising trends, however, tends automatically to produce an overly high and positive correlation. If the linear trend in each variable is calculated, and the trend values are subtracted from the original data, then it appears clearly that there is no relationship whatsoever. A closer look at Figures 1 and 2 indeed shows that there was no causal connection between entering tonnage and demographic development. Population began to grow at an accelerated tempo from 1822, although shipping only began its increase three years later. Between 1830 and 1833, the number of inhabitants remained almost stationary, while in the following decade it rose moderately; traffic on the Scheldt, in contrast, had resumed its previous level by 1832 and within the following six years more than doubled. The opposite also happened: entering tonnage diminished by 40 per cent between 1846 and 1848, while the population grew by 5 per cent; average net migration during this period amounted to 2,000 *per annum*, *i.e.*, three to four times more than in the early 1840s.[17]

It should be noted, moreover, that a rise or fall in the numbers of migrants to Antwerp did not necessarily signify that either more or fewer people were on the road. In 1840, for example, the four chief-towns of Antwerp province, Mechelen, Lier, Turnhout, and Antwerp itself, together received just as many newcomers as in 1837 or 1827. A steadily growing proportion of the migrants, however, chose Mechelen over Antwerp, as appears in the following table.[18]

Numbers of migrants to Antwerp, Mechelen, Lier and Turnhout in 1827, 1837 and 1840

Town	Numbers			Per cent		
	1827	1837	1840	1827	1837	1840
Antwerp	2,299	2,011	1,721	77·1	65·8	56·0
Mechelen	393	588	892	13·2	19·2	29·0
Lier	254	253	241	8·5	8·3	7·8
Turnhout	37	204	220	1·2	6·7	7·2
Total	2,983	3,056	3,074	100·0	100·0	100·0

Whereas in 1827 some 77 per cent of all migrants had gone to the port town, the figure in 1840 was only 56 per cent. Mechelen, on the other hand, attracted steadily more the uprooted people: in 1840 the town gained 29 per cent of the aggregate number, compared with 13 per cent in 1827. For lack of more detailed data it is impossible to explain these remarkable shifts. It does not appear unreasonable however to presume that the creation of new employment opportunities in Mechelen during the second quarter of the nineteenth century had some influence; the *Société anonyme pour la filature de lin mécanique*, a large flax mill, for example, provided work in the late 1830s to hundreds of workers, overwhelmingly women and children.[19]

Thus the metropolis and the smaller cities in the province of Antwerp functioned only as centres of relative attraction during the first half of the nineteenth century. Since the principal objective of most migrants was to find work elsewhere, they were prepared to move to any locality where labour was in fair demand. It follows that shifts in the geographic distribution of employment opportunities shaped patterns of migration. This conclusion corresponds to the findings of historical demographers on the high levels of regional and local mobility among Europeans before large-scale industrialization. As Charles Tilly has recently remarked: 'The landless and land-poor moved frequently, sometimes seasonally, in response to the demand for wage-labour'.[20] Contemporaries themselves said as much. In 1843, the director of poor relief at Antwerp declared that most migrants did not come to Antwerp 'in order to set up in business or to carry on their former trade but quite simply to find in another community one way or another the means of existence denied them in their birthplace'.[21]

Migration to Antwerp was not always direct. The *cartes de sûreté* throw some light on the movements of 606 of the 689 newcomers who were listed in Antwerp's population registers in 1817: 359 or 59·2 per cent had come directly to the town, while 247 or 40·8 per cent declared that they had dwelled in other communities in addition to their birthplaces.[22] Women clearly migrated more purposefully and over shorter distances than did men. In 1817 two-thirds of the female migrants to Antwerp came directly from their places of birth and more than 62 per cent were from the province of Antwerp, while, for their male counterparts, the proportions were respectively 54 per cent and 50 per cent. These remarkable differences were related to the specific occupational choices of female migrants: most of them became housemaids (see page 59 below), for whom towns were the most obvious destination.

Migrants who trekked directly from their birthplace to Antwerp generally came shorter distances than the others. Around 85 per cent of the direct migrants of 1817 had come at most 75 km. from their homes, against 64 per cent of those who had journeyed in stages. Most intermediate communities, however, were closer to Antwerp than the birthplaces of the direct migrants. In other words: those who migrated by stages tended to move to 'more advanced areas'. Although less than half of the indirect migrants were natives of the province of Antwerp, nearly 62 per cent had lived there prior to their entry into the town. The same tendency was evident among those born in more distant areas: more than half of the Brabantines came to Antwerp via a community in the province of Antwerp. Similarly, the Hollanders often moved to 'more advanced' places: 12 out of 20 gave as their last place of residence a community in the province of Antwerp, and six among them even gave a community in the immediate surroundings.

It does not follow that the migrants had planned to settle in Antwerp and that they had selected the intervening communities with that goal in mind. The *cartes de sûreté* noted only the birthplace and the last place of residence. It is possible and even highly probable that a number of migrants had lived in more than one community other than their birthplace and that some of them later left the Scheldt town too, as can be deduced from a list of foreigners on relief who lived in Antwerp in 1846–1855 but were chargeable to other communities.[23] This source allows study of the number of moves made by 759 migrants from their birth to their settlement in Antwerp. Some 64 per cent of the foreigners had been born in the northern Netherlands – half of them in the province of North Brabant, especially the rural area south of Bergen op Zoom, Roosendaal, and Breda, a distance of at most 50 km. from Antwerp. Not surprisingly, nearly 62 per cent of these migrants came directly from their homes to the town. Among married migrants, the proportion was significantly higher than among those single: 53 per cent versus 65 per cent. This (not unexpected) difference can be attributed to the employment of nearly all single migrant females as maids by Antwerp families. Altogether, 291 or 38 per cent of the foreigners had lived in one or more other communities in addition to their place of birth. Only 121 had moved from less advanced communities to centres closer to Antwerp. The remaining 170 had at least once gone to communities further distant from Antwerp than their place of birth or had for lengthy periods lived in the harbour town and left it anew; the second case applied to 83 migrants, of whom 57 were unmarried. Both phenomena point out the insecurity of the uprooted population.[24]

To what extent were 'push factors' at work? Witold Kula has argued that during the Industrial Revolution the uprooted peasant was 'not drawn to the town by the prospect of higher wages. He was driven out of the countryside by hunger.'[25] Does this apply to migrants to Antwerp in the first half of the nineteenth century? The present state of research does not yet permit general conclusions regarding the expulsive forces which drove people from their homes. Data on the origins of the migrants, however, do provide some indications. The registers of the *cartes de sûreté* show that more than half of the migrants who came to the town on the Scheldt in 1817 were born in the province of Antwerp, *i.e.*, in communities a maximum of 50 km. from the town; 30·6 per cent were even born in the immediate surroundings of Antwerp, within 25 km. or less. Including those coming from the province of Brabant, nearly seven out of ten migrants moved less than 75 km. away from their birthplace.[26] Thus, most migration into Antwerp was on a short-distance basis, just as in other western European countries.[27] The poor lists indicate that the recruitment area of the port town grew smaller during the second quarter of the nineteenth century. Of the 1,760 families permanently supported by Antwerp's poor relief in 1855, 579 or 33 per cent of them had at least one parent not born in the town. This percentage closely matches the proportion of immigrants in the total population around the middle of the century, some 36 per cent. From an analysis of the distribution of birthplaces of immigrant heads of household and their spouses on the dole in 1855,[28] it appears that more than 72 per cent among them came from the provinces of Antwerp and Brabant. The immediate surroundings of the town had assumed enormous significance: 39 per cent of the newcomers were born in the district of Antwerp, 9 per cent more than in 1817.

Two features of migration into Antwerp, however, remained unaltered. First, the predominance of the countryside: in 1817 as well as in 1855, nearly 75 per cent of the migrants were born in rural communities. Second, the foremost regions of expulsion were always the same. When the birthplaces of all migrants from the province of Antwerp are represented cartographically, it can be seen that most of the communities were situated south of a northwest/southeast diagonal

Figure 3: Birthplaces of migrants from the province of Antwerp who entered Antwerp in 1817

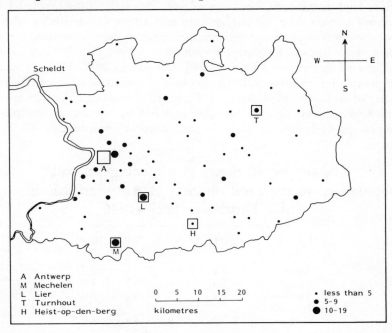

Figure 4: Birthplaces of migrants from the province of Antwerp receiving relief in Antwerp in 1855

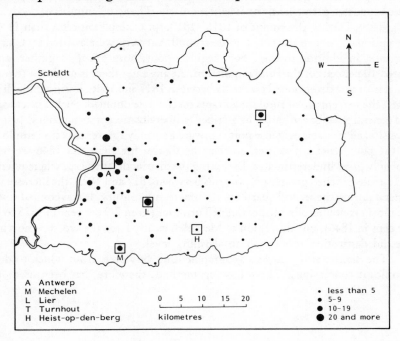

which more or less split the province in two (Figures 3 and 4). How did the two regions differ? Lack of detailed studies on the organization of agrarian production, land distribution, evolution of rent, etc. make it impossible to give conclusive answers. Provisionally, one can only attempt to determine whether or not there was a connection between the extent of the relative surplus population and the degree of geographic mobility.

Censuses carried out by the Charity Bureaux in 1817, 1825, 1836, and 1846 provide information on the proportion of supported needy in the rural districts of Antwerp, Mechelen, and Turnhout.[29] Although the data are not immune to criticism because the criteria applied by the various institutions were not specified, they do allow for some rough comparisons.

The supported needy as percentage of total population, in the rural districts of Antwerp, Mechelen, and Turnhout, 1817–1846

District	1817	1825	1836	1846
Antwerp	3·5	4·0	6·3	7·7
Mechelen	5·1	5·0	6·7	9·9
Turnhout	3·6	2·9	6·2	8·0
Provincial average	4·0	3·9	6·4	8·0

To interpret these figures, it must be remembered that they all relate to people who were supported permanently or at least regularly. The actual number of needy was far greater. During the famine of 1816–1817, for example, not less than 11,493 'exceptional' poor in the countryside around Antwerp were assisted by Charity Bureaux, in addition to the 7,865 'regular' poor; both groups together represented 10 per cent of the rural population. At any rate, there is no doubt that the social situation deteriorated markedly between 1817 and 1846: during these thirty years, the percentage of rural inhabitants on the dole doubled. Such a spectacular and general growth can hardly be ascribed to liberalization of social policy. Just the opposite: all available evidence points toward a steadily stricter selection employed by the poor relief authorities, so that the figures for 1836 and 1846 are most probably gross underestimates. Excepting the district of Antwerp, where poverty had already reached greater proportions between 1817 and 1825, the increase was general during the second quarter of the nineteenth century. It was comparatively the most pronounced in the district of Turnhout (from 2·9 per cent in 1825 to 8·0 per cent in 1846), but the region of Mechelen clearly fared the worst – nowhere else did destitution reach such an alarming level.

The district is too large a geographic unit, however, from which to draw significant conclusions. The following method, therefore, has been used. For

Figure 5: Rural communities in the province of Antwerp in which the proportion of assisted poor out of the local population lay above the district average during at least two of the four years considered (1817, 1825, 1836, and 1846)

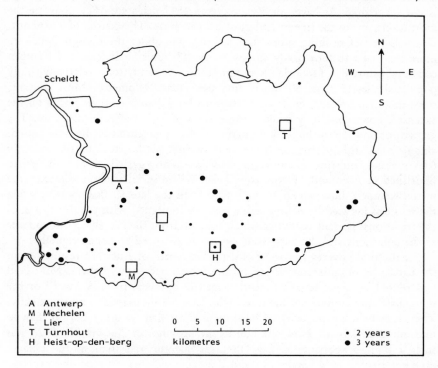

all rural communities, the proportion of the assisted poor out of the local population was calculated for the years 1817, 1825, 1836, and 1846.[30] All villages where the relationship during at least two of the four periods considered lay above the district average were then mapped out (Figure 5). In this way, five regions can be distinguished:

(1) the area to the north of the northwest/southeast diagonal, which apparently was spared from extreme poverty;
(2) six villages in the Scheldt polders north of Antwerp where distinct social problems existed;
(3) the triangle formed by Antwerp, Mechelen, and Heist-op-den-Berg, which contained only a limited number of pauper-concentrations;
(4) the central and south/southeastern portions of the province, where destitution was highly pronounced; and
(5) the southwestern corner of the province, marked by a high degree of

destitution; nearly every community in this area numbered 15 to 20 per cent assisted poor during the dearths of 1816/17 and 1845/46.

The absence of extreme poverty in the first region, which covered the largest area of the district of Turnhout and the eastern part of the district of Antwerp, is not surprising. As baron de Keverberg in 1817 declared: 'The poor are the most numerous in the richest and most fruitful areas. The district of Turnhout, which is in fact nothing more than a heath put under the plough, holds no more than two to four needy among every 100 souls.'[31] Indeed, the Kempen consisted primarily of moorlands and unproductive sandy soils, relatively thinly populated – fewer than 80 inhabitants per square kilometre. Most peasants were small freeholders, far from prosperous but, thanks to their rights on the extensive commons, they could make ends meet, no matter how slimly. The growth of poverty in the second quarter of the nineteenth century was caused, among other things, by the irreversible decline of the rural textile industry (tick-making, knitting of stockings, and flax-spinning), which previously had flourished in Arendonk, Retie, and Dessel.[32] The social situation deteriorated in the Kempen, however, at a quick pace from the late 1840s onwards, when the tensions induced by demographic growth combined with the disruption of the traditional peasant economy which resulted from the parcelling out and sale of the commons and the large-scale clearances financed by urban capital.[33]

Structural poverty in the Scheldt polders north of Antwerp resulted from the particular organization of agriculture which had evolved there. Most land was rented by great tenants, mostly wealthy butchers from Antwerp or the immediate surroundings of the town who fattened thousands of oxen annually. The overwhelming majority of local inhabitants had no other option than to hire out their labour. Nowhere else in the province of Antwerp in 1828 was such a high proportion of day labourers encountered than in the villages of Berendrecht, Lillo, Stabroek, and Zandvliet, 75 per cent on the average, and nowhere else were there so many potential poor, 60 to 90 per cent of the local population.[34]

For lack of information it is at present impossible to explain the relative prosperity of the triangle Antwerp, Mechelen, and Heist-op-den-Berg. 'Relative', because in such villages as Vremde, Kessel, Sint-Katelijne-Waver, and Putte, the potential poor numbered more than 40 per cent.[35] Nor is it clear why so many communal authorities in the centre and south-southeast of the province had permanently to provide some form of assistance to a substantial portion of the population. The extent of destitution in the southwestern corner of the province, in contrast, is easy to explain. Most inhabitants were dispossessed wage labourers engaged in cottage industries, especially linen manufacture, shipbuilding, and brickmaking. The first sector gradually decayed after the turn of the century as a result of Flemish competition, while the other two trades were highly susceptible to climatological and economic fluctuations. According to contemporaries, the precarious living conditions of the local proletariat worsened steadily through the first half of the nineteenth century due to immigration of uprooted cottars from neighbouring areas. By 1828, the potential poor in the Rupelregion represented more than 40 per cent of the total population; in some villages, the proportion even climbed as high as 70 per cent.[36]

Although difficult to interpret, the figures on the number of supported needy indicate that various rural areas in the province of Antwerp in the first half of the nineteenth century had to struggle against a structural and growing social problem. This is borne out by a survey conducted in 1828 at the command of the central government in The Hague. The report, from which some data have already been cited, not only stated how many in every community were considered poor, but it also provided (vague) indications concerning their occupations.[37] From the following summary, two conclusions can be drawn.

The potential poor as percentage of total population in the rural districts of Antwerp, Mechelen, and Turnhout, 1828

District	Casual labourers	Domestic servants	Artisans and journeymen	Miscellaneous labour	Total
Antwerp	24·1	6·5	6·5	1·6	38·7
Mechelen	20·5	11·8	2·1	0·8	35·2
Turnhout	11·8	8·6	5·7	1·0	27·1
Provincial average	19·0	8·8	4·9	1·1	33·8

First, the authorities themselves catalogued nearly 34 per cent of the rural population as potentially poor, of whom the vast majority (4 in 5) were unskilled workers. Taking into account that real wages in the countryside around Antwerp were halved between 1750 and 1850,[38] it comes as no surprise that a growing number had no other solution besides emigration. Second, proletarianization and impoverishment processes reached their greatest proportions in the districts of Antwerp and Mechelen. It might be expected, consequently, that in these areas comparatively more villagers hit the road than in the district of Turnhout. The census of 1840 verifies this deduction.[39]

During a single year, 1840, 2·4 per cent of all rural folk in the province of Antwerp left their homes. When all rural communities in which the level of emigration exceeded the general average are portrayed cartographically (Figure 6), it can be seen that the centres with the highest percentage of emigrants were predominantly situated in the district of Antwerp. It is remarkable, however, that the two other districts more or less matched one another and that the Rupelregion contained few nuclei of emigration. Uprooting was thus not necessarily directly proportional to the level of impoverishment. This is supported by further detailed analysis. As before, all villages have been checked for a possible connection between the percentage of supported needy in 1836 and the percentage

Figure 6: Rural communities in the province of Antwerp
in which the level of emigration exceeded the provincial
average, 1840

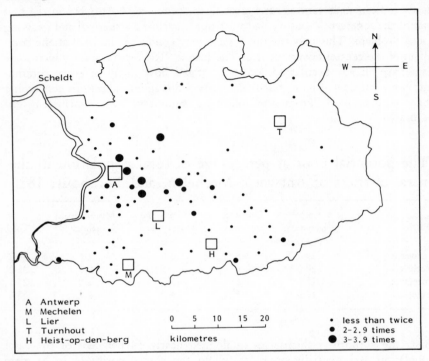

A   Antwerp
M   Mechelen
L   Lier
T   Turnhout
H   Heist-op-den-berg

0   5   10   15   20

kilometres

• less than twice
● 2–2.9 times
● 3–3.9 times

of emigrants in 1840, yielding a correlation coefficient of 0·25. In other words:
only 6 per cent of the variation in emigration can be explained by variations in
poverty. It follows that social need as such was not of a decisive importance.
People obviously did not pull up their roots simply because they faced underemployment or poor wages. Only when they had no other alternative, when
every possibility was exhausted, were they prepared to trek elsewhere. Hence,
only a few native paupers left the Rupelregion. Although circumstances there
were miserable, they did not seem absolutely hopeless: expansion of shipbuilding and brickmaking created new sources of employment, however insufficient
and irregular. The existence of these trades further explains why the Rupelregion witnessed substantial net migration: many country dwellers from neighbouring areas chose to take their chances in communities which had something
to offer and which were not radically different from their homes, rather than
moving to the unknown world of the city.[40]

So long as the socio-economic and demographic characteristics of numerous
rural communities are not thoroughly investigated, it is impossible to explain
why the poor of one village emigrated, while those of another stayed even

though at first glance they were every bit as needy as the first. In any case, it is beyond doubt that most migrants to Antwerp during the first half of the nineteenth century were uprooted countrydwellers who had left their traditional milieu because alternatives were no longer available.[41] How could these people adapt themselves to urban life? What did Antwerp and the immigrants have to offer one another?

CHAPTER 5

Patterns of Settlement

Since migration to Antwerp quickened during the irreversible decline of most of the 'honourable trades' and the rise of port-associated activities in which unskilled labour played a predominant role, it is not rash to deduce that the chances of uprooted countryfolk's finding a job in the town were comparatively greater than in centres based on industrial employment. Work in the harbour, however, required only physical strength, so that all immigrants did not stand an equal chance. Hence, before discussing the occupational distribution of the newcomers, attention must be paid to their demographic composition.

The registers of the *cartes de sûreté* indicate that most migrants were unmarried and in their prime, so that theoretically they had maximum chances for success in Antwerp, particularly the men, who formed the majority.[1] The age structure of the newcomers who were listed in 1817 was as follows:

Age structure of male and female migrants to Antwerp, by percentages, 1817

	Male (N = 365)	Female (N = 324)	All (N = 689)
0–14	1·1	1·5	1·5
15–19	8·2	23·8	15·5
20–24	24·7	36·1	30·0
25–29	22·5	21·3	21·9
30–34	14·0	4·6	9·6
35–39	8·0	5·3	6·7
40–44	9·9	1·9	6·1
45 and over	11·7	5·5	8·9

The small proportion of children is not surprising, since 86 per cent of the migrants were unmarried. The women were in general younger than the men: *c.* 81 per cent of the female migrants belonged to the age group of 15 to 29 versus *c.* 55 per cent of the male newcomers. Conceivably, the dearth of 1816–7 compelled a greater number of young adults to abandon their home villages than could have been the case during ostensibly normal years. There can be no doubt, however, that growing immigration contributed towards Antwerp's more youthful population, as seen in the following table, which distinguishes among three age groups.[2] Within half a century, the proportion of those younger than

Selected age groups as percentages of total population in Antwerp, 1796–1846

Date	0–12 Years of age	12–20 Years of age	20–30 Years of age
1796	23·0	11·4	16·5
1830	24·5	12·6	19·5
1846	25·8	13·4	20·4

30 rose from scarcely 51 per cent to 59·6 per cent out of the total population. It was no accident that the group between 20 and 30 had grown the most: half of the migrants to Antwerp were in that age group.

The continuous flow of immigrants also reduced the enormous excess of women over men registered in Antwerp at the end of the eighteenth century to more modest proportions. There are four censuses distinguishing between native and immigrant populations which are available for the study of the evolution of sex ratios.[3] The data are not wholly comparable, because the sex of

Sex ratio of the Antwerp population, by origin of inhabitants, 1796–1846

Population	Number of females per 100 males			
	1796	1815	1830	1846
Over 12 years of age				
Immigrant	149	149*	132	
Born in Antwerp	131	135*	122	
All	136	140*	126	
Total				
Immigrant		145	130	94
Born in Antwerp		120	113	114
All		126	120	107

*Over 15 years of age

children under 12 was not recorded in 1796 and the age cut-off of young children
was set at 15 in 1815. Nonetheless, several conclusions can be drawn. In 1796,
Antwerp had 136 women over 12 for every 100 men above that age. This great
excess of women was a common characteristic of most European cities of the
ancien régime and is primarily ascribable to the immigration of maids.[4] In Antwerp, the latter represented no less than 12·5 per cent of all female inhabitants
older than 12 at the end of the century; nearly all were born outside the town.[5]
Hence the disparity between the sexes was far more pronounced among immigrants than among the native population: 149 women over 12 per 100 men over
12 as against 131:100. Until 1815, this ratio remained virtually unchanged, thereafter improving rapidly. Between 1815 and 1830, the number of women per 100
men diminished from 126 to 120 and in 1846 had further declined to 107. This
remarkable shift was primarily caused by the spectacular rise in the number of
male immigrants. By the middle of the nineteenth century they were in the majority, whereas 30 years earlier they accounted for scarcely 40 per cent of the total.

What influence did migration have on socio-economic life in Antwerp? It is
well-known that foreign businessmen and their agents settled in the town on the
Scheldt during the first half of the nineteenth century. Although their activities
have never been systematically studied, doubtless many among them played an
important role in commerce, finance, insurance.[6] But this category of migrants
formed a small minority. Calculations based on taxation records show that at the
end of the eighteenth century more than 66 per cent of the immigrant population
over twelve in Antwerp were completely without possessions and wholly reliant
on wage labour.[7] There is no comparable material for the succeeding decades, but
the occupations of the parents of the immigrants of 1817 speak for themselves: 40
per cent were 'peasants' and another 20 per cent day labourers. Such statements,
however, tell us nothing about the impact of immigration on the Antwerp labour
market. Fortunately, the raw data collected by Jos De Belder and Jules Hannes
allow analysis of changes that took place between 1796 and 1830 in the
occupational distribution of native and immigrant populations over 12–13.[8]

This investigation reveals that there were comparatively many more
Antwerp-born than immigrant males with no occupation. In the late eighteenth century, one in seven native men practised no trade as against one in
twenty immigrants. Thirty years later, the respective proportions diverged
even further: nearly a fourth gave no occupation among the Antwerp-born
versus scarcely 10 per cent among the immigrants, a ratio of 2·5:1. Certainly,
the first group had relatively fewer young adults and more elderly than the
second, but the discrepancy in employment was too great simply to be explained
by different age structures. Other factors clearly played a role. Many migrants
who could not get jobs most probably left the town quickly; they could claim
support from the local poor relief only after residence of one year (until 1818)
or more (after 1818). The home village or last place of residence was liable to
contribute for them in the meanwhile, but administrative formalities were time
consuming, and the relief funds allocated by village communities were generally so small that migrants could scarcely live on this rate in town.[9] On the

other hand, most migrants were young and unmarried, so that they had fewer difficulties in finding work than many native inhabitants, especially since uprooted people for obvious reasons were prepared to undertake the heaviest and most poorly-paid jobs – like the foreign workers of the twentieth century.

Indeed in most occupations there was a very close connection between the higher or lower level of skill on the one hand and the greater or lesser proportion of employed migrants on the other. Administration, the professions, and commerce were the only – albeit important – exceptions. The excess of migrants among administrators can perhaps be ascribed to the repeated changes of regime: around one fourth of all men engaged in government were from France or the northern Netherlands. The still greater proportion of migrants in commerce and the professions naturally was closely bound up with the rise of Antwerp as an international harbour; half of the immigrant merchants were born in foreign countries.

All other sectors in which migrants formed the majority were primarily trades reliant on unskilled workers. The bourgeoisie preferred to recruit domestic servants from rural communities because countryfolk 'are more virtuous, more submissive, and more hardworking than born townsmen', as the Chamber of Commerce postulated in 1846.[10] The great number of migrants employed in food processing is to be expected: of all urban jobs, this trade was the least alien for countryfolk. Most of the tasks involved, moreover, required nothing more than physical strength. According to the Medical Commission of Antwerp, work in the breweries and sugar refineries was heavy and exhausting, so that 'only young and robust workers can be considered'. The conclusion of the Commission: 'As a result, the overwhelming majority of the wage labourers employed in this industry come from the country'. Still, the whole of the sector did not become dominated by migrants; they were only a fraction of the independent producers, implying that most owned no capital. Also, few migrants were engaged in tobacco processing – scarcely 15 per cent of the total labour force involved; nearly all the stages in the process could be executed without excessive physical effort.[11]

Nor does the significant presence of migrants in transport cause much surprise: only young, strong men could earn their living hauling goods or at sea. As might be expected, more than half of the sailors were foreigners. As for retailing and distribution, a distinction has to be made between innkeepers, shopkeepers, hawkers, and the like on one side and butchers and barbers on the other side. The first category was 70 per cent migrant, the second only 30 per cent. That so many migrants kept a *cabaret* or a small shop can be explained by a combination of two factors: little skill was required and there was an extensive clientele, since migrants generally tried to stay in contact with one another as much as possible. Although some money was indispensable, wealth was not necessary to begin this sort of business. From the licence fees levied in 1830 it appears that 55 per cent of the inn-keepers and 76 per cent of the shopkeepers belonged to the lowest five tariff classes, paying less than twelve francs *per annum*.[12] For butchers and barbers, things were different: both groups had to be skilled, and butchers, moreover, had to dispose of large sums of money.

Woodworking was the sole industry apart from food processing in which migrants were the majority. Their presence varied strongly, however, from branch to branch. Natives of Antwerp represented 94 per cent of chairmakers, 86 per cent of turners, 85 per cent of brushmakers, 56 per cent of cabinet makers, 55 per cent of cartwrights, and 51 per cent of coopers, while migrants had the majority among sawyers (75 per cent), shipwrights (74 per cent), carpenters (66 per cent), and joiners (62 per cent). All these trades required skill, but, unlike the latter group, the former mainly produced goods for the local market. Most sawyers, carpenters, and joiners, on the other hand, were engaged in shipbuilding, just as the actual shipwrights. Since Antwerp had no tradition in that area, foreign workers had to be employed extensively: 40 to 50 per cent of the migrants engaged in these branches came from foreign lands.[13] The remaining occupations were in effect reserved for the native population. Only in the chemical industry did the number of migrants exceed one third of the total labour force. Nearly all were potters or candlemakers, whose working conditions were considered unhealthy even by contemporaries. The work done by the potters, moreover, was so exhausting that the labourers involved, according to the Medical Commission, had to have 'a very highly developed musculature.'[14]

Why did natives of Antwerp and the migrants more or less balance one another in agriculture and casual labour? As for the first sector, the answer is simple enough: even for a small morsel of land on the outskirts of town, relatively high rents were required, so that a minimum of capital was necessary. Hence, 62 per cent of the market-gardeners were natives of Antwerp, while nearly as many gardeners' men came from rural communities. It is less clear why casual labourers were fairly evenly divided. The solution may be sought in the lack of alternatives for most sons of former textile workers. What else could they do other than try to make a living in the harbour? In any case, the growing immigration of young countryfolk seriously aggravated competition in the 'market for casual labour' – the more so as many migrants switched from domestic service to casual labour: between 1796 and 1830, the proportion employed in the former sector halved, while the percentage engaged in casual labour more than tripled. It was precisely because the 'reserve army' was regularly replenished that the workers involved could achieve no improvements in their conditions. Just the opposite: their real wages sank between 1827 and 1855.

The conclusion of Lynn Lees concerning the Irish in London during the 1830s and 1840s applies equally well to the majority of men migrating to Antwerp in the first half of the nineteenth century: 'They stopped digging peat and potatoes to start unloading ships or transporting bricks. Low-skilled agricultural workers became low-skilled construction and dock labourers.'[15] Even after they had lived in the town for a number of years, migrants did not succeed in improving their occupational status. That at least is suggested by the occupational distribution of male migrants enlisted in 1817 in the Antwerp population registers who can be traced to 1830. Leaving aside those recorded in 1817 as officials, merchants, or professionals, then the following picture emerges:

Occupational classification of single male migrants to Antwerp in 1817, as compared with their occupational classification in 1830, by percentages

	In 1817	In 1830		
Occupation	(N = 311)	Married (N = 93)	Single (N = 51)	All (N = 144)
Casual labour	19·3	21·5	23·6	22·2
Food and drink processing	19·3	21·5	23·6	22·2
Woodworking	13·8	16·1	3·9	11·8
Domestic service	10·6	5·4	19·6	10·4
Retail and distribution	8·0	9·7	5·9	8·3
Clothing trade	7·1	5·4	3·9	4·9
Transport and storage	6·4	6·5	3·9	5·6
Agriculture	5·8	3·2	5·9	4·2
Textiles	3·9	1·1	3·9	3·1
Metalworking	2·6	2·2	0·0	1·4
Miscellaneous labour	4·5	7·4	9·8	8·3

In 1817 as well as 1830, the vast majority were engaged in casual labour, food processing, woodworking, and domestic service. There were only two notable changes. First, most immigrants who married had to give up domestic service, and, second, the number of single migrants employed in woodworking in 1830 lay significantly under the general average of 1817.

The occupational distribution of immigrant women showed two major similarities with that of their male counterparts: unemployment was much less among them than among the native population, and the majority performed unskilled work.[16] In 1796, around 28 per cent of the total female population over twelve consisted of migrants, who held 30 per cent of all available jobs. Thirty years later, the proportions had leapt to 43 and 50 per cent respectively. The impact of female migrants on the labour market thus in growing measure exceeded their demographic weight; but in terms of their occupation, immigrant women could exercise little choice. Domestic service and casual labour together absorbed the largest part of the occupied female migrants: 54 per cent in 1796, 65 per cent in 1830. It should be noted that the latter sector gained in relative importance at the expense of the former. Since a similar shift had taken place among men, it does not seem impossible that indoor servants were increasingly replaced during the first half of the nineteenth century by non-resident personnel hired to perform specific tasks. This would explain why the number of laundry ironers and gardeners' men more than doubled and the number of laundresses nearly tripled between 1796 and 1830. Anyhow, migrant women who could not settle into domestic service or casual labour had great difficulty in finding work. With the exception of the 'happy few' engaged in commerce and retailing, they had to be satisfied with the most poorly paid jobs in the textile and clothing industries. For immigrant women, textile manufacturing meant spinning flax, an occupation learned in the home village. In every other branch of the industry, they were a distinct minority. As for the clothing trade: female immigrants could easily become laundresses, but the more specialized tasks were effectively reserved for native born Antwerp women. No wonder that upward social mobility so seldom was in evidence among migrant women. Only fourteen among those who moved to Antwerp in 1817 and still lived there in 1830 had improved their material situation significantly: eight 'promoted' to housekeepers and six married to someone not dependent on wage labour.

In short, the sources of employment opportunities created by the expansion of shipping and commerce were heavily tapped by newcomers. Nearly half of the casual labourers and the vast majority of the workers engaged in other occupations which required little skill and great strength were recruited from among immigrants. How could it be otherwise? For generations, most native-born men and women had been employed in the textile industry. Given that the transition from weaving or spinning to dock-work made an end of an age-old pattern of family and community life, it is easily understandable that many artisans tried as long as possible to practice their 'honourable' trade – even if that meant under-payment.[17] Besides, only the young and robust among them could choose casual labour, and competition for such jobs was not always to their advantage, for immigrants were 'prepared' to accept the very lowest wages.

The flow of workers from the countryside was thus a *sine qua non* for the development of the port. But did these immigrants find what they were looking for in Antwerp, a livelihood enabling them to settle down permanently? Many historical demographers have stressed that during the Industrial Revolution large towns often functioned as 'way-stations' for the uprooted, who would leave as quickly and sometimes as desperately as they had come. The time lag between disruption of the rural society and the creation of new employment opportunities in the towns was everywhere so great that migrants often had no other choice than to trek hither and yon.[18] As Stephan Thernstrom has remarked: the town 'provided no soil in which to sink roots. It was only one more place in which to carry on the struggle for existence for a few years, until driven onward again'.[19] In Antwerp in particular, where the irregularity of work in the harbour could not be fully compensated (if at all) by supplementary sources of income, it must have been very difficult for people who had been uprooted to support a family. The question then arises: what proportion of the immigrants remained in the port town for good? To that end, all adults who listed Antwerp in 1817 as their 'fixed' abode in the population registers have been traced as far as 1830. No fewer than 94 or 17 per cent of the 544 who can be followed left the city within five years, and 70 others or 13 per cent emigrated between 1822 and 1830. Marital status clearly had some influence on the decision whether or not to trek elsewhere.

Marital status of migrants moving to Antwerp in 1817 and leaving the town before 1830

Marital status	Number of migrants	Per cent of migrants leaving Antwerp
Married before moving to Antwerp	71	23·9
Single male	118	35·6
Single female	185	47·0
Married in Antwerp		
male	103	8·7
female	67	13·4
Total	544	30·1

Single migrants were far more mobile than married couples. This was particularly true for females: nearly one in two female migrants left Antwerp between 1817 and 1830. Since the majority were maids, this is not surprising: many considered their period of service as a necessary evil undertaken to save for the trousseau which would enable them to return to the country to marry.[20] This is verified by an investigation of the destinations of the emigrants concerned: one third of the single adults returned to their birthplace and nearly as many moved to a rural community in the province of Antwerp. It is significant, however, that the respective proportions were even greater among married couples, namely 40 and 37 per cent, indicative of how small their chances were of integration into urban society.

Although no direct evidence is available, there can be no doubt that chronic under-employment kept many migrants from taking root in the town on the Scheldt. Antwerp's commercial circles did set up a commission in 1827 for the support of working-class families affected by the disruption of traffic on the Scheldt during winter-months; the commission organized collections from prominent bankers, merchants, and ship-owners, the proceeds of which were converted to tickets for the purpose of food-stuffs and fuel. In practise, however, the greater part of this aid was reserved not for destitute immigrants but rather for the more or less permanent dockers who carried out essential tasks and were therefore indispensable for the quick loading, unloading, and storage of goods. During the winter of 1828-1829, for example, the commission gave tickets to the following categories of workers: 589 men belonging to a *natie* (dock-company) or regularly employed by one,[21] 309 ship-repairers and caulkers, 72 stevedores, 52 'streetworkers' or longshoremen, 113 labourers whose occupation was not specified, and 139 widows of dockers; all in all 1,274 family heads.[22] Some businessmen may have had genuinely charitable intentions, but it was surely no mere coincidence that such an initiative was undertaken in the very same period which witnessed the first real boom in shipping and the formation of a dockyard proletariat in the true sense. The support commission was most likely considered by business circles as a sort of insurance policy: the core of the reserve army was not only kept alive relatively cheaply during a seasonal depression – it would also be readily available when shipping resumed.

In conclusion, immigrants greatly contributed to Antwerp's vigorous commercial expansion, swelling the ranks of the reserve army necessary for the town to gain decisive competitive advantages within the international transport and distribution network. The glut of casual labour, however, tended to intensify the adverse effects of de-industrialization. The poor relief authorities' statement of 1829 'that the social burden grows in proportion to the improvement of the economic situation of the town and the rise in its income' was not paradoxical.[23] The degradation of the textile workers, who in growing measure had been thrown out of work, joined with the influx of impoverished country-dwellers, who stood a comparatively better chance of finding a job in the new economic sectors: it was the conjunction of both of these processes which enabled employers to put downward pressure on wages and which condemned the lower classes, whether born in Antwerp or immigrant, to extreme poverty – the more so as commercial growth and the population explosion resulted in a grinding struggle for living space.

PART III

The Housing Question

CHAPTER 6

The Struggle for Living Space

Accelerating migration to Antwerp swelled the demand for housing. Nonetheless, the number of private dwellings both *intra* and *extra muros* rose from only some 10,500 in 1797 to 13,689 in 1856, a mere 30 per cent increase, even though the population had doubled during the same period.[1] Nor was this phenomenon restricted to Antwerp. Nearly every large town in western and central Europe faced a growing discrepancy between supply and demand. Although Paris held some 25 per cent more inhabitants in 1826 than in 1817, the number of houses had increased by only 10 per cent. In 1850, Amsterdam accommodated 45 per cent more families than a hundred years earlier, while the number of dwellings had scarcely risen by 5 per cent. In the English and German metropoles, too, the need for living accommodation became more pressing than ever before.[2]

The housing question in nineteenth-century towns is often analytically reduced to some unavoidable imbalance between demographic growth and new building. Periods of accelerated urbanization, it is argued, are inevitably accompanied by tensions in the market for housing: supply lags behind the exceptional demand which results from massive immigration. Antwerp shows that such interpretations need revision. The structural lack of suitable proletarian housing resulted from the mal-allotment of urban living space combined with the reluctance of entrepreneurs to invest in buildings for workers, and was exacerbated by the space newly-devoted to the commercial and residential needs of the élites. Moreover, the growth of proletarian ghettos reflected the élites' desire for social isolation from the lower classes.

Certainly, in a city fast approaching saturation point, an increase in population created problems in the use of the remaining space. The shortage of housing must be attributed in part to Antwerp's role as a military stronghold, which hindered expansion of urban land area. Since no buildings could be erected within a distance of 585 metres from the fortifications, the bourgeoisie could not establish new residential quarters, unlike the upper classes of London, Paris, and other metropolitan areas in which city centres were progressively relinquished to the working population.[3] This situation lasted until the early 1860s, when the antiquated Spanish walls were demolished and replaced by a new ring of fortifications, sextupling the surface area of the town.[4] Antwerp also differed from other metropoles because of the almost complete absence of high buildings: in 1846 barely 22 per cent of all houses had two or more floors.[5] Most dwellings dated from the later middle ages and the sixteenth century,[6] and this large reservoir of old houses covered no less than 97 per cent of the city area suitable for building.[7] The housing shortage, however, was caused not so much by some supposed natural scarcity of space as by pressure from the élites to ensure that the penalties – in spatial terms – of demographic growth were not shared out equally.

The rise of shipping and commerce added to the need for harbour installations, railway lines, warehouses, and other economic facilities, which entailed both new building and the displacement of citizens. Nearly all public works carried out during the first half of the nineteenth century were accompanied by demolition of old houses. This was especially the case with the construction of the Bonaparte dock in 1804–1806, the Royal Staple House in 1830–1834, the new fish market in 1841–1842, and the *Rijnspoorweg* with its large goods-station in the 1840s.[8] The creation of commercial facilities naturally increased rents on land and housing in neighbouring streets, and because of this, many existing residents had to leave their homes. Ever greater numbers of needy people settled into the fifth ward.[9] Indeed, the population *extra muros* almost tripled between 1830 and 1846, and the number of dwellings more than doubled, all building codes to the contrary. Nor was there any talk of planning. Paving was not laid, and water mains were totally absent. Whole parcels of land along old country roads were simply stuffed with primitive wooden barracks without sanitation.[10] In 1860, the director of the Charity Bureau wrote to the municipal authorities: 'The fifth ward greatly resembles a hut camp, and so many hovels are built with such shoddy materials that after a few years they fall into decay.'[11]

Many workers, however, could not allow themselves to live far from the city centre. This was true not only for transport and dock workers, for whom it was of crucial importance to be as close as possible to the loading and unloading sites, but also for seamstresses, laundresses, and ironers, who had to stay within a short walking-distance of their customers, and for retailers such as pedlers and hawkers who had to live in the neighbourhood of markets and warehouses.[12] Hence, relatively few migrants settled into the fourth ward: the majority of the newcomers practised trades which either provided bed-and-board with bourgeois families or which compelled them to remain in the economic heart of the town, where not only the harbour installations and commercial facilities but also the wood-working and food-processing industries were situated. The following table sheds some light on the spatial distribution of the immigrant population in 1830.[13]

Number of migrants over 13 years of age per 100 natives of Antwerp over 13 in each ward, 1830

Ward	Total population over 13			Working population over 13		
	Males	Females	All	Males	Females	All
I	80	91	86	118	174	137
II	75	78	77	80	83	81
III	75	86	81	88	112	98
IV	56	57	56	64	68	66
V	80	89	84	104	163	119

The explanation for the large proportion of migrants *extra muros* is plain enough: the men were employed in agriculture (or, rather, market gardening) and nearly all the active women worked as domestics – generally with rich families who had summer cottages in the neighbourhood of the Markgravelei. Within the town itself, the third and especially the first ward displayed the highest concentrations of migrants. In ward III, domestic service formed the most frequent female occupation, but in ward I there were many migrant women occupied as retailers, shop girls, and seamstresses, while their male counterparts were predominantly engaged in transport, casual labour, retailing, food processing and wood-working, in that order.

The upper classes protected their neighbourhoods from overcrowding. Since they could not move to new residential areas, they absorbed space and forced the proletariat back into certain streets. This process was accelerated by a ruthless policy of demolition. Although no statistical information is presently available, other data indicate that new construction in the second and third wards took place at the expense of dwelling space for the poor. To cite a single eyewitness: in 1854, one high official deplored the fact that nearly all 'fine mansions have been raised on the ruins of old and humble dwellings.'[14] Business motives may have played a role in this development: by building valuable houses, the new élites made their wealth safe and raised their credit-worthiness. Their main objectives, however, were distancing themselves from the proletariat and augmenting their prestige. Every aspect of the bourgeois way of life – housing, clothing, speech, recreation, and so forth – was deployed to provide overwhelming evidence of 'natural' superiority. Since first-class citizens ought only to encounter their equals, segregation became a requisite to assure the security of the inhabitants of the middle-class areas.[15] In less than fifty years, urban space was restructured to conform to the process of social polarization. Changes between 1797 and 1845 in *per capita* living space show that the contrasts between the different parts of the town were greatly accentuated.[16]

Average built-up area in Antwerp, 1797–1845 (square metres per head)

Ward	1797	1815	1829	1845
I	26	24	19	17
II	45	42	31	30
III	35	34	25	28
IV	37	34	24	20
All	36	33	25	24

In interpreting these figures, it ought to be noted that the built-up areas included courtyards, small gardens, warehouses, and industrial buildings besides dwellings. The averages given for the first and fourth wards are certainly overestimates, for in 1829 they included 144 and 138 buildings, respectively, with purely economic functions.[17] It is clear that, within a half century, noticeable deterioration had taken place: the average *per capita* living space diminished by 33 per cent. The Dutch régime of 1815–1830 witnessed the sharpest decline, some 2 per cent *per annum*, versus 0·5 per cent in the preceeding period and less than 0·3 per cent between 1829 and 1845. Although it was a general phenomenon, some parts of the town fared worse than others. In the fourth ward, the decline amounted to *c.* 46 per cent, against only 20 per cent in the third. By the middle of the century, individual living space had become most cramped in wards I and IV: a person there had a mere 17 and 20 square metres, respectively – around a third less than the inhabitants of wards II and III. The same factors applied in the question of population per house.[18]

Average number of persons per house in Antwerp, 1797–1846

Ward	Persons per house			Percentage shift	
	1797	1830	1846	1796–1830	1830–1846
I	4·76	7·17	6·55	+51	−8·6
II	4·70	6·45	6·45	+37	0·0
III	4·97	6·48	6·35	+30	−2·0
IV	5·03	7·04	7·45	+40	+5·8
All	4·88	6·80	6·77	+39	−0·4

Between 1797 and 1830 the average number of persons per house rose by 39 per cent. The growth was most pronounced in wards I and IV: in 1830, each dwelling lodged seven people on average compared to five at the end of the eighteenth century. The period 1830–1846 saw both a slight diminution in the general level of overcrowding and an accentuation of the contrast between different parts of the town. The first change can be attributed to two factors: the number of houses *intra muros* grew by 13 per cent and, at the same time, increasingly more people moved to the fifth ward. By mid-century, spatial segregation within the town had been carried much further than the table suggests. Leaving empty dwellings out of consideration, population per house in 1846 amounted to:

I	II	III	IV	All wards
8·25	7·35	6·97	8·25	7·76

Clearly extreme overcrowding characterized wards I and IV. At first sight it may seem that an average of eight persons per house would not be excessive, but the overwhelming majority of the dwellings had only one or two rooms. In comparison with wards I and IV, the situation in other sections of the city was relatively favourable, especially since most houses with two or three floors were in wards II and III.

The discrepancy between the two series of averages calculated from the 1846 data shows that 'housing shortage' was a relative concept. Despite the high level of overcrowding in some areas of the town, no fewer than 1,461 houses, or 13 per cent of the total, stood empty in that year.[19] The explanation is that the bulk of new dwellings were financially out of the reach of the proletariat. Working-class houses planned by the town council in 1849 were never erected because most wage-labourers simply could not afford to spend 3·20 francs a week on rent. As the Charity Bureau remarked: 'With a few changes these little houses could be offered to two or three families, and there would certainly be a demand for them, but then the goal of improved hygiene would of necessity have to be abandoned'.[20] Since public authorities were not prepared to contribute financially, it is not surprising that the good burghers refused to help the working population to acquire proper dwelling places. Only a minority of wage-labourers could pay the rents which were deemed a normal return on investment, so that building contractors clearly saw that there were no profits to be had from such projects.[21] Housing, of course, fulfilled an important function as a place of reproduction and recuperation for the labour force, but, due to the continuous and massive supply of cheap and docile migrants, this factor was not significant in setting wages. Hence, during the nineteenth century few workers' dwellings were built which could be considered decent, *i.e.* houses constructed of materials of such quality that they could be kept in repair without excessive cost, which had sufficient space to provide necessary air and light for all members of the family, and the rent of which lay within the financial grasp of the working population. Shortage of suitable proletarian housing was inherent to an economic system in which the supply was determined exclusively by purchasing power.

It comes as no surprise, then, that the geography of class became more and more distinctive across the Antwerp landscape during the first half of the nineteenth century. By calculating the location quotients of Antwerp's wards *intra muros* by occupational groups, it is possible to investigate in rough terms whether any connection existed between the level of overcrowding in the ward and its socio-economic profile. Five occupations can be taken as signals of bourgeois residence patterns: administration, rentiers, the professions, commerce and banking, and domestic service. In the retail trades and transport, the lower middle-class was strongly represented; according to the licence fees, those engaged in these trades came from both the highest as well as the lowest tax brackets, but the majority was concentrated in the middle levels.[22] Casual labour, textile manufacturing, and lacework can be labelled proletarian activities. Although the wards were administrative units in the first instance and occupations provide only vague indications, the location quotients show that the social groups were far from evenly spread throughout the town in 1830.[23] The third ward had an undeniably bourgeois character: for administrators, rentiers, professionals, merchants, bankers, and domestics, the relevant values far exceeded a quotient of one, indicating a much stronger level of concentration of these occupations in the district than in Antwerp as a whole. The very low levels for casual labour, textile manufacturing, and laceworking indicate the opposite. The fourth ward showed quite the reverse: proletarian occupations were excessively represented compared to the proportion of the working population living in that part of town, while bourgeois occupations produced very low quotients. The other wards had a more mixed appearance. The lower middle class, however, was primarily concentrated in the first ward – not surprisingly, for the district bordered on the most important section of the roads and docks; most markets and nearly 40 per cent of all warehouses were at hand. For the same reasons, the concentration of transport workers in the first ward was particularly great. It should be noted that the levels of occupational concentration and of overcrowding more or less coincided. The population per house was much greater in the fourth ward, where the proletariat predominated, than in the third ward, where the bourgeoisie was most strongly represented. When domestic servants are excluded, the number of persons per house in 1830 amounted to scarcely 5·8 in the third ward versus 6·9 in the fourth. The census of 1846 provides no information concerning occupational distribution in the different wards. From the license fees, however, it appears that bourgeois residences in the second ward increased in significance between 1827 and 1842. While the level of concentration of commerce and the professions in the other sections of town remained practically unchanged, the respective values in the second ward rose from 0·98 to 1·27.[24]

Further exploration into the social topography of Antwerp in the first half of the nineteenth century demands geographic units covering far smaller areas than the wards. Unfortunately, the latter formed the administrative basis for which all sorts of information was assembled by contemporaries. The sole solution is to turn to the poor lists of 1827 and 1855, which noted the address of

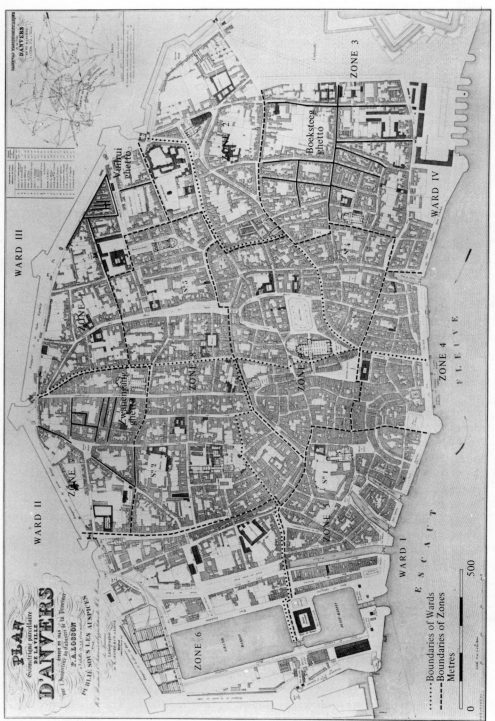

Figure 7: Antwerp streets with heavy concentrations of paupers, 1827 and 1855

every family on relief. Statistical analysis of the data allows division of the town *intra muros* into nine zones according to the level of concentration of paupers (see Figure 7). Since the poor lists of 1780 have only been partially preserved, they cannot be used for comparative material. Jos De Belder, however, was able to calculate the number of slum dwellings in every street by means of the land tax levied in 1797.[25] When his data are also arranged by zone, the following picture emerges:

Spatial distribution of slum dwellings (1797) and supported Antwerp families (1827 and 1855), by percentages

Zone	Slum dwellings 1797 N = 2,049	Supported families 1827 N = 1,360	Supported families 1855 N = 1,589
1	13·22	14·93	14·98
2	3·76	3·82	2·64
3	32·90	38·67	39·14
4	2·79	3·38	6·86
5	9·96	10·74	8·50
6	7·07	2·61	2·33
7	19·13	14·04	12·46
8	7·22	5·81	4·91
9	3·95	6·00	8·18

More than 60 per cent of all slums recorded in 1797 and all families supported in 1827 and 1855 were to be found in Zones 1, 3, and 7; Zone 3, which covered a large area of the fourth ward, accounted for 33 to 39 per cent of the total. Zone 5 took an intermediate position and the remaining zones were characterized throughout the period by relatively low concentrations of paupers. Yet, in the second quarter of the nineteenth century, there were some significant shifts. By 1855, the proportion of families on relief living in Zones 4 and 9, which bordered on Zone 3, had increased sharply, while it had diminished in Zones 2, 6 and 8. Although the data are not wholly comparable, the land tax of 1797 suggests that the first quarter of the century witnessed a similar shift. Thus, it seems indisputable that spatial segregation in Antwerp grew steadily greater. While a growing number of needy was herded together into certain sections of town, the bourgeois features of other neighbourhoods became more and more pronounced.

Taking those streets with exceptional concentrations of paupers separately, three ghettos can be distinguished, lodging around 50 per cent of the families on relief in 1827 and 1855 (see Figure 7). The largest ghetto was the Boeksteeg, in Zone 3. It covered no fewer than eleven streets, occupied by 400 to 500 families on the dole: the Boeksteeg itself, five streets to the west (Arme

Beukelaarstraat, Vlierstraat, Prekersstraat, Lepelstraat, and Lange Ridderstraat) and five to the east (Schoytestraat, Bogaerdestraat, Steenbergstraat, Sint-Rochusstraat, and Sint-Jansstraat); the whole area was laced with small alleys and culs-de-sac. The ghetto of the Zwanengang in Zone 7 consisted of six streets inhabited by *c.* 150 families on relief: Zwanengang, Grote Kauwenberg, Paradijsstraat ('Paradise Street'!), Rozenstraat, Sint-Annastraat, and (Korte and Lange) Winkelstraat. The ghetto of the Vuilrui ('Rubbish Street') in Zone 1, finally, covered five streets with concentrations of paupers: Vuilrui, Gezond-straat ('Healthy Street'), Meistraat, Bontemantelstraat, and Sint-Jorisvest.[26] The ghettos in Zones 1 and 7 were relatively small, but the Boeksteegghetto extended its tentacles over the whole of Zone 3. It should be noted that the latter increasingly expanded, as appears from the growing proportion of assisted families in the neighbouring Zones 4 and 9; nearly all of these people lived in streets close to Zone 3. Spatial segregation thus showed two distinct faces: on the one hand, paupers living in more or less mixed areas were gradually driven to distinct ghettos within these areas; on the other hand, there was a general expulsive process in which one particular section of the town was increasingly allotted the function of an urban slum. A glance at Figure 7 confirms this: the ghettos of the Zwanengang and the Vuilrui formed mere fractions of the built-up area of wards II and III, whereas the Boeksteegghetto consisted of half of ward IV.

These conclusions are reinforced by a map sketched on orders of the municipal authorities after the cholera epidemic of 1866, showing all houses with one or more incidences of disease.[27] The body of the contagion was situated in the fourth ward; although the epidemic took most of its victims from among inhabitants of the Boeksteegghetto, it spread far outside that area. The second and third wards were largely spared and the few cases were primarily concentrated in the ghettos of the Zwanengang and Vuilrui. The appearance of contagion in the first ward is to be explained by a combination of factors: no single area of town contained so many small canals, brooks, and other watercourses nor counted so many cheap lodging houses and brothels.[28]

From the middle of the nineteenth century, some members of the establishment began to have doubts about the desirability of 'ghettofication'. They argued that spatial segregation held more dangers than advantages: social disparities were clear for everyone to see; social tensions were augmented, not diminished. When the municipal authorities of Antwerp drew up a plan in 1849 to build workers' cottages near the Boeksteegghetto, one of the members of the municipal council remarked that it would be preferable to spread the dwellings over the whole of the town, 'so that they would be surrounded by housing inhabited by moral individuals'.[29] This point of view, however, had not the least chance of being put into practice so long as the working population was not a paying clientele, that is, before the twentieth century. Meanwhile the bourgeoisie preferred to separate itself from the lower classes.

Although quantitative data are scarce, there can be little doubt that numerous western and central European towns saw comparable tendencies towards spatial segregation during the nineteenth century. By 1875, no less than 88 per cent of the population of Berlin lived in districts where the average number of persons per room varied between 2·0 and 2·6; the remaining 12 per cent concentrated in residential zones where only 0·9 to 1·5 had to share a room.[30] Just as in Antwerp, spatial segregation was made worse in many towns by the execution of large-scale public works. In and around the metropoles, more and more railroads and stations were built, canals and docks dug, new traffic arteries built, markets created, commercial and industrial blocks built. These improvements of the urban infrastructure were nearly always accompanied by the razing of numerous old buildings. In London, for example, around 100,000 people were pushed out of their homes between 1830 and 1880 as a result of the broadening of existing streets or the opening of new ones, while around 76,000 others had to make way for the railroads between 1853 and 1901.[31] Such thorough transformation of the urban landscape went hand in hand with extraordinary speculation in real estate. Two Parisian examples: in 1857, a single square metre of unbuilt land on the Boulevard de Sebastopol cost forty times more than it had two years earlier, and on the Avenue de l'Opéra the price multiplied fifty fold between 1860 and 1865. While landowners, bankers, governmental officials, and political appointees made fortunes off town planning, the lower classes were increasingly dumped into the overpopulated slum quarters.[32] Street clearances had equally disastrous social consequences. For the proletariat, the bourgeois attack on 'contagion, criminality, and prostitution' amounted to a further disappearance of their miserable slums, and, in most cases, the time lag between razing and rebuilding was too great to provide the expelled inhabitants with proper accommodation. Rents in the new buildings were so high that wage labourers could seldom afford them. When the Jordaan construction company drove 103 families out of their slums in Amsterdam at the end of the nineteenth century in order to make way for new premises, the director had to concede that this did not solve the demand for housing. Just the opposite: 'From the very outset it was clear that none of the new dwellings could be rented for under 1·70 guilders per week, so that those who had previously paid 0·60 to 1·70 guilders could not return as tenants'. Of the 103 evicted families, there were in the end only 9 in a position to occupy a Jordaan house; all of the others 'ended up at about the same rent in other slums, and it must be admitted that some of these hovels were even more miserable than the previous ones', the director declared.[33] In short, urban development took place in this period nearly everywhere at the expense of the proletariat.[34] As the Belgian sociologist *avant la lettre* Edouard Ducpétiaux wrote in 1844:

> far from benefitting the wage labourer, such schemes turn into a new source of misery, for, ceaselessly followed by the demolisher's hammer, daily he sees the circle shrink within which he is allowed to breath. What is the consequence? Rent for housing in the nastiest hovel rises in relation to the competition of the poor to get into it; the lodgings which sufficed in former times for a single family must now be shared by two and more households.[35]

CHAPTER 7

Living Like Pigs

The previous chapter has shown that the social consequences of Antwerp's economic transformation were aggravated not only by the flow of workers from the countryside but also by the restructuring of urban space. The housing question, however, was more than one of displacement and demographic redistribution, or one of ghettos and social segregation. As long as their living standard did not improve – denying them the purchasing power needed for better housing – the lower classes were forced into fierce competition for the cheapest possible lodgings. Since demand far exceeded supply, more and more working-class families herded together in one-room dwellings. The growing pressure on available accommodation not only worsened proletarian housing conditions; it also enabled landlords to exploit their tenants' poverty by covering otherwise unproductive sites with slums, subdividing and overcrowding the tenements, and raising rents.

New lodgings were indeed created for the proletariat, but this construction consisted primarily of slums wholly lacking in the most elementary hygienic facilities. Profit maximization meant erection of as many living units as possible with the poorest and cheapest materials on the least possible surface area. Since land facing the street was the most expensive, narrow parcels were lined on both sides with houses; back gardens and courtyards of older buildings were built up on three sides. These dwellings connected with the public street via narrow, dark alleys, usually closed off by a small door. The buildings along or through which the back premises were accessible were often turned into inns, so that their rental could be hiked up – the entrepreneur could count on numerous clients.

Between 1797 and 1842 the number of blind alleys *intra muros* grew from 116 to 207 and the number of slums situated in such culs-de-sac from 731 to 1,519; no less than 40 per cent lay in the fourth ward. Each alley contained seven dwellings on the average, but in some the number leapt to 30 and more.[1] The slums expanded rapidly *extra muros* as well. Around 1800 there was only one blind alley in the fifth ward, with five dwellings. Sixty years later, the number had risen to 62, with 370 slums inhabited by *c.* 1,800 people, nearly a sixth of the total population.[2] To exploit space to the maximum, the houses were more and more often built back-to-back, further depriving their inhabitants of light and ventilation. The surface area of back-to-backs in general amounted to twenty square metres, consisting of cellar, one room, and attic. The *Nieuwstad* (New Town), a series of workers' dwellings in the ghetto of the Vuilrui erected by one Beukelaar around 1820, gives an idea of the congestion: the 'colony', as it was known to contemporaries, was accessible only via a single door and had three parallel alleys on each side of which were built single room dwellings. By 1837, more than one thousand crowded into the ninety back-to-backs of the 'colony'. Each person had two square metres.[3]

Overcrowding was not limited to blind alleys, as can be seen from an investigation of living space available to families which in 1827 were regularly assisted by the Charity Bureau. The method employed: the houses occupied by these families were traced in the cadastral registers of 1834; only a fifth belonged to the same tariff category as the dwellings in alleyways, back gardens, and inner courtyards, signifying that the overwhelming majority of the supported families rented one or more rooms in larger houses. Then, on the basis of the cadastral survey, the total surface area of the dwellings was calculated, and the number of inhabitants drawn from the population registers of 1830.

Number of square metres per person in houses occupied by supported Antwerp families, about 1830

Number of square metres per person	Number of houses	Per cent
Less than 1	13	1·7
1–5	420	53·5
5–10	214	27·3
10–15	77	9·8
15–20	25	3·2
20 and more	36	4·5
Total	785	100·0

In 55 per cent of the houses, less than 6 square metres was available per person. Considering that the height of each story seldom exceeded 2·5 metres, the crowded living conditions of the lower classes were nothing less than dehumanizing. In addition, in most cases members of different families were packed together: only one third of the slums in blind alleys were inhabited in 1842 by single families.[4]

The worsening of housing conditions in Antwerp can be deduced from a comparison of the land tax of 1797 and the cadaster of 1829, which noted the net income of all houses, *i.e.* the average rental value less 25 per cent for maintenance and restoration. Since dwellings in blind alleys in 1829 were generally assessed together, the same has been done for 1797. Jointly with Jos De Belder, the 54 tariff categories of 1829 were grouped into six: the first of slums with two rooms at most, the second of modest dwellings with two to four rooms, the third of medium-sized houses of around eight rooms, and the remaining of comfortable middle class houses and mansions.[5] The percentage distribution per ward *intra muros* was as follows:

Percentage distribution of houses, according to their taxable income, at Antwerp in 1797 and 1829

Category	Taxable Income (in francs)	Per cent of houses				
		I	II	III	IV	All wards
1797	$N =$	2,332	1,973	1,990	2,882	9,117
1	less than 50	9·2	25·6	13·1	24·6	18·4
2	50–99	33·3	26·8	13·1	24·6	18·4
3	100–149	25·3	20·4	19·2	15·1	19·8
4	150–249	17·2	14·2	14·7	12·4	14·5
5	250–499	11·4	6·6	9·8	6·0	8·3
6	500 and more	3·6	6·4	7·7	3·3	5·0
1829	$N =$	2,154	1,939	2,083	3,089	9,265
1	less than 56	13·9	30·1	18·8	35·0	25·4
2	56–111	25·9	22·0	21·8	29·2	24·3
3	112–168	29·6	23·5	24·1	18·9	23·5
4	169–280	15·3	10·3	11·5	6·8	10·6
5	281–561	12·6	8·6	15·3	7·4	10·6
6	562 and more	2·7	5·5	8·5	2·7	4·6

Two significant shifts had taken place. In the first place, the proportion of the poorest dwellings (category 1) rose spectacularly: from *c.* 18 per cent in 1797 to *c.* 25 per cent in 1829. This growth must in reality have been much greater, for slums in blind alleys represented nearly 15 per cent of the total housing supply in 1829, against scarcely 7·5 per cent in 1797. The expansion of category 1 was primarily induced by the decay of many houses belonging to category 2: on the eve of the Belgian Revolution of 1830, their share of the total number of housing units had fallen from one third to a quarter. In the second place, contrasts among the different parts of town became much more pronounced. Although the proportion of the poorest dwellings rose overall, nowhere else reached the levels of the fourth ward: 35 per cent (up 10 per cent), versus 30 per cent (up 4·5 per cent) in the second ward and an average of 16 per cent (up 5 per cent) in the other districts. The accentuation of these contrasts was also mirrored in the evolution of houses belonging to categories 4–6. In the third ward, their number rose from 32·2 per cent to 35·5 per cent while declining from 21·7 per cent to 16·9 per cent in the fourth ward.

It would be an endless task to present here the hundreds of reports drawn up by the town's architect, Pierre Bourla, and the Public Health Committee concerning the living conditions of the lower classes in the middle of the nineteenth century.[6] Two examples should suffice. In the third ward, a cellar 5·5 × 3·15 m. and 1·9 m. high lodged no fewer than ten people, including six children. This subterranean hole was described by a police commissioner as follows: 'Daylight enters through a barred window which does not open and through two small windows under vent-holes; it is only via these vents that air comes into this kennel, in which ten pass the night. Water oozes from the walls, and one breathes constantly a musty, decaying stench'.[7] Nor were the poor living in houses of two or three stories much better off. In the fourth ward, the Medical Commission found a house in which two families crowded into the first floor, four on the second, and six on the third; 'there are two rooms on the third floor, one of which is inhabited by six and the other by five persons right under the roof, with no windows, lit only by some glazed tiles'. None of the floors had sanitary facilities.[8] This house was not exceptional. As five physicians wrote the provincial governor in 1844:

> A house in Antwerp is nearly always inhabited by several working families, each of which generally has only a single room. Understandable then is the filth and that the air is laden and thick with a foul odour, especially in the winter when they burn low-grade oil and keep the windows shut against the cold. The insalubrity of such dwellings is a fact beyond dispute.[9]

As for hygienic facilities in the proletarian quarters, in 1849 the municipality admitted that

> a great number of dwellings, especially those in blind alleys, do not have a tap nor even a cistern; few have cesspools, and those which do usually have the man-hole in one of the rooms. Most dwellings are much too small and usually filled with foul, stinking air. Few houses have drains for roof water; rain and household water stagnate since the sludge-wells are never cleaned, their drains are decrepit, and they are usually in the open air.[10]

A year later, the Public Health Committee, following a thorough investigation, came to the disconcerting conclusion that 110 of the 207 blind alleys *intra muros* were uninhabitable. They lodged more than a thousand families... Although the *Comité* declared that the living conditions of the working classes

in the other parts of town were little better, it judged that cleaning up the culs-
de-sac was the most pressing task. Yet everything remained as it was. The
town council, it is true, proclaimed a number of hygienic regulations and set
fines for their infringement, but nothing was done about overcrowding.[11]

In the other major Belgian towns, proletarian housing was equally pitiable.
In Brussels, the average number per house rose from 7·2 in 1829 to 9·7 in
1846; by that time no less than 45 per cent of all families had to make do with
a single room. The Public Health Committee drew up one alarming report
after another, to no effect: 'In the miserable slums where the workers herd
together, everything is sacrificed to the greed of the landlords. Any repair which
would be to the benefit only of the health and well-being of the tenants and
which does not have the exclusive goal of preventing the total ruin of the dwelling
is foregone'. In the following decades the situation deteriorated further.
According to the poor relief authorities, even stables were fitted up as dwelling
places. Around 1890, one high official plainly declared: 'The labouring classes
are undoubtedly less well housed than in former times. Their living space has
shrunk and still shrinks, from day to day'.[12] Ghent's working population was
no better off. The well documented report drafted in 1845 by two outraged
physicians, Mareska and Heyman, on the dehumanizing housing conditions of
the proletariat did not compel intervention by local authorities. The Public
Health Committee set up after the cholera epidemic of 1849 did draw up hygienic regulations for slumlords, but they had no effective means to enforce them.
In 1866, Ghent had no less than 674 blind alleys, inhabited by c. 28,000 people,
around one-fourth of the total population; at least 150 of these alleys were
in fact unfit for habitation and 200 others lacked the most elementary sanitary
provisions.[13]

Similar situations existed in German, English, French, and Dutch towns.
In Berlin, the average number per house rose from 30 to 49 between 1815 and
1860. According to the census of 1875, 10 per cent lived in cellars. Ten years
later, the town government established that more than half of the tenements
were single rooms.[14] In much of London, a medical official wrote in the 1860s,
'between 60 and 70 per cent of the population are compelled to live in one
small overcrowded room, in which every domestic operation has to be carried
on; in it birth and death takes [sic] place; there plays the infant, there lies the
corpse; it is lived in by day, and slept in by night'. He did not exaggerate; the
census of 1891 showed that nearly 20 per cent of the whole population of London lived more than one to a room; in the centre, it was even 40 per cent.[15] In
Paris, too, overcrowding reached greater proportions than ever before. In
1846, 60 per cent of households supported by the Charity Bureau had to make do
with a single room. Thirty years later, Dr. Jacques Bertillon, head of the statistical
service, concluded that 14 per cent of *all* Parisians lived in overcrowded rooms,
i.e., where the number of family members was two times greater than the number
of rooms available to them. Nor was the situation much rosier in other French
towns. An inquest carried out by the *Office du Travail* (Office of Labour) in
1906 concerning living conditions in 50 provincial centres brought to light that

200,000 tenements, 20 per cent of the total, consisted of single rooms; scarcely 32,000, or 16 per cent, were inhabited by single individuals. That the percentage of slums was significantly greater is indicated by samples taken by the *Statistique Générale de France* in 1910, whereby the level of overcrowding as well as the quality of housing was taken into consideration. Although particularly conservative definitions were employed, they concluded that, in all towns of more than 100,000, 49 per cent of the population was housed in dehumanizing circumstances.[16] Dutch towns gave an equally pitiful picture. In the Amsterdam of 1858, more than 200,000 persons, nearly 9 per cent of the total population, lived in cellars each containing four to five people. Fifteen years later, a commission reported that 73 per cent of these cellars were thoroughly unsuitable for human habitation. One in five was less than 1·6 metres high. The census of 31 December, 1899 registered 1,088,736 housing units in the whole country, of which 307,937, or 28·5 per cent, were single-room dwellings, 334,355, or 30·5 per cent, double-room. Nearly 14 per cent of all Dutch families had to divide a floor among four or more persons.[17]

There is abundant evidence to show that in many European towns the housing conditions of the proletariat deteriorated significantly because rack-renting functioned as the primary outlet for the profiteering instincts of intermediate social strata. Fearing extra expenditures, these small investors blocked all initiatives towards slum-clearance, and even the least effort to improve sanitary conditions.[18] Antwerp's nineteenth-century municipal authorities never made a serious effort to determine which social groups busied themselves with exploiting working-class lodgings. For example, when the police drew up a list of all blind alleys *intra muros* in 1842, they noted in detail the number of dwellings but systematically failed to register the names of the owners – a conscious failure, as demonstrated by Bourla's repeated protests that the 'houseknackers' were in fact well-known.[19] Fortunately, private papers deposited in public collections permit the identification of some 200 slumlords who were active in the 1840s and 1850s. Around 70 per cent were registered voters or paid license fees, implying that they were not impecunious. The licensees, however, did not belong to the upper classes: none paid for licences in the higher tariff categories. As for the remaining 30 per cent, only fragmentary data are at hand, but these occupations have been noted: one shopkeeper (owning 15 slum dwellings), one tailor's foreman (9), two masons (3 and 2), one pastry chef (3), one chimney-sweep (2), and one embroiderer (1). Although the sample is small, it suggests that the exploitation of slum dwellings was predominantly a lower middle-class business. For obvious reasons: participation in commerce and finance entailed risks, while investment in real estate – given the acute shortage of housing – was both secure and profitable.[20] Moreover, shopkeepers, retailers, and the like, because of their daily contacts with the lower classes, were well placed to tackle the numerous problems, especially irregular payment, arising from renting out accommodation to working families.[21]

The reactions of house-owners to the sanitary regulations promulgated in mid-century are most revealing. When several Belgian towns experienced political turmoil in February and March 1848 and then, a few months later, faced a cholera epidemic which took many lives, the Minister of the Interior, Charles Rogier, spurred local authorities to investigate 'the origins of the moral degradation and the physiological decay of the working classes'.[22] Antwerp's municipal government set up a *Comité de Salubrité publique* (Public Health Committee) to draw up a detailed report on housing conditions. Bourla, who not only was a great architect but a man of conscience, tried to convince the members of the *Comité* that strong measures and regulations were required to put an end to the worst abuses. He argued that everyone needed at least fourteen m^3 of living space and proposed that all dwellings lacking the most elementary hygienic facilities be evacuated immediately.[23] The *Comité*, however, resolutely refused 'to resolve officially how many inhabitants each tenement and each room might lodge or to forbid that they be occupied by an exceptional number of people'. Although it was 'highly desirable to limit the number of inhabitants of these tenements and their small and low rooms, since health and morality would improve . . . such limitations must come about as a result of advice and the paternalistic influence of the local administration, not through compulsion and official regulation'.[24] Quite simply, the propertied classes held the better end of the stick. The town government ultimately resolved that health measures should be carried out in such a way that the material interests of houseowners be affected as little as possible.[25] But of course the two interests were irreconcilable. In 1855 the poor relief authorities wrote to the mayor that most houseowners merely avoided the sanctions by interpreting literally the official directives without taking into account their intentions. Pumps were installed, but of such poor quality that they broke down after short use; drains were covered, but not sufficiently deepened, so that the alleys still frequently flooded with heavy rain; latrines were built but were so shoddy as to be unusable. And even these supposed improvements were confined to 45 of the 110 slums which had been declared uninhabitable.[26]

This was but one side of the coin. The other – even worse – side was the exorbitant increase in rents.[27] After stabilizing at a relatively low level in the seventeenth and eighteenth centuries, they rose far more rapidly than did food prices from 1805. The economic difficulties and demographic decline of the second decade of the nineteenth century brought a short breathing space, but during the 1820s, a time of commercial expansion and large scale immigration, rents rose at breakneck speed. By 1829, real prices were 150 per cent higher than around 1800. Thereafter they stabilized, due to the movement of a large number of paupers to the fifth ward and perhaps also to the growth of cheap hotels *intra muros*. Between 1827 and the middle of the 1870s, the number of boarding houses rose from scarcely 100 to more than 500.[28] In general, these establishments could accommodate only 10 to 20, but some offered sleeping room for 50 or more. The rented space often amounted to nothing more than a bed (or part of one) in a crowded dormitory; according to his or her means, the tenant received a bed with or without mattress, a sack of straw or some rags for a pillow. Many doss-houses functioned as transit barracks for poor migrants from Germany and eastern Europe on their way to the New World, but from the inquest of 1874 it appears that a large number of 'sedentary' day labourers also had to make do with a resting place in such *hôtels des miracles*.[29]

Shortly after the cholera epidemic of 1866, which took nearly 3,000 lives, the Medical Commission of Antwerp wrote: 'Rent is so high that the majority of the working population is obliged to dwell in the most miserable of lodgings, and many among them in dark and dank cellars'.[30] The growing number of slums shows that the proletariat indeed tried to counter extraordinary price increases by moving into the cheapest possible tenements. Did their efforts, their acceptance of extreme overcrowding, enable them to hold expenditure on rent at more or less the same level? To answer this question, the percentage shift in the real rent paid by Antwerp's assisted needy between 1780 and 1850 has been calculated.

Average weekly rent, expressed in kg. of rye bread, paid by supported Antwerp families, in 1780 and 1850

No. of Members	No. of families		Rent (kg. of rye bread)		Percentage shift
	1780	1850	1780	1850	
1	208	714	2·890	5·412	+ 87
2	131	330	4·080	7·882	+ 93
3	59	249	5·270	8·000	+ 52
4	44	246	5·440	8·706	+ 60
5	41	180	6·630	9·765	+ 47
6	29	163	6·630	10·235	+ 54
7	13	207	7·480	10·706	+ 43
8	5	123	9·350	11·529	+ 23
9	4	67	9·520	11·294	+ 19
10	1	35	9·520	11·824	+ 24

That the price rise remained under the urban average proves that the lower classes had moved into lodgings that were much smaller and inferior. Nonetheless, they had to spend much more on rent in the mid-nineteenth century than seventy years earlier: single individuals and aged couples *c.* 90 per cent more, families of 3–7 *c.* 50 per cent more, larger households *c.* 20 per cent more. The growth, thus, was inversely proportional to family size, indicative of an exceptional demand for the cheapest housing, especially single rooms. The price rise hit even harder because the real incomes of the families concerned diminished 10 to 30 per cent between 1780 and 1850.[31] This combination meant that rent absorbed a steadily greater proportion of the worker's budget. Whereas the lower classes around 1780 devoted at most 17 per cent of their real income on rent, the proportion 70 years later varied between 19 and 46 per cent. Despite

Per cent of real weekly income spent on rent by supported Antwerp families, in 1780 and 1850

No. of Members	Average weekly income (kg. of rye bread)		Rent (kg. of rye bread)		Per cent	
	1780	1850	1780	1850	1780	1850
1	16·660	11·765	2·890	5·412	17·3	46·0
2	28·560	20·588	4·080	7·882	14·3	38·3
3	31·280	26·471	5·270	8·000	16·8	30·2
4	40·800	29·412	5·440	8·706	13·3	29·6
5	45·220	29·412	6·630	9·765	14·7	33·2
6	46·240	38·235	6·630	10·235	14·3	26·8
7	55·760	50·000	7·480	10·706	13·4	21·4
8	57·460	52·941	9·350	11·529	16·3	21·8
9	71·740	58·824	9·520	11·294	13·3	19·2
10	68·000	58·824	9·520	11·824	14·0	20·1

deterioration of their living conditions, the aged in the mid-nineteenth century paid out on rent nearly three times more than at the end of the *ancien régime*, families of three to six around twice as much, and larger households averaged one half as much. No wonder that wage labourers were always on the look-out for cheap lodgings and that many of them were compelled to move repeatedly. Of the 201 couples married in 1830 and still in Antwerp in 1846, 175 had changed addresses at least once. The average was four moves per family, but 54, or 31 per cent of the mobile couples, changed their residence five times or more – thirteen families even ten times or more.[32]

From the correspondence of the Charity Bureau it can be seen that the weekly payment of rent was one of the most acute problems faced by the poor. For example, the widow Johanna Catharina Verheyen wrote despondently in 1832: 'The reasons why I've moved once again are the following. They want me to pay even more, because I earn a bit more at the moment. That's very difficult for me, since I have had to live so long on credit. I hope things won't go on the same way, for frequent moves bring extra costs'.[33] Numerous letters to the same effect show that moving due to sudden increases in rent was frequent in Antwerp during the first half of the nineteenth century. Since non-payment in such cases was common enough, it can be presumed that slumlords were inclined to demand more from new tenants.

Thus, during the most dramatic phase of Antwerp's economic transformation, the changing profile of urban space catalyzed the further deterioration of proletarian living conditions. The expansion of the port sector increased the need for commercial facilities, and this entailed the construction of new buildings and the demolition of others. For military reasons the available space could not be expanded, and therefore a substantial rise in land prices and house rents followed. Rents also rose under the pressure of the continuous influx of uprooted countrydwellers. The growth of the proletariat did indeed increase the demand for housing, but the extreme poverty of the labouring masses made the construction of new, decent dwellings within the reach of low-income groups an unattractive undertaking for businessmen. Since the ascendant élites refused to face the filth and stench of the 'barbarians', they did all they could to secure their neighbourhoods from overcrowding. Consequently the lower classes were driven to separate areas or streets, which turned into ghettos. Intermediate social strata were quite successful in exploiting this situation. They profited from the growing demand for cheap lodgings, subdividing old houses into one-room dwellings, filling back-gardens and courtyards with hovels, and renting out their unsanitary tenements for as much as they could get. The result was a steady worsening of housing conditions. Why make repairs when new tenants lined up to take the place of the old tenant? The combination of all these factors implied that the poor had to spend an increasingly large part of their declining incomes on rental of dwellings unfit for human beings. The housing question wrought by impoverishment produced further impoverishment. The implications were serious, for every penny the poor had to give up for rent was a penny less for other needs.

PART IV

Measurements of
Pauperization

CHAPTER 8

Food Consumption

The social costs of Antwerp's economic transformation were very high indeed. The incomes of many families were drained on two accounts: women and children were thrown out of work, while adjustments to wages were not sufficient to match the rise in food-prices. These difficulties were compounded by the ever harder struggle for living space, which sent house-rents soaring. However the question remains: what impact did these developments have on the level of poverty? How many labourers were living at or below the subsistence minimum, and did their proportion of the total population grow? If so, when, and at what rate? The available evidence for study does not include family budgets, nor the average earnings of the proletariat as a whole, but there are statistics with a bearing on working-class diet which do permit an alternative approach.

The quantity and types of foodstuffs consumed are perhaps the best criteria for objective measurement of the standard of living in the period under study.[1] Historians of France and Belgium, in contrast to their colleagues studying other regions, are particularly inclined to this method, since they have available a highly reliable source of information: the *octrois*, indirect taxes reinstated shortly before or after 1800 in the majority of towns of more than 5,000 inhabitants and levied on a number of products consumed within their jurisdictions.[2] In Antwerp, collection of the taxes began in April 1800. Five categories of merchandise were taxed: drinks (beer, wine, brandy, gin, and liqueurs), food (fish, meat, vinegar), fodder (hay, straw, and oats), fuel (coal, charcoal, and firewood), and other goods (soap). Many products were to be added in the following years: rye and wheat from 1819, oysters from 1843, game and poultry from 1845, and so on. The tax was due on all quantities of products intended for local consumption, whether harvested, grown, quarried, or manufactured on the spot or imported from elsewhere. All other goods were exempt.[3]

Although there were some incidents of fraud,[4] it was impossible to evade Antwerp's *octrois* on a large scale. All essential foodstuffs had to be imported, since there was no open space *intra muros* available for cultivation of grain or for grazing; even vegetable gardens and orchards were rare within the town. Supervision of the town's provisions was easy because of its topography: inland, the town was completely walled with entry only via closely watched bridges and gates, while the riverside was guarded by a small army of officials who inspected the contents of every ship immediately after arrival. The owners of goods in transit had to pay the *octrois*, receiving repayment only on submission of proof that the quantity and quality of goods exported corresponded precisely with the data previously noted by the tax collectors.[5]

The system was abolished in Belgium by a royal decree of 20 July 1860, so that the evidence from Antwerp theoretically covers the period 1800–1859. Unfortunately, not all the registers have survived. Leaving aside several smaller gaps, consumption of meat, beer, and wine can be traced from 1807, salt fish from 1813, gin from 1815, and grain from 1827. With the exception of rye and wheat, the periods are sufficiently long to reveal some general trends. Since the bulk of the quantitative data to be derived from Antwerp's *octrois* has already been published and analyzed,[6] a short summary of the most significant conclusions will suffice here.

The average *per capita* consumption of meat (beef, veal, mutton, and pork)

Figure 8: Average *per capita* consumption of meat and salted fish (kilograms) in Antwerp, 1807–1859

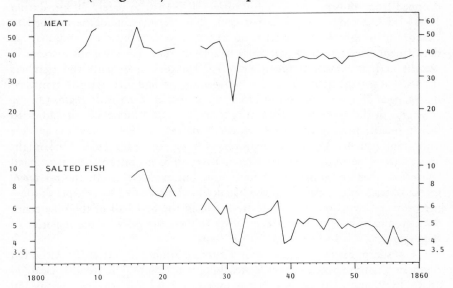

Figure 9: Average *per capita* consumption of beer and wine (litres) in Antwerp, 1807–1859

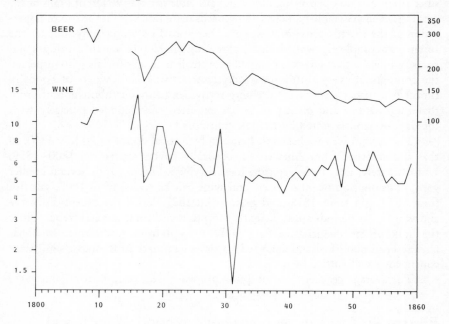

dropped from 48·6 kg. *per annum* during 1807–1810 to barely 38 kg. during 1850–1859, a reduction of 22 per cent. This decline cannot be ascribed to changes in weight of livestock: from five surveys held by the communal tax department between 1829 and 1850 it appears that there was no increase in weight and simultaneous investigation of livestock merchants and butchers shows, moreover, that the ratio between gross and net weight remained unchanged. Nor were more fish eaten to compensate for the decrease. On the contrary: in the space of scarcely fifty years, *per capita* intake of salt and dried fish (primarily herring and stockfish) nearly halved; in 1850–1859, the average inhabitant had 4·3 kg. *per annum*, versus 8 kg. in 1815–1822. One might argue that these figures are unrepresentative, since no information is at hand concerning the consumption of fresh fish, but without doubt the *per capita* intake of cod, sole, turbot, and the like declined markedly, for receipts of the 5 per cent tax levied on the sale of fresh fish in the first half of the nineteenth century diminished by 15 per cent, even though the price of the majority of these sorts of fish had risen by 20 per cent.

Consumption of grain can only be traced from 1827 to 1859. Although the period is too short to draw far-reaching conclusions, the trend is clear: in 1850–1859, annual consumption amounted to 156 litres *per capita* versus 160 litres in 1827–1836, *i.e.* a decline of around 2·5 per cent. A far greater drop appears to have taken place earlier, for five isolated references indicate that during the first two decades of the nineteenth century, an annual average of 180 to 195 litres of rye and wheat were consumed per person. Thus the total decline over the whole period must have amounted to between 13 and 20 per cent.

As for alcoholic beverages, beer, wine, and gin alone need to be considered; so little liqueur, rum, brandy, etc., was drunk that they can be ignored. The drop of consumption of beer was nothing less than spectacular: the annual average dropped from 307 litres a head in 1807–1810 to 130 litres in 1850–1859, a decline of more than 57 per cent. The *per capita* consumption of wine fell strikingly as well: after the middle of the century, it amounted to scarcely 5·5 litres a year, while 50 years earlier it had varied between 10 and 12 litres. The average *per capita* consumption of gin cannot strictly be determined, because distillers, unlike brewers, were not taxed on the basis of production actually brought to market but on the amount of raw materials used. All their efforts to the contrary, public authorities never discovered precisely how many litres of gin could be obtained from a hectolitre of mash. Until around 1840, the ratios given by the distillers roughly corresponded to those of the tax collectors: a minimum of five and a maximum of seven litres of gin per hectolitre of raw materials. There-after their points of view diverged. According to the officials, the yield of some distillers rose during the forties and fifties to 9 or 10 litres, while the entrepreneurs concerned maintained that they still did not exceed 6 litres. In either case, it is clear that average *per capita* consumption of gin at Antwerp in the first half of the nineteenth century did not rise. Even if the communal taxing service had been right, *i.e.* if a ratio of nine or ten litres of gin per hectolitre of mash is accepted as a basis for calculations after 1840, then average consumption amounted to at most 7·9 litres *per capita per annum* in 1850–1859, versus *c.* 8·4 litres in 1815–1824.

The declining *per capita* consumption of essential foodstuffs such as grain (between 13 and 20 per cent), meat (22 per cent), salt fish (46 per cent), and beer (57 per cent) can only be interpreted in one way: the absolute impoverishment of broad sections of the population. This conclusion is reinforced by an investigation of the amounts of bread, meat, butter, and beer consumed in 1815–1816 and 1859–1860 in five charitable institutions: the Foundling Hospital, housing girls under eleven and boys under twelve; the *Maagdenhuis*, an orphanage for girls aged eleven to twenty; the *Knechtjeshuis*, an orphanage for boys between twelve and eighteen years old; the Mental Hospital, housing adults only; and the Sint-Elisabeth Hospital which cared almost exclusively for the needy. In both 1815–1816 and 1859–1860, these five institutions together housed some 920 inmates, of whom around 600, or 65 per cent, were older than twenty.[7] These data regarding consumption of foodstuffs thus bear upon a fairly large number of internees, all belonging to the same social group but sharply differentiated by age and sex.

Between 1815–1816 and 1859–1860, the average *per capita* consumption of bread, meat, butter, and beer fell by 17, 21, 32 and 43 per cent, respectively

Average consumption of bread, meat, butter, and beer *per
capita per annum* in five charitable institutions at Antwerp,
1815–1816 and 1859–1860

	1815–1816				1859–1860			
	Bread* (kg.)	Meat (kg.)	Butter (kg.)	Beer (litres)	Bread* (kg.)	Meat (kg.)	Butter (kg.)	Beer (litres)
Foundling hospital	144·2	25·2	17·2	141·6	167·9	18·6	9·8	118·3
Boys' orphanage	227·8	40·9	19·3	303·3	236·5	28·7	16·8	96·4
Girls' orphanage	161·3	30·3	17·2	248·9	149·6	32·1	15·0	75·2
Mental hospital	224·5	32·5	16·8	344·2	173·4	53·3	11·3	307·3
Sint-Elisabeth's hospital	179·6	146·7	14·6	332·9	119·0	101·8	5·1	171·2
Average	184·7	81·7	17·0	290·0	153·6	64·4	11·6	164·3

* Mixed loaves consisting of half rye and half wheat.

– shifts on the same order as those calculated for the town as a whole on the basis of the *octrois*. One might suppose that the decline in the quantity of food consumed in these institutions was primarily induced by a deterioration of their financial means, but that simply begs the question, which calls for an explanation for the authorities' unwillingness to provide more funds for orphanages and hospitals. The solution must be sought in the general erosion of living conditions in Antwerp, which widened the gulf between the average diet of the urban population and that provided in charitable institutions. Hence it was considered necessary to bring the latter into line with the former. Nevertheless, some public officials felt that the inmates were still too well fed. Although the *per capita* consumption of bread, butter, and beer in the *Maagdenhuis* had been drastically limited, an inspector of the communal health service remarked cynically in 1858: 'I can state that these charming orphan girls are delicately fed. There is no better treatment in a boarding school for young ladies'.[8]

Were substitutes available for the lost meat, fish, bread, and beer? For meat and fish: no. According to the director of Antwerp's tax department, *per capita* consumption of butter in the late forties amounted to scarcely 10 kg. a year, a figure in the same range as the national average (9 to 11 kg., *c.* 1855).[9] Although no statistical information is available for Antwerp, without any doubt the consumption of other foodstuffs with large proportions of fat and animal proteins was minimal. From evidence relating to twelve Belgian towns with a total of 300,000 inhabitants, it appears that average consumption of cheese and edible oils in 1843 was respectively one litre and one half litre *per capita per annum*.[10] Not surprisingly, more and more people were compelled to make do with meat and fish of dubious quality. In 1832, the committee entrusted with the regulation of foodstuffs reported to Antwerp's municipal authorities: 'At the cattle mart on Saturday and Sunday morning meat and sausages of poor quality are sold to the poor at low prices; the sausages cost only two stivers a pound, which makes it quite obvious how tainted they are and detrimental to health'.[11] The same year, the committee complained about the laxity of the authorities in permitting public sale of rotten fish, all health regulations to the contrary. In the Boeksteegghetto, spoiled food lay, sometimes days at a time, in the stalls of the fishmongers. The municipal government, however, refused to intervene, because strict measures 'would only hurt those of our citizens who usually buy these foods'.[12] By 1844 the situation had not improved: the Medical Board declared that the mass of the population seldom ate meat; the only animal products which wage labourers could allow themselves were entrails, lungs, blood sausage, mussels, and scraps of stockfish.[13]

Since complaints about the low quality and high price of meat grew steadily more numerous, the town government resolved in 1851 to investigate the matter. The majority of the members of the commission judged that there was little or nothing remarkable about the meat trade. They declared that three categories of butchers were distinguishable, whose average prices varied considerably: 1 kg. of first quality beef cost *c.* 0·94 francs, while the third category sold for *c.* 0·5 francs. Gross profit amounted to around 25 per cent, certainly not excessive, taking into consideration the great quantity of scraps such as blood, entrails, and the like. The rapid growth of the number of butchers (from 76 in 1845 to 116 in 1850) was ascribed by the majority to the growth in the population and the flood of German emigrants embarking at Antwerp for America. Some members of the commission wholly disagreed with this point of view; their minority report argued that retail prices of meat of every quality were higher in Antwerp than elsewhere and that, since 1830, they had progressively risen despite the decline in wholesale prices. Moreover, entrails and other scraps could scarcely be written off as a loss since they were sold at great profits to the lower classes. In the end, they refuted the majority's explanation for the growing number of butchers: the population had scarcely grown 10 per cent between 1845 and 1850 and the emigrants to America were too few and too poor to have had much of an impact. According to the minority, things were just the reverse: exceptional profit margins had brought about an expansion of the retail trade in meat, which had in turn led to pricing agreements among the butchers. To correct such abuses, the minority proposed to set meat prices from week to week and to erect a communal abbatoir where the working classes would be able to obtain provisions. The town government, however, agreed with the majority, who argued that such measures, 'although salutary from the social point of the view, are destructive to the whole of society, which cannot exist without the free commercial and industrial activity of individuals'.[14]

As for grains, a distinction must be made between wheat and rye. While the average *per capita* consumption of the former rose by more than 20 per cent, the latter dropped by more than 60 per cent between 1827 and 1859, because the lower classes in growing number switched from rye to potatoes, which were far cheaper. As early as 1807, the prefect of the *département des Deux-Nèthes*

Figure 10: Average *per capita* consumption of grain for bread (litres) in Antwerp, 1827–1859

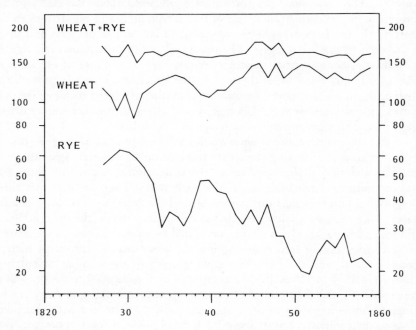

stated that 'the people have received considerable relief by the lowering of the price of potatoes, as this vegetable has become their principal food, which greatly diminishes the consumption of grain'. With specific regard to Antwerp, the Charity Bureau noted in 1805 'that if the potato has not yet replaced bread, at least it has become here a matter of prime necessity'.[15] Forty years later the transition was complete. In 1846, Antwerp's Medical Commission reported to the central government that the lower classes seldom ate bread any longer, and in 1848 the Chamber of Commerce explained that 'the majority of labourers live exclusively on potatoes'.[16] The growing importance of the so-called 'miracle tuber' in the diet of the working classes is borne out by quantitative data too. In 1814, according to the Charity Bureau, at least 107 1/7 sacks of potatoes were required to feed 3,000 poor for a single week; given that a sack held some 100 kg., this signifies around 510 grams of potatoes a person a day. A half-century later, 920 people in charitable institutions each received 700 grams a day.[17]

The *per capita* consumption of alcoholic beverages dropped during the first half of the nineteenth century from *c.* 330 litres to *c.* 140 litres a year. Obviously, the latter quantity – scarcely 0·4 litres a day – was completely inadequate; in a moderate climate, a person needs at least one litre of liquid a day to survive. Hence, the mass of the Antwerp population had to substitute something for beer. Well-water was brackish owing to the proximity of the Scheldt and tap-water drawn from the Schijn had become so polluted by the early nineteenth century that it was suitable only for industrial purposes.[18] Although quantitative information is lacking, there can be no doubt that consumption of milk was minimal. In 1859 the Antwerp physician F. de Wachter wrote that 'even the propertied classes only exceptionally drink milk'.[19] According to contemporaries, labourers could compensate for the drastic limitation on consumption of beer only by drinking more coffee.[20] National averages reveal a clear trend: the *per capita* consumption of coffee rose from 1·5 grams a day at the end of the *ancien régime* to *c*. 12 grams in the later fifties.[21] At least four or five grams are needed for one cup (about 0·15 litres); 12 grams would make two or three cups. However, coffee can be adulterated with a substitute in a ratio of four to one. If it is assumed that in the middle of the nineteenth century coffee was adulterated with chicory to the maximum, there was an average *per capita* consumption of about ten cups or about 1·5 litres of coffee substitute per day.[22] From the point of view of caloric values, the transformation was disastrous, for beer was an important source of nutrition in pre-industrial society: one litre of the lowest quality provided fifteen times more calories than the same amount of coffee. It is true that the use of sugar rose a little in the first half of the nineteenth century, but it in no way compensated for the loss of calories due to the decline in the volume of beer drunk. By 1860, every inhabitant of Belgium consumed on average only nine grams of sugar a year.[23]

The consumption of beer from inside and beer from outside the town evolved in opposite directions, just as did rye and wheat. While the *per capita* consumption of cheap beer brewed inside Antwerp dropped by more than 80 per cent between 1807 and 1859, that of expensive imported beer rose by around 20 per cent. These radically divergent trends attest to Antwerp's experience not only of impoverishment but also of social polarization during the first half of the nineteenth century. The enormous drop in the consumption of rye and locally-brewed beer demonstrates the impoverishment of broad segments of the population; more and more people were reduced to potatoes and coffee substitutes, the cheapest means of subsistence. Moderate increases in the consumption of wheat and imported beer, on the other hand, indicates both an absolute and a relative increase in the numbers of the propertied. The divergence of these consumption curves thus reflects an accentuation of social contrasts.[24]

The evolution of gin poses a problem. It has been shown that whatever ratio is taken as a basis for calculation, the average intake of this drink at Antwerp did not rise during the first half of the nineteenth century. Although the revenue service was convinced that the receipts of the distilleries after 1840 were far higher than their owners reported, it had to admit that *per capita* consumption declined from year to year. In 1850 the director even declared that, as things were going, 'gin would end up disappearing from the list of objects taxed'.[25] Besides, the decline in the number of distilleries – from more than forty in the early nineteenth to four in 1859 – was so sharp that it cannot be ascribed purely and simply to an increase in productivity.[26] Yet, the complaints of contemporaries over the extraordinary consumption of gin by the lower classes grew more and more numerous. In 1838, one high official declared that in Antwerp gin was no longer drunk from small glasses, but from quarter litres.[27] Six years later, the Medical Commission reported that 'the overwhelming majority of adult labourers drink gin, and a large number of them drink to excess'.[28] Although such pronouncements must be treated with care, the innumerable police warrants for drunkenness and the many orders prohibiting the hawking of spirits indicate that a large number of wage labourers drowned their sorrows in gin.[29] Moreover it cannot be a mere accident that in 1858 Antwerp's most popular poet, Andries de Weerdt, devoted one of his tunes to *Kwak*, Gin:

> They always talk of drinking
> and when they set to work
> there goes with clinking
> a drink before their work,
> and in between up to six times three.
> And no sooner the afternoon is over,
> again the pub they enter.[30]

The explanation for this apparent paradox must be sought in the large scale dilution and adulteration of alcoholic beverages. In 1844, an Antwerp police commissioner wrote to the town authorities: 'I have long heard complaints about the adulteration of spirits, especially gin. These misdeeds are not the work of the distillers but of the retailers who sell in small lots to the taverners. It is they who stretch two barrels out of a single barrel of gin by adding water and sulphuric acid'.[31] The *Commission du Travail*, instituted by the central government in 1886 to investigate the living conditions of the working classes, came to the same conclusion. In every town, spirits were heavily diluted. In Antwerp, according to the commission, 'gin' was sold which consisted of water, vitriol, and pepper; in Brussels, potatoes, beet roots, and wine-lees were often the primary ingredients; in Vilvoorde it was pepper, ether, and sal ammoniac; etc. In these circumstances it is not surprising that consumers got drunk quickly and became aggressive, nor that they frequently came down with painful and sometimes even fatal illnesses.[32]

Since the foodstuffs subject to taxation were not numerous, it is not possible on the basis of the *octrois* to reconstruct comprehensively the average daily diet of the population of Antwerp in the first half of the nineteenth century. The available data, however, can be supplemented with information drawn from institutional records and some national consumption figures.[33] As noted earlier, in 1814 the Charity Bureau needed around 10,714 kg. of potatoes to feed 3,000 poor a week, *i.e.* 510 grams per person per day. In order to check whether this quantity was representative for Antwerp's population as a whole, the following method was used: between 1550 and 1830, the average *per capita* consumption of bread at Antwerp declined from 470 to 340 grams a day, a diminution of some 28 per cent (nearly the same percentage as has been calculated for Ghent). Assuming that the missing bread was wholly replaced by potatoes, then *per capita* consumption was $\frac{(410 \times 100)}{70}$ or 586 grams of potatoes a day around 1830. Since it is more than likely that the declining consumption of other foodstuffs led to an expansion of potato consumption, an average intake of around 600 grams per person per day is an acceptable estimate. From the accounts of charitable institutions it can be deduced that this quantity had risen to 700 grams thirty years later. The same sources provide data concerning the consumption of butter: 47 grams *per capita per diem* in 1815–1816, 32 in 1859–1860. As for eggs: in the Sint-Elisabeth hospital a patient received about two eggs a week in 1858–1860, versus about five in 1815–1822. For lack of other information, national consumption figures for coffee show a rise from nine grams per person per day around 1830 to twelve grams during the period 1857–1859.

In short, the available sources contain, first, accurate figures on the consumption of rye, wheat, meat, salt fish and alcoholic drinks[34] and, second, fairly reliable figures regarding the consumption of potatoes, butter, eggs and coffee. The lack of information about other foods is not a serious handicap, since their average *per capita* consumption was minimal. Two periods have been distinguished: 1820–1829 and 1850–1859. The termination of the relevant data necessitated the choice of the last decade, while the years 1820–1829 have been chosen because, first, exact figures for grain consumption are only available from 1827 and, second, the sources concerning the period 1807–1819 for the other products contain too many gaps for reliable decennial averages to be calculated. From this investigation, it appears that the ration per person and per day fell from 2,592 calories in 1820–1829 to 2,267 in 1850–1859, a diminution of 12·5 per cent.[35] Although *per capita* consumption in Antwerp was substantially lower around 1860 than around 1820, it was still sufficient to supply vital needs. Nutritional specialists agree that a daily diet of 1,800 to 2,000 calories is a physiological minimum. At the same time it is accepted that an average intake of 2,200 to 2,400 calories per head is necessary to satisfy the requirements of a normally distributed population. Nevertheless, three remarks must be made.

In the first place, caloric needs vary considerably according to sex, age, and labour conditions. Consequently, the changes in the demographic composition of Antwerp's population in the first half of the nineteenth century must be considered. Chapter 5 has shown that continuous immigration not only reduced the excessive numbers of women of the late eighteenth century to more modest proportions but also greatly rejuvenated the population. It is obvious that these drastic changes had an important bearing on *per capita* food consumption: men eat more than women; old people eat less than young people. The same number of inhabitants in the 1850s would therefore have required substantially more calories than their predecessors in the 1820s. Taking into account the approximate ratios proposed by most nutritionists,[36] the quantities of calories needed daily by the different age categories, grouped by sex, in 1830 and 1856 have been investigated. All data were added together and the sum divided by the number of inhabitants. The result was then compared with the average daily diet every person actually had at his disposal in 1820–1829 and 1850–1859. About 1856 the average *per capita* deficiency amounted to no less than 215 calories per day as against barely 100 calories about 1830. Even this figure is probably too favourable, because it has been assumed that everybody did only moderately strenuous work, which was certainly not the case for the majority of Antwerp's population at the time.

In the second place, a proper amount of calories alone is not sufficient; the composition of the food is equally important. Therefore, protein, fat, and carbohydrate intake has been calculated for 1820–1829 and 1850–1859.[37] The *per capita* diet deteriorated qualitatively as well as quantitatively over this period. During the 1850s, carbohydrates provided some 71·5 per cent of the calories, versus 67 per cent during the twenties: this change took place primarily at the expense of fats, the proportion of which declined from 15·5 to 12 per cent. It is generally accepted that a balanced diet must consist of 15 per cent proteins, 25–30 per cent fat, and 55–60 per cent carbohydrate. The daily diet of Antwerp's population thus showed a gross and growing deficiency of fats during the first half of the nineteenth century. The same holds for animal proteins: in 1820–1829 they comprised 45 per cent of all proteins consumed, in 1850–1859 scarcely 38 per cent. For an adult, the latter quantity just barely satisfied minimal needs, but for children it was completely insufficient. Since no information is available concerning consumption of milk, vegetables, and fruit it is difficult to generalize about the intake of vitamins and minerals. Yet without doubt the calcium/phosphor ratio was poorly balanced: it varied between 0·25 and 0·30, while most nutritionists believe that it ought to be at least 0·6 for adults and 1 to 1·5 for children and pregnant women. The results were all the more serious because the diet as a whole provided barely half the requisite amount of Vitamin D. This deficiency, coupled with the absence of sunlight, often caused rickets (skeletal calcification with associated deformities). The children of the poor were prone to such illnesses, especially when they had to spend their days largely in confined and dark rooms. Many of them had crooked spinal columns, bowed legs, and ossified joints. To cite but two eyewitnesses: in 1804 the prefect of the *département des Deux-Nèthes* wrote that in the *Maagdenhuis* 'the majority of orphan girls have poor health and are malformed', and forty years later the reporter for the Medical Commission noted that 'many workers are below normal height and have bones not of the usual rectitude'.[38] The near total absence of Vitamin A undoubtedly explains the high incidence of visual impairment among the lower classes: around half of the cripples registered in the poor lists of 1850 suffered from either defective sight or total blindness. Evidently visual impairments were aggravated by certain occupations such as lacework and embroidery, but the great number of men among the blind or nearly blind paupers (some 40 per cent of the total) clearly indicates the determining influence of their diet.

Finally, it should be noted that an 'average' *per capita* diet estimation does not correspond to any social reality. Owing to lack of adequate sources, it is impossible to reconstitute the actual diet of the different social classes in Antwerp. The admirable investigator Edouard Ducpétiaux did compile various 'typical' budgets of working-class families in 1854, but they can hardly be considered as representative.[39] It is therefore better to turn to the Antwerp poor lists for the (low price) years 1780 and 1850. The following method was used. The wages of all family members were added together and supplemented with the aid provided by the Charity Bureau. The families and their total incomes were then divided according to the number of family members. Next, the average amount paid for rent was subtracted from average family income, relief included, after which the remaining sum was converted into the food which provided the highest number of calories per price unit, namely rye bread in 1780 and potatoes in 1850.

Average caloric intake, *per capita* and per day, of supported Antwerp poor in 1780 and 1850

Number of members	Number of families		No. of calories *per capita* and per day		Percentage shift
	1780	1850	1780	1850	
1	208	714	3,675	1,863	−50·5
2	131	330	3,342	1,863	−44·2
3	59	249	2,365	1,806	−23·8
4	44	246	2,145	1,530	−28·7
5	41	180	2,106	1,177	−44·1
6	29	163	1,819	1,385	−23·9
7	13	207	1,883	1,653	−12·2
8	5	123	1,641	1,530	−6·8
9	4	67	1,886	1,560	−17·3
10	1	35	1,594	1,395	−12·5

The evidence is plain: the eighteenth-century recipient of relief was indisputably far better off than his counterpart in the middle of the nineteenth century. Whereas most people on the dole around 1780 had an average daily intake of 3,000 calories, this quantity had been reduced seventy years later to barely 1,700, a decrease of almost 43 per cent. If it is assumed that every adult, *i.e.*, every person over nineteen, consumed a minimum of 2,000 calories per day, each child had a mere 1,230 calories in 1850. This figure is incredibly low – even taking into account that more than 50 per cent of the children were under ten. At the end of the eighteenth century the poorest sections of the Antwerp population had sufficient food, so that they could spend money on other things. In the middle of the nineteenth century, on the other hand, they lived on the verge of starvation. Even if they did not spend a single penny on fuel and clothing they still went hungry, and a diet of potatoes meant a severe lack of animal proteins, fats, and vitamins A and D.

Qualitative evidence fully confirms these figures. In 1847 François Digand divided the population of the town into five social categories, relating each to a specified diet. At the bottom of the ladder were the needy, *i.e.*, all those who had no savings and worked only irregularly; their starvation rations consisted of potatoes, rye bread, and some scrawny vegetables. The poor followed, equally lacking in possessions but managing to find work for most of the year. They ate little besides potatoes, rye bread, coffee heavily dosed with chicory, and sometimes (but seldom) a bit of bacon. Skilled labourers, who generally had a little to spare, had potatoes, mixed loaves, vegetables, a piece of bacon, and a more expensive cut of meat on Sundays; now and then they even had a glass of beer. According to Digand, these three groups – who together comprised the overwhelming majority of the population – bought hardly any food-stuffs which were not subject to the *octrois*. The lower middle class of small proprietors and small businessmen, in contrast, consumed conspicuously, while the rich bourgeoisie had nearly all luxuries to themselves.[40]

A detailed report on poverty in Antwerp, drawn up by the Charity Bureau in 1860, reiterated the assertions of Digand concerning the diet of the labouring poor: 'Black bread, potatoes, and coffee are the 'favourite' foods of the working class. The poor and even the workers seldom if ever eat a piece of meat'.[41] Although the 1860s witnessed economic expansion the shopping basket of the lower classes was just as restricted as before. In 1867 the Medical Commission declared: 'The customary diet of the labouring poor consists of rye bread in the morning with a dab of butter or grease and thin ersatz coffee; at midday, potatoes, sometimes with a bit of nasty fish or meat – scraps of hake, stockfish, herring, lungs, intestines, udders, and so on; in the evenings it's usually black bread and ersatz coffee'.[42] Two years later, *De Werker* wrote that the proletariat 'lacks, sometimes for months at a time, such essential foods as meat' and that 'bread-and-butter has become a luxury'.[43]

Antwerp's bourgeoisie at mid-century was fully aware that thousands lived in hunger. In December 1853, Mayor J.F. Loos founded an Association for Disbursing Cheap Soup,[44] which from 1854 sold soup daily for 0·05 to 0·08 francs a litre at a number of locations in the town. A kettle of 500 to 600 litres of the cheapest soup contained 10 kg. meat, 5 kg. fat, 50 kg. potatoes, 15 kg. rice, 5 kg. carrots, 4 kg. onions, 10 bunches of leeks, 5 litres of salt, and some pepper; the more expensive sorts included additional vegetables and meat.[45] The Association was subsidized by the town government, but the bulk of its expenses were met by private persons, who bought most of the soup (75 per cent) in the form of meal tickets to be dispensed to the needy. But this was a drop in the ocean: between 1854 and 1874, an average of 125,000 litres of soup were ladled out each year, scarcely enough to provide 350 families with one litre a day.[46]

Taking everything into account, it makes little sense to study hypothetical workers' budgets drawn up by contemporaries. That they all showed a serious deficit, however, indicates that nineteenth-century specialists in domestic economy themselves realized that the incomes of the lower classes did not nearly suffice to provide the most elementary needs. A single example: in 1841, the

Charity Bureau estimated the weekly expenses of a poor family of two adults with five children at a strict minimum of 10·20 francs, while the average income of such families in fact amounted to a mere 8·50 francs.[47] The rent estimated by the Bureau, 1·92 francs, corresponded closely to the average amount paid by assisted families of seven in 1850, 1·82 francs. According to the director, food cost at least 6·14 francs, of which 3·20 went on rye bread and 2·94 on other items. Presuming that the latter was spent on the cheapest of foodstuffs, potatoes, then each family member had a total of some 1,500 calories a day – nearly the same amount calculated for 1850. The remaining 2·14 francs had to go on the replacement of worn clothing (1·15 francs) and on the purchase of a small amount of fuel and oil (0·96 francs); that, however, was out of the question, since food and rent alone cost more than eight francs, so that, in reality, scarcely half a franc could be devoted to other purposes. The poor, in other words, faced the dilemma of either buying some secondary products and as a result suffering even more from hunger, or eating more but forfeiting all expenditure on clothing, heat, and light. Basically, the 'choice' made no difference: the margin was so thin that these families suffered permanent malnutrition.[48] To cite Andries de Weerdt once again:

> Those who managed to survive
> being ordinary labouring men
> they can say, I have been tortured
> for getting the food, the pots and pans,
> I have eaten sour scraps
> the baddest stuff instead of bread.
> And that's the reason why
> so many were doomed to die.[49]

Antwerp was not exceptional. In Ghent, the average *per capita* consumption of meat, salt fish, and beer fell during the first half of the nineteenth century by 16 per cent, 50 per cent, and 57 per cent, respectively. By 1850, the daily intake of calories, alcoholic beverages aside, amounted to only 2,056 per person in the pre-eminent industrial centre of Flanders, *i.e.*, nearly the same quantity as in Antwerp.[50] In Brussels, too, a comparable shift took place: between 1807–1810 and 1850–1859, the *per capita* consumption of meat declined by 22 per cent and that of beer by 45 per cent.[51] So far no investigation has been made into the long-term transformation of consumption patterns in other Belgian towns. Two series of data, however, suggest that Antwerp, Brussels, and Ghent were not characterized by especially low food consumption and that the deterioration of living standards was a general phenomenon.

In 1847, Eduard Stevens published the results of an inquest into the average consumption of meat in eleven Belgian towns during 1836–1845.[52] Since the sample contains Antwerp, Brussels, and Ghent, it is possible to verify Stevens' estimates. For Brussels and Antwerp, he estimated 47·2 and 35·0 kg. *per capita per annum*, respectively, while the actual consumption of meat was 48·1 and 37·4, in other words only 2 to 7 per cent more than the quantities calculated by Stevens. Consumption of meat in Ghent, in contrast, was slightly overestimated: 39·8 versus 38·4 kg. Altogether the figures given by Stevens are thoroughly plausible.

Average *per capita* meat consumption in selected Belgian towns about 1840, according to Eduard Stevens (kg.)

Tournai	55·5
Mons	55·1
Brussels	47·2
Mechelen	40·3
Ghent	39·8
Leuven	38·6
Antwerp	35·0
Namur	34·4
Liège	33·6
Bruges	31·2
Verviers	28·9

Bruges excepted, *per capita* consumption of meat was nowhere so low as in Liège and Verviers, the two most important manufacturing centres of the Walloon provinces in the second quarter of the nineteenth century; it is a myth that industrialization was paired to rising living standards. This conclusion is reinforced by the investigations of Edouard Ducpétiaux, according to whom the average consumption of meat in the province of Liège around 1850 varied between 4·5 and 25 kg. per person per year. The latter quantity was consumed only by the best-paid workers; others had to be satisfied with 4·5 to 10 kg. In the province of Hainaut, *per capita* consumption of meat was even lower than in the vicinity of Liège: 13 kg. a year on the average or scarcely 36 grams a day.[53] In Ghent, things were no different. According to the physicians Mareska and Heyman, who published a detailed report in 1846 on the living conditions of workers employed in the cotton factories, 19 per cent of them were never able to eat meat, and 29 per cent only once a week.[54] One cannot but agree with Ducpétiaux' clear words of 1855:

> To the physiologists and chemists who have calculated the amounts of nitrogen and carbon that foods must contain for subsistence, it is maintained that the population multiplies and propagates even though the nutritional conditions are not fulfilled. However, it is ignored or overlooked that this population lives miserably, that it wastes away, that scrofula and rickets strike it with an ineffaceable stigma, that its stature gets smaller, that its strength diminishes, that diseases and epidemics continuously decimate its overcrowded ranks. To what causes must this

degeneration – which is manifest to all who are willing to see and which it would be vain to deny – be imputed, if not in the first place to the unsoundness and the insufficiency of diet, which in turn are nothing but the results of the imbalance between the resources of the working classes and the basic necessities of life?[55]

CHAPTER 9

On Relief: Numbers

Given the drastic deterioration – both quantitative and qualitative – in the average daily diet, it is arguable that more and more proletarian families were living below the subsistence minimum. Nonetheless, Antwerp's mortality rate did not leap upwards during the first half of the nineteenth century,[1] indicating that the poor had other means of survival than wages. What were those sources of income? The most obvious answer would be that ever greater numbers resorted to institutionalized forms of relief. Thanks to exceptionally rich archives, the proportion of supported needy within the total population can be calculated for the whole period 1800–1860, providing an excellent theoretical measure of the impoverishment process. However various factors complicate the interpretation of these figures and limit their usefulness. Before drawing conclusions from aggregate data on the beneficiaries of outdoor relief, it is necessary to trace three parallel lines of development: the annual receipts of the Charity Bureau; the selection criteria employed by this institution; and the allowances it distributed among the different categories of the urban poor.

The French poor law of 1796 reorganized public relief in the southern Netherlands, the basic outlines of the system remaining in force until 1925. In each 'commune' two secular institutions under the supervision of the municipal authorities were created: Commissions for the Civil Hospices, entrusted with the administration of all charitable foundations and hospitals, and Charity Bureaux, controlling outdoor relief. Although this reorganization brought no radical break with the existing situation in Antwerp, it was some time before the almoners ceased their task. On 20 January 1799 the *Nieuwe Bestiering* was definitively replaced by the Charity Bureau, which received the full income of charitable institutions designated for outdoor relief.[2] With debts far in excess of income, the municipal authorities organized in 1800 an 'octroi municipal et de bienfaisance' to provide funds for public assistance; only a fraction of the proceeds, however, actually went to poor relief. In the period 1811–13, the *octrois* raised *c.* 2,750,000 francs, of which barely 752,000 (27 per cent) went to the Charity Bureau and the Commission for the Civil Hospices; some forty years later, the proportion had declined to less than 20 per cent.[3] Nonetheless, the Charity Bureau was largely dependent on these subsidies: between 1811 and 1860, they constituted more than half the total annual receipts, whereas only 30 to 40 per cent derived from real estate with which the institution had been endowed. The illiberality of the bourgeoisie can be deduced from entries under 'alms and gifts' in the Bureau's accounts. From *c.* 10 per cent in the second decade of the nineteenth century, the proportion of income from this source dwindled to *c.* 1 per cent of total annual receipts in the forties and fifties. Only during severe economic crisis were the upper classes prepared to make greater financial efforts. That was the case in 1845 and 1847, when alms and gifts accounted for more than 8 per cent of revenue. The tax on amusements brought little or nothing; this 'poor money' (*armengeld*), temporarily instituted in 1796 and made permanent by an Imperial decree in 1809,[4] amounted initially to only 10 per cent of the ticket price of public dances and plays. Although the rate was raised to 25 per cent in 1822, the Charity Bureau seldom got more than 1,000 francs a year, *i.e.*, at most 0·5 per cent of the finances which the institution disposed. All other sources of income, derived chiefly from the sale of medicinal aids prepared in the Sint Elisabeth Hospital and manufactured goods produced in the *ateliers de charité*, represented a mere 5 per cent of the total.[5]

Although the annual receipts of the Charity Bureau rose from *c.* 179,000 francs in the years 1811–1820 to *c.* 310,000 by the late fifties, the administration had to deal with a chronic and growing shortage of funds. Shortly after the creation of the new institution, complaints came over the insufficiency of the subsidies provided by the authorities. On 6 October, 1803, the director wrote to the communal council:

> The lives and well-being of thousands are at stake, something sufficiently important, it seems to us, that it should not be an object of indifference. If one learns that the poor are dying of hunger and malnutrition, that the poor are overcome by the cold because they have nothing to bundle up in, that still others are the victims of illness caused by the severity of the seasons, then one must assume responsibility.[6]

But moral indignation changed nothing. Though the Charity Bureau might argue that the receipts of *octrois* had been designated for public assistance, the municipal administration resolutely refused to devote a larger percentage to poor relief on the pretext that the almoners' inclinations were too liberal. The almoners answered sharply that they were constantly at work regulating the needy: 'All those capable of working are struck from the poor lists; only the elderly, the lame, the widowed, and the orphaned are effectively supported'. In these circumstances, they continued, for we who undertake a thankless and costly task, who regularly put our health at risk visiting the poor in their homes, who must neglect our own businesses, it is painful indeed to state that we waste a great deal of our time pleading for the things which should be allowed to us so that we can honourably fulfill our duties.[7]

Many other letters to the same effect could be cited. The entire correspondence of the Charity Bureau with the municipal government was one continuous lament about the insufficient finances of the institution. Until 1822, the Bureau more or less succeeded in balancing its budget, but thereafter expenditure nearly

Figure 11: Annual receipts and expenditure (in francs) of the Antwerp Charity Bureau, 1811–1860

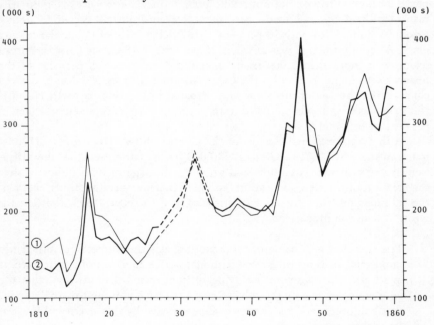

1 Receipts   2 Expenditure

always exceeded receipts (Figure 11), so that one loan after another had to be raised. Although the town council provided greater subsidies over the years (the annual average rose from *c.* 86,000 francs in 1811–1820 to *c.* 152,000 in 1851–1860), the Bureau never received enough substantially to assuage social problems. The growing disparity between the rising number of the needy on one hand and available funds on the other obliged the institution to limit public support more and more. There were two ways to do it: either employ stricter selection criteria, so that fewer of the needy could lay claims to aid, or diminish allowances in order to assist as many paupers as possible.

Both the *Nieuwe Bestiering* and the Charity Bureau had as their goal the provision of material aid to all persons unable to provide for their own subsistence. What did this mean in practice? Besides the orphaned and the aged, the ill and the lame, the ranks of the needy were considered to include wage labourers who could not find employment, families which through accidents beyond their control had no means of subsistence, and widows, widowers, and other heads of families with many children but an income which did not suffice to provide the most basic expenses for food and rent.[8] Implicitly, all wage labourers were potentially needy, according to the administrators of poor relief. The definitions which they used, however, were ambiguous. The *Nieuwe Bestiering* took the position that the elderly and lame could be considered for public assistance only if they were entirely incapable of working. The directors were also of the opinion that the able-bodied unemployed should not be permanently supported: regular help was reserved for those who could not labour because of physical infirmities or for large families. For the latter, the regulations of 1799 stipulated that parents themselves had to provide for the subsistence of at least two children.[9]

The replacement of the *Nieuwe Bestiering* by the Charity Bureau led to reevaluation of the criteria for relief. Henceforth, only families with at least three children to support could claim permanent assistance; all other families were excluded unless they could demonstrate that it was impossible for them to make ends meet. As for widows and widowers: those who had two children to support would receive regular relief only if the second child was under six, while those with three or more only received help for boys and girls under twelve. The poor-law administration was prepared to deviate from the new rules in exceptional circumstances such as famine, but the daily allowance could not exceed seven stivers in the summer and eight in winter, no matter how large the family.[10]

In 1823, screws were tightened once again. Permanent relief was henceforth reserved for families with at least four children and whose head of household earned no more than three guilders per week. To mitigate the blow, the Charity Bureau would provide more temporary relief than in the past, especially during the winter months; those who did not satisfy the new conditions might submit an application for such temporary allowances, on the presumption that, through illness or structural unemployment, they had no income.[11]

In 1837 the eligibility criteria were changed for the third time. From then on, poor families had to have at least five children under twelve and the prime breadwinner could earn no more than 1·65 francs a day to enjoy permanent support. Single adults had to be over seventy and infirm; if still in good physical condition, they had to be satisfied with assistance during the winter only.

The rest of the needy were excluded, unless a thorough investigation showed that they could not provide for their own subsistence.[12]

Clearly the Charity Bureau did all it could to limit the most demanding group, namely the recipients of permanent relief. Even so, the institution could not hold its expenses at a stable level, let alone reduce them. Every time more restrictive standards were applied, the number of families which fulfilled the new conditions soon surpassed the previous level. Hence the poor relief authorities were obliged gradually to lower the allowances they provided. Between 1779 and 1850, the maximum sum granted to families permanently supported changed six times; three nominal decreases (1781, 1826 and 1837) and three nominal increases (1799, 1805 and 1841), the latter insufficient to compensate for rising food prices. While the daily needs of widows and widowers without children during the period 1780–1789 were estimated at the equivalent of 2·6 kg. of ryebread, during the decade 1840–1849 they had to make do with less than 2·2 kg., a reduction of 15 per cent. For elderly couples the drop was of the same order: *c*. 3·7 kg. of ryebread in the forties against 4·3 kg. at the end of the eighteenth century, a decline of 14 per cent. As for needy families with children to support: in 1779, the maximum allowance for seven persons was established at 17 stivers a week, the equivalent of 1½ kg. of ryebread per day; by the mid-nineteenth century, dole amounted to at most 1·50 francs a week, just enough to buy one kg. of ryebread a day.[13]

But that was not all. Since the increase in subsidies granted by the municipal government lagged far behind the growth in the numbers needing relief, the Charity Bureau could not even disburse at the level it itself had established. In 1800, the director informed the municipal council that actual allowances lay well below official norms and that, as a result, the needy were justifiably disaffected and embittered. 'The arrogance one sees in their eyes makes one fear unpleasant scenes', one almoner remarked in 1801. Year after year, the same complaints were voiced. A few days before the revision of allowances in 1805, the Charity Bureau declared that it was totally inadequate: the new allowances lay only 10 per cent above the earlier ones, whereas at least 25 per cent was required simply to keep pace with inflation. The financial situation of the institution was by then so bad that new petitioners for relief had to wait until a place became vacant.[14] During the 1810s, the gap between theory and practice widened even further. Although the calls upon poor relief emphasized the need for more funds to save the many paupers from starvation, the authorities refused to provide additional funds. According to the town council, the Charity Bureau could make great savings by providing soup rather than money, since the needy were supposed not to spend their incomes in a rational fashion. The almoners replied indignantly that families on relief could scarcely pay rent, let alone make 'irrational' purchases, and one could hardly ask human beings to live exclusively on soup.[15] It was all to no effect. The town council did not insist on the soup kitchens, but it was not prepared to grant more subsidies, so that the Charity Bureau had to lower family allowances. By 1820, poor relief had turned into a farce. Some paupers even borrowed children to obtain higher allowances. The

Figure 12: Index of real *per capita* allowances received by permanent dole-drawers in Antwerp, 1811–1860

(1811 = 360 grams of rye a day = 100)

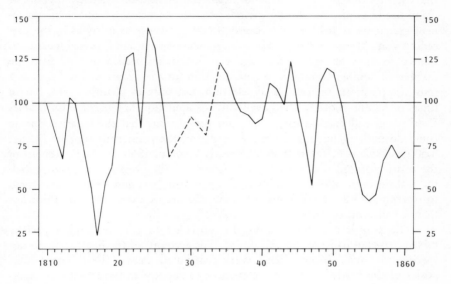

Charity Bureau reacted harshly against such practices, but admitted that the families involved could hardly be blamed since the progressive retrenchment of allowances spurred them to deception.[16]

The following decades brought no improvement. From a report drawn up in 1839, it appears that single elderly persons received only two francs a week, although due three francs. Two years later the poor-law administration declared that relief funds should be divided among so many needy that each would receive a pittance. By 1860 the situation had become hopeless. To cite the almoners themselves:

> The aid provided by the Charity Bureau is in most cases absolutely inadequate; it suffices not even to pay for a part of their rent . . . it is an inexplicable mystery to us how most of these families manage to stay alive.[17]

The accounts of the Charity Bureau allow investigation of amounts permanent dole-drawers received between 1811 and 1860.[18] All amounts have been converted into kg. of rye, indexed against 1811 base levels; the *per capita* allowance was at that time equivalent to 132 kg. of rye or some 360 grams a day. Figure 12 shows that this level was matched or exceeded in only 15 of the 45 years for which information is available. It also shows that real *per capita* allowances were smallest when need was greatest. During the famine of 1817, for example, the index fell to 24 points, *i.e.* less than 87 grams of rye per person per day. That the purchasing power of *per capita* allowances had been severely reduced between 1817 and 1847 must be ascribed to a radical change in the policy carried out by the Charity Bureau. Until around 1825, the institution tried to support as many needy as possible during periods of crisis. Hence the number of permanent recipients in 1817 leapt to nearly 4,600, *i.e.* twice as many as in the preceding year. Impoverishment was however too massive and financial means too limited to carry on in this manner. The poor relief needed to hold firm the number of families coming into consideration for the *secours continuel* and, as a result, applied stricter criteria of selection, not only in plentiful years but in times of famine too. By 1850 even this manipulation had become untenable. Destitution had reached such enormous proportions that the Charity Bureau could do nothing but register more people on the permanent support lists: *c.* 5,500 in 1852, *c.* 6,500 in 1856, and nearly 7,000 in 1860. Since the receipts of the institution did not rise proportionately and the price of rye skyrocketed, the real *per capita* allowance fell sharply: between 1851 and 1860, it amounted to scarcely 85 kg. of rye a year or some 230 grams a day, *i.e.*, one third less than a half century earlier.

The poor-law administration also provided support in kind, especially mixed loaves of half rye and half wheat. The accounts of the institution do not specify how such disbursements were distributed among the different categories of the needy. The amount devoted to support in kind however represented, throughout this period, only 25 per cent of all expenditure on outdoor relief, meaning that there could be no question of compensation for rising prices. This conclusion is supported by an investigation of the quantities of bread distributed to permanent recipients in 1780, 1804 and 1850.[19]

Percentage distribution of mixed loaves among supported Antwerp poor in 1780, 1804 and 1850

Kilograms of bread per week	Single persons			Aged couples			Families of five		
	1780	1804	1850	1780	1804	1850	1780	1804	1850
Less than 5	6·4	50·9	47·4	0·0	22·9	41·9	0·0	25·0	36·4
5–10	22·5	30·9	52·6	28·6	60·0	54·9	55·6	37·5	63·6
10–15	71·1	16·4	0·0	28·6	11·5	3·2	44·4	37·5	0·0
15–20	0·0	1·8	0·0	14·2	2·8	0·0	0·0	0·0	0·0
20 or more	0·0	0·0	0·0	28·6	2·8	0·0	0·0	0·0	0·0

Between 1780 and 1850, a radical transformation had taken place: while at the end of the *ancien régime*, scarcely 29 per cent of single persons and old-aged couples received less than 10 kg. of bread per week, all the former and nearly 97 per cent of the latter were in this situation by the mid-nineteenth century. Families of five faced an equally spectacular decline in their weekly allowances in kind: in 1780, 44 per cent of them had more than ten kg of bread and none less than five; in 1850, the proportions were reversed.

Innumerable letters written by the poor themselves or by professional letter-writers on their request attest to the human dramas caused by the systematic retrenchment of poor relief. In 1832, a widow with five children petitioned the Charity Bureau piteously for a small increase in her weekly allowance. Since the poor relief handed her only 0·40 francs and a kg. of bread, she had to endure 'the most unbearable misery which any human being ever suffered'. She could no longer pay her rent and was threatened with eviction, so that 'we'll all die like dogs on the street'.[20] In 1845, a family with three children received only 1 franc a week from the Charity Bureau, even though their total income from wages barely reached 4 francs, of which 2·36 went on rent; as a result of the failure of the potato harvest, their vegetable patch had provided almost nothing that year.[21] In June 1846 the neighbours of an 80 year-old widow wrote to the Bureau that the woman would starve if her allowance was not raised; the 1·75 francs a week was her sole source of income. Since she had to spend 1·25 a week on rent, only 0·50 remained for food – the daily equivalent of 300 grams of ryebread or 650 grams of potatoes.[22]

These were the lucky ones. Other needy claimants were not left to their fate by the poor relief; they were directed to the *secours casuel* or the *secours accidentel*. With the former, they received regular support (mainly during the winter months), but the amount was not fixed to any standard. With the latter they were assisted only in exceptional circumstances, such as disease, famine, and so on. Since the Charity Bureau was unable to provide an adequate allowance to even the most privileged group, it is no surprise that the institution provided the rest with a pittance. In 1850 the director wrote to the town government that subsidies designated for the *secours casuel* barely provided a few hundred people with a minimal quantity of bread daily.[23] He was not exaggerating: between 1851 and 1860 the temporary recipients of aid received an average of 3·40 francs a year, the equivalent of 22 kg. of rye in years of plenty and 11 kg. in years of dearth, some 420 or 210 grams a week respectively.

There is no point in calculating the average *per capita* allowance of the needy who were referred to the *secours accidentel*, for, after subtracting expenses for regular assistance (the *secours continuel* and *secours casuel*) the Charity Bureau had virtually nothing left over. In fact, the occasional recipients of relief were put on something resembling a waiting-list: the poor-law authorities recognized their need but could provide material help only to those among them who stood on the verge of starvation; others had to wait until they met the criteria for regular assistance, *i.e.*, having the requisite number of children or being very old. As impoverishment advanced and the Charity Bureau, through lack of finances, applied increasingly stricter criteria, a growing number of families were brought into this category. By 1810 it had reached such enormous proportions that the poor relief authorities no longer bothered to collect detailed demographic and occupational data on the families concerned, and frequently official reports gave their numbers in round figures.

For these reasons, separate figures for each of the categories of the assisted needy will not be given here. Regular recipients of relief, for example, were not necessarily the most impoverished inhabitants of Antwerp: many other families were as badly or even worse off, but did not fulfill the conditions to be eligible for the *secours continuel*. Since selection criteria were repeatedly changed, it is impossible to draw significant conclusions from the fluctuations in the numbers of regular recipients. Hence all supported indigents have been counted together, irrespective of the form of support they received. Only in this way can confusion caused by largely artificial shifts within and among the various categories be overcome.

Although comparison of the available data is not without difficulties,[24] some general trends can be charted. Between 1773 and 1815 the recipients of outdoor relief, as a percentage of the total population, grew from 11 per cent to nearly 18 per cent. During the dearth of 1816–1817, coupled to an economic crisis, the number receiving support reached greater proportions than ever before: in 1817, on average 23·5 per cent of all inhabitants needed assistance from the Charity Bureau. Despite the drastic fall in food-prices during the following years, the percentage of recipients remained at this high level. The explanation is that the textile industry had lost all importance by 1820, while the activity of the port stagnated due to structural difficulties of commerce after the separation from France. Between 1818 and 1824, Antwerp's poor relief authorities reiterated that the vast majority of labourers could not find work; the wages of laceworkers, moreover, were so low that they did not suffice even to keep a single person alive.[25]

The gradual reduction of the supported needy as a percentage of the total population between 1823 and 1829 (from *c*. 23 per cent to *c*. 19 per cent) was caused primarily by the application of stricter selection criteria, by which many families were no longer eligible for public support. It is possible that the trend was also affected by the growth of traffic on the Scheldt, which presumably had a favourable influence on employment opportunities, though this factor was certainly not decisive. Indeed, the percentage receiving support began to drop before the commercial expansion made itself felt and, in 1829, when a record number of ships entered the harbour, the Charity Bureau informed the town government that poverty had reached previously unknown levels. The poor relief authorities admitted that the growth of trade had brought great profits and created employment possibilities for the lower classes, but added that during the winter months shipping often came to a standstill and that work in the harbour required great physical strength. Thus, the directors continued, the numbers requesting support sky-rocketted in every bad season, while ever more children, women, and the elderly had to petition for public assistance. That the number of recipients nonetheless remained constant (and thus in decline in relation to the growing population) was, according to the Charity Bureau, purely and simply the result of its policy of severe retrenchment: 'We have in recent years used every possible means to slash expenses, and we have even gone so far as to strike families with four children from the poor lists'.[26]

The succeeding three decades brought no improvement: the beneficiaries

Figure 13: The recipients of outdoor relief as a percentage of total population in Antwerp, 1773–1860

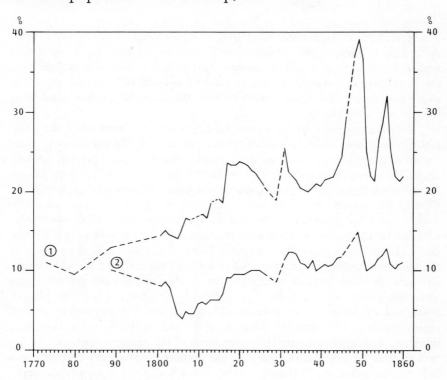

1 All recipients of outdoor relief
2 Recipients of permanent support

of outdoor relief in 'normal' years always represented 20 to 25 per cent of the population. And even these proportions give too rosy a picture of the social problem, as the almoners repeatedly emphasized. Again and again they argued that the actual number of the needy was double the recorded figure and that they had to leave out thousands of families for lack of funds.[27] When in 1843, a year of economic recovery, the authorities refused yet again to raise the subsidies, the poor relief officials wrote despondently:

> We regret as much as you do that the number of the needy and their misery reach ever greater proportions, that the needs of the poor grow as they do, that the expenses for mitigating them a little (to say nothing of relieving them) continue to exceed your expectations as well as ours . . . but we have frequently shown you a fact which is clear to all, a fact recognized by most communal administrations, a fact about which members of

our legislative assemblies speak with concern, a fact that is not peculiar to Belgium but is felt even more keenly in England and France, namely the growth of *pauperism*.[28]

The fearful crisis of 1845 and succeeding years indicates that they were right. According to Ducpétiaux, no less than 39 per cent of Antwerp's population needed assistance in one way or another. This ratio does not seem exaggerated, for 32 per cent of inhabitants received outdoor relief in 1856, when, according to the correspondence of the Charity Bureau, the situation was less threatening than in the late 1840s.[29]

Three conclusions can be drawn. First, poverty, as measured by the number of beneficiaries of outdoor relief, grew most strongly during the early nineteenth century: from *c.* 14·5 per cent around 1800 to *c.* 23·5 per cent around 1820. The explanation undoubtedly lies in the irreversible decline of the labour intensive textile industry. Second, despite the policy of retrenchment which the Charity Bureau was forced to carry out, the proportion of supported needy within the total population remained fairly constant until 1860; obviously, commercial expansion in this period offered insufficient compensation for the decay of nearly every industrial activity. Third, the actual number of needy in the mid-nineteenth century amounted to some 40 per cent of Antwerp's population, as deduced from an estimate of poor relief in 1845 (42 per cent), the unverifiable but clearly credible figure given by Ducpétiaux for 1849 (39 per cent), and a calculation, obtained by adding together *all* categories of assisted needy, for 1856 (37 per cent). Thus since the end of the eighteenth century, when the authorities estimated the proportion of the needy in the total population at 20 to 22 per cent the indigent had doubled. No wonder that *per capita* food consumption fell so sharply in the first half of the nineteenth century.

Although a large amount of statistical material has been published on the number of indigents receiving relief in other Belgian towns during the Industrial Revolution, it cannot be used to draw meaningful comparisons with the data from Antwerp. This would only be possible if the selection criteria applied by poor law authorities in the towns involved were known. Contemporaries themselves were conscious that significant differences existed from province to province and from place to place. But they were mainly interested in the financial aspects of public support and, as a result, did not record the norms which local Charity Bureaux applied to the poor lists. Even the admirable sociologist *avant la lettre* Edouard Ducpétiaux, who devoted numerous books and articles on poverty, paid no attention to the divergence of eligibility criteria. The same is true for the few historians who have attempted to discover the extent of poverty in nineteenth-century Belgian towns. They have provided a great deal of quantitative data but have not specified what 'siphoning mechanisms' the different poor relief authorities employed to limit the number of those supported, so that it is not clear to which categories of poor their figures relate.[30]

It is however beyond doubt that the proportion of the supported needy in Belgium's urban population grew significantly during the century after 1750.

At Ghent, the time-lag between the decay of traditional industry and the rise of cotton manufacture entailed under- or even unemployment for many artisans, so that the poor-law authorities had to assist more and more inhabitants: 13 per cent in 1793, against 7 per cent fifty years earlier. Although precise data are lacking, it can be assumed that the spectacular boom of the cotton industry in the period 1795–1810 was matched by a drop in the number receiving dole. The demand for workers far exceeded the supply, leading on one hand to wage rises and on the other hand to stronger relief regulations. After 1810 the social situation again worsened. Accelerating migration to Ghent augmented the labour pool, while demand diminished as a result of further mechanization; the concurrence of both processes enabled entrepreneurs to depress wages significantly. Moreover, the cotton industry faced recurrent crises, so that workers were repeatedly thrown out of work. The result was that, by 1850, the Charity Bureau supported no less than 33 per cent of the population of Ghent, half of them on a permanent basis; the actual number of needy at that point was estimated at 41 per cent, *i.e.*, nearly twice as many as at the end of the *ancien régime*.[31]

Liège, the largest town in the Walloon provinces and the preeminent centre of metallurgy in Belgium, witnessed the same expansion of poverty. Although heavy engineering and coal mining developed at a rapid pace, it did not yet compensate for the decline in the older economic sectors. The implications were all the more serious because the crisis of nail manufacture and other domestic industries in the surrounding countryside forced many cottars to leave their home villages and swell the ranks of the urban proletariat. Whereas the Liège Charity Bureau in 1808 had supported 'only' 8 per cent of the inhabitants, the proportion amounted to nearly 14 per cent a decade later, and by 1850 it had risen to 27 per cent.[32]

In Brussels, too, steadily more working-class families required public assistance. Although the capital played an essential role in the industrialization of Belgium through banking institutions and the creation of a dense network of railways, hardly any factories were set up in the city itself; Brussels' capitalists and government officials preferred more profitable investment elsewhere in the country. The presence of a large number of nobles and well-to-do foreigners as well as political and administrative centralization after 1830 stimulated the development of a variety of 'sweated trades', but the continuing immigration of impoverished artisans and uprooted country dwellers encouraged the underpayment of the workers. No wonder that the proportion of supported needy in the population as a whole rose from 15 per cent in 1782 to more than 30 per cent in the late 1830s. By 1845, their number had risen such that the Charity Bureau had to apply for stricter selection criteria: rather than giving a pittance to ever more paupers, the directorate resolved henceforth to provide financial aid only to the aged and infirm on one side and to very large families on the other. The number on the dole fell within five years to 20 per cent.[33]

Medium-sized and small centres fared no better. At Mechelen, the proportion of supported-needy remained at the same level during the French régime, but rose progressively thereafter: to 16 per cent in 1829, nearly 20 per cent in 1836, and more than 23 per cent at mid century.[34] In Ath, Hainaut, the increase was of the same order: from 8–9 per cent in 1772 to 23·5 per cent around 1850. Mons and Tournai, two other towns in Hainaut, experienced a similar fate: whereas at the end of the eighteenth century barely 12 per cent of the inhabitants received public assistance, the proportion in 1850 amounted to nearly 29 per cent for Mons and 39 per cent for Tournai.[35] At Namur, finally, the numbers on the dole in 1811 represented some 31 per cent of the total population, and during the second quarter of the nineteenth century no less than 40 per cent.[36]

It should be emphasized that these figures are not strictly comparable, since too little information is available on the criteria employed by the various Charity Bureaux. That the *trend* everywhere was the same, however, points unequivocally to growing social problems. This conclusion is supported by well-documented national averages calculated by two contemporaries, Adolphe Quetelet and Edouard Ducpétiaux. During the famine of 1816/17, one in eight inhabitants of the southern Netherlands received public support, one in seven in the 'normal' year 1823, and one in five at mid-century.[37] The commission set up by the Belgian government in 1848 to investigate the causes of this growing destitution hit the mark when they declared that

> Pauperism, as distinct from poverty, is essentially a plague of modern times. Present day society has created new forms of suffering. There have been poor people in every period of history, but pauperism has not always and everywhere existed. One understands by that concept the presence in one state of exceptional numbers of the poor dependent on public support.[38]

PART V

The Labouring Poor

CHAPTER 10

On Relief: Occupations

That between 1820 and 1860 more than 20 per cent of the population of Antwerp in normal years and nearly twice as many in times of crisis depended upon public assistance clearly indicates that pauperism was not a marginal problem. A question arises, however, whether the *permanent* recipients of relief formed a distinct social category with its own specific characteristics. Did they constitute a *lumpenproletariat*, as some historians have argued,[1] or were they an integral part of the working class? To answer this question, one must turn to the poor lists which, *inter alia*, registered the marital status, age, physical condition, and occupation of every person in receipt of the *secours continuel*. On the basis of these data, it is possible to study in considerable detail the demographic composition and occupational structure of those on relief.

The earliest poor list dates from 1780. Unfortunately it is distinctly incomplete: the surviving sections cover only 13 of the 32 wards into which the town was at that time divided by the poor law authorities. On the assumption that the number of recipients of permanent relief remained unchanged since 1773, the 1,524 paupers registered in the fragmentary list of 1780 represented some 50 per cent of the total. The poor lists of 1827 and 1855 have been chosen because they were, respectively, the earliest and the latest complete nineteenth-century registrations yet traced.

It ought to be noted that the poor lists seldom distinguished between childless widowers and single adult males, that they do not always specify the sex and age of the children, and that they never mention co-resident lodgers. Nonetheless, systematic analysis of these sources reveals several demographic characteristics of the assisted population. Four types of families have been distinguished for this purpose:

A   elderly widows and widowers or single individuals without resident children;

B elderly couples without resident children;
C widows and widowers or single individuals with resident children;
D married couples with resident children.

The distribution of these family types was as follows:

Types of Antwerp families receiving permanent relief, by percentages, in 1780, 1827 and 1855

Type		1780	1827	1855
	N =	638	1,374	1,760
A		44·7	40·8	32·8
B		16·6	8·4	5·4
C		17·9	18·0	34·4
D		20·8	32·8	27·4

Undoubtedly the most striking revelation of the poor lists is the spectacular growth of types C and D, rising from a combined share of *c.* 39 per cent in 1780 to *c.* 62 per cent in 1855. Figures included in the annual reports of the Charity Bureau also reveal this shift. The number of married couples with resident children in receipt of regular support (the *secours continuel* and *secours casuel*) quintupled between 1806 and 1843, while the number of other families only doubled during the same period.[2] Between 1780 and 1827 only type D gained in importance (from *c.* 21 per cent to *c.* 33 per cent), while the relative decline of families without children in the second quarter of the nineteenth century augmented type C; the proportion of type D even diminished somewhat during this period. How is the strongly rising proportion in the poor lists of widowed or single persons with resident children (from 18 per cent in 1827 to more than 34 per cent in 1855) to be explained? Although the deaths of many heads of household or couples during the cholera epidemics (1848–1849 and the mid-fifties) may have played a role, the solution must be sought primarily in the spectacular growth of unemployment among women and children during the second quarter of the nineteenth century. Because of the irreversible decline of the textile industry, more and more women from the lower classes faced the most severe misery after the loss of their family's principal wage-earner: many simply had no means of subsistence at all, and those who did work seldom earned enough to feed their children. Half of all widows who had children to feed and who in 1855 received permanent support called upon the Charity Bureau in the year in which they lost their husband or during the subsequent year; the average term was six months. Old age played only a minor role, for most of the widows concerned (61 per cent) were under 55.

Taking into account the growing proportion of types C and D, it comes as no surprise that the average number of children per family rose significantly. The following table, however, reveals some contrasts regarding periodization.

Mean number of children per supported Antwerp family in 1780, 1827 and 1855

	1780	1827	1855
Percentage of families having no children (A + B)	61·3	49·3	38·2
Mean number of children			
– all families	1·01	2·19	2·28
– childless families excepted	2·62	4·30	3·72
– widowed or single persons with children (C)	2·13	3·17	2·93
– married couples with children (D)	3·05	4·94	4·73

Between 1780 and 1827, the average number of children per family doubled. The causes for this rise were two-fold: fewer childless heads of household (types A and B) and, above all, more children living with the other families; for type C the increase amounted to nearly 49 per cent, for type D no less than 62 per cent. By 1855, the average number of children had barely risen above the level of 1827, which suggests that the Charity Bureau did not stick rigidly to the new criteria. One must remember that the minimum number of children required to be considered for the *secours continuel* was set in 1827 at 4 and in 1837 at 5 per married couple. The poor lists show that in 1827 the Charity Bureau adhered quite strongly to the official regulations: only 31 per cent of the married couples had fewer than 4 children (versus 73 per cent in 1780). Around the middle of the century, by contrast, only half the married couples satisfied the norm of 1837. The extent and the intensity of destitution had clearly reached such extreme proportions that the poor law authorities could do nothing other than show greater flexibility.

Fewer single individuals and more children: the combination of the two factors led to larger family size and a more youthful supported population. The average number of persons per family rose from 2·39 in 1780 to 3·60 in 1827 and 3·63 in 1855, and the proportion of recipients of relief 65 or older decreased from 23 per cent in 1780 to less than 10 per cent in 1855, while the population in the age group 0–14 rose from 34 per cent to 44 per cent (the ratio of the latter to the former, in other words, jumped from 1·5 to 4·5). Considering only heads of household, around 1855 one in two was younger than 55, versus one in three around 1780. In the mid-nineteenth century, even young couples with three or four children were no longer secure against utter destitution: the underpayment or chronic under-employment of the primary breadwinner could make such families totally dependent upon public assistance.

Percentage distribution of supported Antwerp families and their members, in 1780, 1827 and 1855

Persons per family		Families			Family members		
		1780	1827	1855	1780	1827	1855
	N =	638	1,374	1,760	1,524	4,947	6,395
1–2		69·0	51·3	46·4	39·0	17·2	16·5
3–5		22·7	17·1	28·3	37·0	18·9	29·8
6–8		7·7	26·7	18·9	20·9	51·0	36·3
9 or more		0·7	4·9	6·4	3·1	12·9	17·4

Within three quarters of a century, then, the demographic composition of the supported population changed radically. At the end of the *ancien régime*, 61 per cent of the supported families consisted of elderly couples, widows and widowers 65 or older (many of whom suffered from serious ailments) *without* resident children. In 1855, in contrast, relatively young couples and widows 54 or younger *with* resident children constituted the majority, respectively 24 and 31 per cent of the total. A quarter of the families receiving the *secours continuel* in the mid-nineteenth century had six or more members, against only 8 per cent in the late eighteenth century.

These shifts illustrate in a striking way the disastrous social consequences of Antwerp's economic transformation. In the late eighteenth century, only a limited number of large families knew severe misery, because nearly all the members earned a living. Parents with two or three children under 5 were generally worse off than those who had five or six aged 5–14, since the latter children usually contributed to family income. By the mid-nineteenth century, in contrast, most large families led a miserable existence: in many cases the spouse was out of work and the children could seldom earn their keep prior to the age of 15. Moreover married couples now had to have at least five children in order to be considered for permanent support instead of two at the end of the *ancien régime*. The concurrence of the two changes – the diminution of employment opportunities for women and above all children, plus the stricter selection criteria employed by the Charity Bureau – meant that many working-class families faced material need. Their poverty, however, was greater the more young children they had. The policy carried out by the Charity Bureau, thus, was in no sense arbitrary; it was a necessary option considering the limited financial means at the disposal of the institution along with the radical changes in the economic roles of family members among the lower classes. The poor relief authorities had to deny the *secours continuel* to most parents with two or three young children – even though they were just as needy as their predecessors had been in 1780 – because otherwise too little money would be left over to save

larger families from starvation. If the couples with five or more children permanently assisted by the Charity Bureau in 1850 had had to make do without this
outside help, they would have had on average scarcely 1,000 calories per person
per day.

Given the employment opportunities actually available during the period
under study, the families registered on the poor lists cannot be accused of idleness. On the contrary: in 1827, employed persons of 15 or older amounted to
86 per cent of the total supported population of that age group, although the
comparable figure for the urban population as a whole (three years later) was
only 61 per cent.[3] The overwhelming majority of paupers, moreover, worked
in the most labour intensive sectors of economic life. The new generation did
not vegetate in branches of industry in decline but switched over resolutely to
more promising trades: only when there was no other alternative did they follow in their parents' footsteps. This is borne out by an analysis of the changes
in the occupational structure of the supported population.

Between 1780 and 1855, two not unexpected transformations took place
in the distribution of occupations among the male heads of household in receipt
of permanent relief.[4] In the first place, the number of textile workers dropped
from 42 per cent to less than 10 per cent. In the second place, the occupations
which directly or indirectly were dependent on shipping expanded significantly.
In 1855 casual labour provided subsistence for nearly 23 per cent of all male
heads of household, against 2·5 per cent in 1780, while the proportion of those
engaged in the retail trades and transport more than doubled. The aggregate
number of wood and metal workers rose equally significantly: from *c.* 2 per
cent in 1780 to *c.* 8 per cent in 1855. If all casual labourers are considered
dockers and included in the percentages of those employed in the transport,
wood and metal trades, then 43·5 per cent of male heads of household in receipt
of permanent support in the mid-nineteenth century lived off port-associated
activities. Seventy years previously these sectors had accounted for barely 10 per
cent, so that the expansion of shipping and commerce had created sufficient
employment opportunities for adult men to compensate for the collapse of the
textile industry. Thus the proportion of male heads of household who gave no
occupation remained nearly unchanged between 1780 and 1855; it fluctuated
between 11 and 15 per cent. It should be noted that, in 1780 as in 1855, more
than 15 per cent of men on relief were engaged in the clothing trade, whereas
the proportion of men over 12 or 13 employed in this sector dwindled from
10·2 per cent in 1796 to 3·4 per cent in 1846. This comes as no surprise. The
clothing sector was one of the few significant traditional industries in which
physical stamina played no role; hence it 'attracted' wage labourers who had
weak constitutions.[5]

In order to study in greater detail the impact of the transition from textile
centre to port town on the employment opportunities of the male labouring
force, three age-groups have been distinguished.[6] As could be expected, younger
men switched much more quickly than their elders to more promising trades.
Between 1780 and 1827, the proportion of textile workers in the 20–54

age-group was reduced to a third of its earlier extent, while it was barely halved in the 55–64 age group and diminished by less than a third among those 65 and over. As for the percentage of casual labourers, this grew ten-fold in the 20–54 age group, quintupled among those 55–64, and tripled among the elderly.

The reorientation was not painless. A great proportion of individuals had more than one occupation: in 1827 nearly one-third of the casual labourers aged 20–54 declared that they had an additional job; most tried to make ends meet as mason's helpers or hawkers when they could not find work in the port. By 1855 however nearly all casual labourers had a single trade: that of docker. By then, textile manufacturing had lost all significance for men of 55 and older. Those fit enough were employed on the docks; the rest tried to earn their daily bread at tailoring, retailing, or various odd jobs such as running errands and carrying packages for middle-class families.

Two conclusions can be drawn from these data. In the first place, the vast majority of male heads of household in receipt of permanent support were regularly engaged in the most dynamic sectors. When textile manufacturing decayed at an increasing pace and the harbour with its associated activities began to determine the future, strong young men left the traditional industries. Their destitution, therefore, cannot be blamed on a lack of adaptability. In the second place, the decline of the textile industry undoubtedly had dramatic consequences for older men. Most of them, it is true, remained at work; but they had increasingly to be satisfied with various forms of underpaid work and even 'disguised' begging. From the poor list of 1855 it appears that a male hawker, 55 or older, rarely if ever earned more than half a franc a day, the equivalent of around 2 kg. of ryebread.

The economic transformation of Antwerp also brought drastic changes in the occupations of adult women in receipt of permanent relief.[7] Until the late 1820s, most women held their heads above water. The proportion of lace-workers and embroiderers declined markedly (from 68·5 per cent to *c.* 47 per cent), but this drop was partially compensated by growth in retailing, the clothing trades, and casual labour. But it grew steadily more difficult to gain a place in the labour market, as evidenced by the large number of women with a second job: no less than 150, *c.* 12 per cent of the total. Nearly all these women gave lace-work, spinning, or sewing as their principal occupation; as a sideline they did casual labour (40), hawked fish, fruit, rags, etc. (28), cared for the children of other poor families (20), or performed any sort of odd job. The second quarter of the nineteenth century represented a turning point. The total collapse of textile manufacturing and the bursting of the tulle 'bubble' brought massive unemployment. By 1855, more than 45 per cent of the women on relief had been expelled from the labour market. As for the employed female population, only a minority could make a living from casual labour with its supposedly adequate wages; the others were concentrated in economic sectors like lacework, retailing, and the clothing trades, where earnings were extremely low.

Between 1780 and 1827 the proportion of laceworkers and embroiderers diminished much less among younger women than among their elders (55 and older). By 1827, younger workers had overwhelmingly switched to embroidery on tulle, while the older on the whole made traditional pillow-lace. In the textile industry, the opposite occurred: only half the younger women remained, while the proportion among the other age groups remained virtually unchanged. That is no surprise, given that cotton spinning was almost the only branch of Antwerp's textile industry which employed large numbers of women, and it had no future in the 1820s. Older women, however, could less easily switch to other economic sectors; they had to carry on in their trade until they ceased work. Even so, a quarter century later, the number of female lace and textile workers, 65 and older, fell to less than one fourth of its earlier extent. Only two trades retained any hold over this age group: retailing and the clothing sector. That around 1855 unemployment was nearly as great among the young as among the older women must be attributed to the congestion of the labour market. Only the strongest and healthiest women were considered for casual labour: nearly all the rest had to compete for a few last-resort jobs.[8]

The move from textile manufacturing to casual or intermittent forms of employment posed every woman with a further difficult problem: since they now had to work outside the home, they could no longer care for their children during the day. The situation was all the more serious because the diminishing value of support payments compelled ever more poor families to put their elderly family members in charitable institutions or board them out with people in the countryside. The combined effect of these factors largely explains the success of the infant schools created by the *Société d'Ecoles gardiennes*. This association, founded in 1839 by the wives of some of the most prominent of Antwerp's businessmen with a view to teaching young children 'manners', opened four nursery schools between 1840 and 1849, where paupers could send sons and daughters aged 2 to 6 between 7 a.m. and 7 p.m. each day. By the mid-nineteenth century, these institutions catered for 1,160 infants, nearly 14 per cent of all children in the age group. Although the distribution of free food (mainly soup) was undoubtedly an additional stimulus to attend, the great increase must be ascribed fundamentally to the growing number of women who worked outside the home and, as a result, needed a crèche for their youngsters. It is worth noting that the headmistresses of the nursery schools, according to the Antwerp Medical Commission, gave too little attention to physical training; the Commission found matters in a deplorable state, since a strong constitution was an absolute necessity 'for children who belong to a social class the vast majority of which must later provide for their subsistence by bodily vigour'.[9]

The fall in the level of employment among child paupers was nothing short of catastrophic.[10] Whereas in 1780 six out of ten children aged 5–14 practised or were apprenticed in a trade, 70 years later the proportion had shrunk to one in ten. This drastic diminution must be ascribed to the decline of the cotton industry and of lace-work, which at the end of the *ancien régime* had occupied the bulk of child paupers (respectively 54 per cent of the boys and 60 per cent of the girls). By the mid-nineteenth century, child labour had little significance in Antwerp. Only the producers of sewing-silk and sail cloth, paper manufacturers, tobacco twisters, and – above all – cigar makers hired young children. For the Chamber of Commerce, the existence of these few enterprises was nonetheless sufficient reason to reject any regulation of child labour. In 1846 the governors judged, it is true, 'that children who cannot read or write should only be recruited before their tenth birthday on condition that they continue to benefit from some education', but they hastened to add that a prohibition of child labour was totally unnecessary, since the businesses involved 'only provided tasks which are not exhausting and which cannot be deemed deleterious for the development of the physique'. The Antwerp Medical Commission heartily agreed and went a step further: children could be put to work in the factories after their eighth birthday, because 'work can be considered the gymnastics of the poor; it prevents the children from becoming vagrants; and the wages they earn are frequently a valuable source of income for the family of the needy labourer'.[11]

Growing unemployment explains why more and more poor citizens sent their sons to school. Until 1833, Antwerp had only one primary school (founded in 1819), where some 300 boys received free education. In 1833, two new institutions opened, and a decade after the passage of the first Primary Education Act in 1842 two more had followed. By 1855 the total number of pupils had risen to 2,328, nearly 40 per cent of all male children aged 7 to 14.[12] Although the 1842 Act stipulated that daughters as well as sons of poor families had a right to free education, it was not until 1849 that a girls' school was opened in Antwerp. The explanation for this delay, perhaps, is that many pauper children went to private schools where they learned to make pillow-lace so long as that trade seemed to offer any future opportunity.[13] It is, in any case, striking that the bourgeoisie made efforts for the schooling of young girls from the lower classes only after the lace industry had collapsed. The number of pupils attending the primary school founded in 1849 rose so fast that the municipality was forced to open a second institution in 1856, where 800 immediately matriculated.[14]

The poor lists also indicate that in the mid-nineteenth century most female adolescents (15 and older) still contributed to family income. The level of their employment was only slightly lower than at the end of the *ancien régime* (80 per cent instead of 92 per cent), a remarkable figure given that unemployment among other age groups had reached a very much higher level. By 1855, less than 12 per cent of girls aged 5 to 14 and only 55 per cent of women 20–54 were in employment. The explanation lies in the short-term resurrection of the lace industry during the 1840s: almost half of the girls aged 15 or older on the poor list of 1855 were lace-workers. For the succeeding generation, however, there was no comparable opportunity.

As could be expected, the overwhelming majority of male adolescents were in work. The economic transformation of Antwerp, however, resulted in drastic changes in occupational structure. Whereas in 1780, nearly 58 per cent of all boys 15 or older were engaged in in textile manufacturing, the proportion had fallen to barely 10 per cent by 1855. Port-associated activities now played an important role: casual labour absorbed about 17 per cent of the youthful labour force in the mid-nineteenth century, the tobacco industry 9 per cent, wood and metal working nearly as much, and transport around 5 per cent; seventy years earler, no child of parents on relief was employed in these sectors.

Although the available sources do not permit a thorough study of inter-generational occupational mobility, several trends can be deduced. The civil birth registers of 1827 give the occupations of the fathers of male heads of household aged between 20 and 40 and in receipt of permanent relief. Marriage records could not be used for this purpose because the fathers of most subjects were already dead at the time of their son's marriage. Only 117 sons, or one fourth of the total, could be traced in the civil birth registers. The explanation is that most were born either before 1792 (*i.e.* prior to the institution of the civil registrar's office) or outside Antwerp. This sample shows that no more than 21 per cent of the sons were engaged in the same economic sectors as their fathers; the great majority followed a completely different path. Only casual labourers were an exception: 13 of the 26 fathers on day wages had sons with the same occupation. Leaving this category aside, the rate of continuity was barely 11 per cent. If the occupational structure of fathers and sons is compared, then it shows that the latter were much more concentrated in occupations requir-ing little or no skill than the former: whereas only one in five fathers earned a livelihood from casual labour, one in two sons did; three-fourths of the son/day-labourers came from families of textile workers.

The occupations 'chosen' by the sons of the male heads of household who received permanent support in 1827 have also been examined. For this, marriage acts have been assembled of all sons who married in the period 1842–1857. No fewer than 266, or nearly 60 per cent, were traced; the remaining male children emigrated (30 per cent), did not marry (16 per cent), or had died (4 per cent).[15] If the father was alive at the time of the son's marriage, current occupation has been noted; if not, the job he held in 1827 is used. The contrast with the first sample is striking: nearly one in two sons listed at his marriage the same occu-pation as his father. The continuity was highest for casual labourers: 75 per cent. Then followed the building trades (*c.* 60 per cent), the tailors and cobblers (*c.* 50 per cent), and retailers (*c.* 35 per cent). This comes as no surprise: the period of dramatic change in occupational opportunities had passed. The genera-tion born shortly before or after 1800 could enter the same sectors as the preced-ing generation only at the risk of structural unemployment; the vast majority realized that very well and chose work in the harbour instead of textile manu-facturing. For the generation marrying between 1842 and 1857, things were wholly different: since occupational opportunities during the second quarter of the nineteenth century remained largely unchanged, many adult sons now remained in the same occupation as their fathers.

In short, the available evidence shows that destitution was not limited to any particular category of labourers. During critical phases of the life cycle or during periods of prolonged unemployment, most proletarians had to turn to outsiders for help. Their enrollment on the poor lists, however, did not depend on the severity of their poverty but upon the selection criteria applied by the Charity Bureau. This institutional 'filter' also explains why those 'eligible' did not receive public assistance for long. Between 1855 and 1859, the poor relief authorities noted in detail why given families no longer came into consideration for the *secours continuel*. At the end of 1859, the remaining families were transferred by the directorate to a new register, which in turn was maintained up to 1865. These sources show that in 1860 around 44 per cent of families who in 1855 had received permanent support for at most two years had already disappeared from the poor list; in 1865 the ratio had risen to no less than 85 per cent. The following table summarizes the factors which led to removal from the list between 1855 and 1860.[16]

Reasons why Antwerp families in receipt of permanent relief were struck off the poor list between 1855 and 1860

Cause	Number of families	Per cent of total
Death of head of household and/or wife		
– widowed or single person	212	32·8
– one parent	54	8·4
– both parents	16	2·5
Changes in the size or structure of families where parents alive		
– child over 12 years of age	91	14·1
– return of husband	50	7·8
– death of one child	22	3·4
Aged person removed to a charitable institution or boarded out	139	21·6
Others		
– emigration	23	3·6
– 'rising family income'	12	1·9
– 'bad conduct'	26	4·0
Total	645	100·2

Taking into account the composition of the supported population, it comes as no surprise that death was the prime reason for removal (282 cases, nearly 44 per cent of the total). Healthy men whose partners died were no longer considered eligible for permanent support because their wages, according to the relieving-officers, sufficed to keep them and their children alive. Nearly all orphan boys younger than 19 and orphan girls younger than 21 were placed by the poor law authorities in charitable institutions; beyond those ages orphans had to look after themselves. A second category disappeared from the poor list through the changed size and structure of the family (163 cases or 25 per cent of the total). The Charity Bureau struck off 91 parents of whom both were employed, because one of their children passed the crucial age of 12, and 22 other couples were similarly treated because one of their children had died. Permanent support was also denied when the head of household rejoined his wife and children after a voluntary or involuntary absence (imprisonment, for example), whether or not he now had a job; the families concerned could at best turn to the *secours casuel*. A third group consisted of the elderly who could no longer care for themselves and could not rely upon married children or relatives; these were placed by the poor relief in a civil hospice, or lodged with farming families. The fourth and last category of families disappeared from the poor list for highly diverse reasons. One should have no illusions about the 'rising family income' cited by the poor law administration; this most often meant that one of the children had his or her first job. And under the term 'bad conduct' someone caught begging or repeatedly drunk or found guilty of prostitution could not lodge a claim for permanent support, no matter how great his or her material need.[17]

Of all family types, parents with numerous children enjoyed the greatest number of consecutive years permanent support, as can be seen from a comparison between the poor lists of 1827 and 1834. No less than 80 per cent of the parents with four or more children who in 1827 received the *secours continuel* still appeared on the poor lists seven years later. In three out of four cases, the birth of one or more children was the cause of the continuing support; the remaining registered families in 1834 were supported on account of the death or illness of the prime breadwinner.

Removal from the poor lists was not irrevocable. From the moment that a family met the eligibility criteria anew it once again received permanent support. Thus some families with five children who in 1855 received permanent assistance were, in the course of the following ten years, first struck off because one of the children had died or reached the age of twelve, and later re-registered following the birth of another child. A second example: of 519 parents with four or more children mentioned in the poor lists of 1827 and 1834, 88 heads of household or wives, *i.e.* around 17 per cent, were found on the list of 1855–1860, although their children had by this time left home; all had been widowed and, as a result of old age and/or permanent poor health, earned little or nothing.

Since no continuous series of sources is available, it cannot be precisely determined how many children of permanent recipients had themselves to call upon public assistance after they married. Comparison of the poor lists of 1827 and 1855, to investigate which sons and daughters born between 1823 and 1827 (of parents with at least four children and in receipt of the *secours continuel*) were themselves dependent on permanent support thirty years later, gives a rough indication. All the relevant children – 684 – are traceable in the civil registers up to 1860. By then, 77 had died and 36 had emigrated, while 178 others were unmarried. Of the 197 married sons and 196 daughters, no more than 28 and 29 (14·2 per cent and 14·8 per cent) respectively appeared on the poor list of 1855–1860. One-third of these families had then to be supported because they had five or more children under 12, another third because the spouse had died and the widow remained with two or more youngsters, and the remaining group because the head of household was absent or ill.

The recipients of public assistance, thus, did not come from a distinct social category with specific characteristics; they did not constitute a *lumpenproletariat*. Rather they were that continuously changing portion of the lower classes which satisfied the formal requirements for public assistance. Both the registration of working class families on the poor list and their later removal were determined by the interaction of the standards applied by the Charity Bureau and the life cycle of the families concerned; the number of children, their ages, and their health were of crucial importance, not destitution as such, since the majority of workers were destitute. Lacking adequate socio-economic data, it is impossible to discern what proportion of Antwerp's proletariat lived at various stages under or near the poverty line.[18] But there is no doubt that destitution was a real hazard for almost all working-class families and that most at certain stages were dependent upon public assistance. None remained long on the poor list, but the majority reached it sooner or later, and generally more than once.

Contemporaries were themselves quite conscious of the structural vulnerability of the proletariat. When the *Commission du Travail*, installed by the central government, asked the communal authorities in 1886 how many workers required public support, one of Antwerp's representatives answered that the recipients of relief comprised one-third of the total population and that all belonged to the working class. 'The material situation of the wage labourer is, unfortunately enough, so miserable', he declared, 'that he is obliged to enter his name on the poor list in case of illness or unemployment.'[19] Most *litterati* too considered destitution endemic to wage labour. The study of nineteenth-century Flemish drama indicates that playwrights had no doubt about the causal connection: one was poor *because* one was working class.[20]

CHAPTER 11

Philanthropy, Respectability and Social Control

The previous chapter showed that the supported needy were not necessarily the most impoverished members of the working class. Many people lived in as great or even worse misery but, acording to the increasingly restrictive criteria applied by the Charity Bureau, they were ineligible for relief because they had too few children, were too young, had no incurable illness, or had 'misbehaved'. How did these families survive? Could they rely upon private charity?

Although the poor law authorities felt it necessary to dampen the ardour of the 'indiscriminate alms-giver', they could not forbid visits by parish priests and propertied laymen to the needy, providing them with material aid. The recipients, however, had to inform the Charity Bureau of the amount and frequency of these donations if they were in receipt of public assistance; otherwise they were subject to sanctions. The poor list of 1827 is the only source which sheds light on the importance of charity dispensed on an individual basis. The officers systematically noted which recipients of the *secours continuel* were additionally helped by private parties who were neither relatives nor neighbours. Two conclusions can be drawn from these data. In the first place, it is clear that this form of assistance had little significance. Scarcely 9 per cent of all the families concerned could rely on benefactors who regularly put their hands in their pockets. These families, moreover, were far from pampered: they received fortnightly the monetary equivalent of about three kg. of ryebread. In the second place, the clerics as well as the laymen were interested almost exclusively in the 'deserving poor', *i.e.*, the elderly, the sick, the lame. In eight out of ten cases, they confined their charity to single individuals or childless couples aged 65 and over; nearly all had one or another disease or infirmity.

Proportion of Antwerp families receiving public assistance in 1827 which could also rely on private charity, categorized by marital status and presence of children

	Families supported by		Of all, proportion in receipt of charities %	All families N (100%)
	clerics %	laymen %		
No children present:				
widows and spinsters	5·1	9·9	15·0	487
widowers and bachelors	2·7	5·4	8·1	74
married couples	7·0	8·7	15·7	115
Children present:				
widows	2·3	3·6	5·9	220
widowers	0·0	0·0	0·0	27
married couples	1·1	1·6	2·7	451
All	3·3	5·6	8·9	1,374

Any needy person who received no material aid from the poor relief authorities could appeal to a benevolent society. It is a hopeless task to describe in detail all the charitable actions undertaken by members of the upper classes. There were many such initiatives, but in general they were discontinuous and limited in scope. Middle-class groups organized balls, concerts, and theatrical performances, the proceeds of which were used to buy food for the poor. Similarly, they assembled art-objects which, over the course of several weeks, were displayed in coffeehouses or the homes of do-gooders and then sold to the public. But one should not over-estimate the importance of these charitable activities. During the hard winter of 1845–1846, funds raised by such auctions for the needy barely sufficed to provide 200 kg. of ryebread daily for six months.[1]

The *Société de Saint-Vincent de Paul* was in fact the only private institution in Antwerp in the mid-nineteenth century which regularly provided support to a large group of (select) indigents. The idea of uniting pious laymen in pursuit of their salvation by disbursing alms – '*Dieu comme but, les pauvres comme moyen*', 'God our goal, the poor our means' – originated in France. The first Society of St. Vincent was founded in Paris in 1833 by students led by Frédéric Ozanam, later well-known as a literary historian.[2] It was an extraordinarily successful undertaking: by 1848, the Society had 100 branches in France and 94 in other countries, 29 of which were in Belgium, where they were introduced on the initiative of Cardinal Engelbert Sterckx.[3] The branch in Antwerp, founded on 6 October 1846, had 40 active members by 1847, operating in 3 of the 7 parishes *intra muros*. Eight years later, their number had more than quadrupled, and every parish, including those outside the walls, had its own *conférence*.[4]

Nearly all the 'Messieurs de Saint-Vincent' belonged to the nobility and the upper bourgeoisie: rentiers, businessmen, doctors, lawyers, magistrates. Only Roman Catholics with unimpeachable reputations were considered for membership, committing themselves to a weekly donation, the amount of which was kept secret. Why did a significant portion of the élite – the Society recruited hundreds of notables during the 1850s who provided financial assist-ance without personally disbursing alms – join a charitable institution with a pronounced religious character? In 1864, Charles Périn, a jurist and professor at Leuven, explained that

> in every society, no matter how free and prosperous, there shall always be alongside the rich and powerful the poor and powerless; the latter shall always need assistance, not only of a material sort, but also of the moral sort, not only temporary and contingent support, but also continuing help, embracing the whole of life in all its phases. Such help we call pat-ronage. It is through the exercise of charity within the framework of patronage that the higher classes shall be seen to be the bearers of the man-date of Heaven and the representatives of Divine Providence, bearers of the Divine Sovereignty, the foremost sign of which is goodness.[5]

Philanthropy, in other words, was *the* instrument supporting the existing social order, an order instituted by God. Indeed, 'to bind the populace to the solidarity and unity of social life, there are only two paths: submission to an order strictly determined by law, or mutual agreement'.[6] The Belgian historian Jan Art very properly observed that the links between Church and bourgeoisie in the nine-teenth century must be seen in contractual terms. Both parties drew advantages from their cooperation. The bourgeoisie legitimated its authority through the Church and in return made available to it significant financial resources, thus offering the Church the possibility of reversing the decay which had begun under the French régime and rebuilding an apparatus of authority. In short, the upper classes stimulated the religiosity of the workers, and the priests threatened them with excommunication if they did not accept the superiority of the bourgeoisie.[7] Even the Liberals, who ruled from 1847 to 1884 almost without a break, supported this policy out of class solidarity. In 1851 one of their leaders, Joseph Lebeau, openly declared that the services of the clergy on the social plane could not be estimated highly enough. The Liberals, it is true, did not regard wholly favourably any preaching which propounded acquired wealth and power as signs of God, because such preaching all too easily sug-gested that the duty of charity was linked to 'election'. However the Liberals considered the indoctrination of the proletariat by the clergy as an indispen-sable contribution to the neutralization of class antagonisms.[8]

The *Société de Saint-Vincent de Paul* was very active in Antwerp. They funded charity schools, provided patronage for young workers, founded lend-ing libraries and so forth. But the foremost task of the members was visiting the poor. They investigated every aspect of the daily life of families ineligible for public assistance: were they born in Antwerp or immigrants? If immigrants, from whence and why had they come to the town? Was the head of the household in regular work? If not, why not? How old were his wife and children? Did they practise a trade? Did the parents keep the home clean? Did every member of the family have decent clothes for work and school and church? Did they have enough beds so that parents and children, boys and girls could sleep apart? Was there a crucifix in the home, an image of Our Lady, a prayer book? Were the parents married, and was it a marriage sanctioned by the Church? Could they produce a marriage certificate? Had the children been baptized, and in which town, village, parish? Did they go to school, or were they learning a trade? Had those over 12 had their first communion? Could they answer the catechism? The 'Messieurs' listened, friendly and attentive, noted all, and promised to put in a good word for them at the next meeting of the Society. Should the petition be granted, that family henceforth received – on different days at different times – a weekly visit from two delegates who, while they distributed alms, investigated the material circumstances and morality of the parents and their children, tendered advice, dispensed words of hope and comfort, and preached.[9]

It has not been possible to locate the registers containing the names and other data regarding the pauper families, but the annual reports of the Society show that only in exceptional circumstances did they receive financial assistance.[10] Clothing made up the lion's share of the alms. Even during the crisis of 1845–1846, more than half the relief funds were directed towards the purchase of 'proper' dresses, pants, skirts, shoes, and the like. As for the distribution of food tickets: no less than 90 per cent of the monies thus spent went on rice, beans, peas and meat-soup; only 10 per cent went on bread. The policy of the Society was clearly directed to the uplifting of these families: distinguishing them from the rest of the poor by their clothing and their diet, transforming them into examples of respectability.

How effective was this form of philanthropy? Lack of sources makes it impossible to assess its religious and moral impact, but the annual reports leave no doubt that material assistance provided by the Society was quite modest. The number of pauper families who were clients of the Society rose from 152 in 1847 to 266 in 1848 and thereafter to an average of 538 in 1854–1856, the high point of the charity; by 1860 it had fallen to 408 and during the following decade hovered around 350. Assuming that each of these were families of three or four, then some 1,500 to 2,000 poor received alms from the Society in the mid-1850s, *i.e.*, barely 2 per cent of Antwerp's population. And even for these the charity was minimal: during the crisis of 1845–1846, each family received an average of 53 centimes a week, one fourth the amount which the poor relief authorities disbursed to families in receipt of the *secours continuel*. Around 27 centimes were given in the form of clothing. The detailed investigations of Ducpétiaux show that a labouring family during the 1840s and 1850s needed at least 80 centimes a week to clothe themselves properly; a pair of wooden shoes cost 0·45 francs, woollen socks of poor quality 1·40 francs, an adult's cotton shirt 1·50 to 2 francs and a cheap pair of trousers or a dress 3 to 3·50 francs.[11] The least that one can say is that the clothing allowances provided by the 'Messieurs de Saint-Vincent' did not afford anything beyond the ordinary. The weekly ration card gave even less occasion to rejoice: the average value was 22 centimes, not even the equivalent of a kg. of ryebread. That hundreds of poor families were prepared week after week to tolerate the visit of two well intentioned mini-inquisitors in exchange for such pittances is highly revealing. One must however do justice to these do-gooders: their liberality in dispensing crucifixes, holy prints, paternosters and religious medallions was limitless.

Other benevolent societies seldom provided direct and regular support to the needy. Their few clients were generally invalids or *pauvres honteux*, people who had known better days and who had lost their last savings by an unlucky turn of events. The *Société des Dames de la Charité*, founded and governed by women from the highest social circles, took some unemployed workers under its wing during the famine of 1845–1847, but that was exceptional. The annual contribution of their members and the receipts of their charity balls supported a limited number of 'deserving' poor (around 125 in the 1850s), generally providing for the education of the children. In 1834 the *Dames*, including the countess of Nevele and the baronesses Osy-Knyff and della Faille de Terbruggen, established a commission for the financing of Sunday schools. They had considerable success: in 1838, some 3,000 pauper children between 12 and 25 took lessons every Sunday morning; by 1844, their number had grown to more than 4,000. Nowhere were submissiveness and pliancy so deeply imprinted, as the irrepressible crusader Melchior Kramp stated in 1838:

> They seek to impell into these children's hearts and spirits those views of society and ethical principles which – along with religion – set up for the rest of their lives an unbreachable barrier both to the desperation caused by adversity and to the perfidious insinuations used by miscreants to subvert the working class.[12]

The *Société d'épargne pour l'achat de provisions d'hiver* deserves special mention. The goal of this organization, founded in 1850 at the instigation of the municipal authorities, was to enable the needy to buy potatoes and coal cheaply during the winter. The funds came from two sources. All propertied burghers were asked to become honorary members of the Society and to provide an annual contribution of at least three francs. Then, working-class families who were considered for active membership each had to provide at least half a franc a week between 1 April and 31 October. With these funds, foodstuffs and fuel were bought at wholesale prices in the summer, and from 1 November shared among the active members in proportion to their deposits. Two years after its formation, the association, which was administered by prominent merchants, financiers, and manufacturers, numbered more than 700 honorary members, around a fifth of the propertied inhabitants of Antwerp. Success must largely be ascribed to the fact that the bourgeoisie felt confident that they were not wasting their money: a minimal weekly contribution of half a franc meant that genuine paupers were excluded from participation. Supplementary admission requirements limited active membership to the proletarian élite: the administrators only accepted wage labourers who sent their children to school regularly and who had never been implicated in theft, extortion, fraud, or conspiracy. Between 1850 and 1860, some 1,350 working class families could satisfy all the requirements; each of them bought annually an average of 92 kg. of potatoes and 8 hl. of coal at a discount.[13]

There is no doubt that some members of the upper classes sincerely sympathized with the poor and dispensed alms for purely humanitarian reasons. That does not, however, disprove that the philanthropy of the bourgeoisie as a whole was clearly less informed by altruism than by the conviction that paternalistic initiatives contributed to the justification of the existing social order. To cite a contemporary: 'Philanthropy is the soul of civilization . . . it makes the needy understand the necessity of maintaining social inequality; it erects a dam against the riotious passions emanating from their humble position; it dispels their immoderate desire to break out'.[14] Indiscriminate almsgiving was obviously the wrong path. That would only release the supposedly natural inclinations of the proletariat towards laziness and indifference and, moreover, give the impression that the needy had a right to the benevolence of the rich. Most philanthropists were in full agreement with the poor relief authorities who declared outright in 1850: 'The foremost cause of poverty is misbehaviour. Let us raise the morality of the lower classes, imbuing decent behaviour and appearance, love of family, resignation and courage in the face of adversity, and sobriety in all circumstances; thereby shall we erect the only dyke which can resist the high waters of destitution'.[15]

Hence, benevolent societies concerned themselves almost exclusively with those whose misery was the result of individual misfortune and who proved receptive to moral improvement. The bread of charity had not only to be repaid with submissive and inexhaustible gratitude,[16] but also by the practice of virtues preached by their benefactors. In order to put these families on the right path, their personal hygiene, the orderliness of their dwellings, their recreation, and the attendance of their children at school had to be regulated closely and continuously. Due to lack of sources, it cannot be said whether this patronage – the new key-word – had the desired effects, but the poor relief authorities were themselves convinced that philanthropic associations were doing outstanding work. In 1847 the directorate established in every parish a *comité de charité*, comprising the parish priest, who presided, and a limited number of propertied laymen (preferably members of charitable societies) appointed by the mayor and aldermen upon the nomination of the poor relief authorities. These committees were to oversee the moral conduct of families in receipt of public assistance, to instill in them the love of work, to inspect their living quarters, and to investigate whether good use was made of their support payments. They paid particular attention to the education of the young: they compelled pauper children to attend school, or at least Sunday school; older boys had to be apprenticed in the factories or with a craftsman; and the most promising adolescents were provided with small sums for the purchase of tools. In short, 'a well intentioned patronage was exercised for the children of the poor until they attained their majority'. Even the *Dames de la Charité* could join these committees; they took care of pregnant women, widows, babies, young women.[17] Protest against this patronage was out of the question; as the almoners clearly stipulated, 'by entering the poor lists, the needy are considered to be minors and are for that reason automatically subject to the custody of the administration'.[18] The address given by a school child at an awards ceremony in 1859 summarized the goals of the benevolent societies:

> We are all children born of indigent parents. The sweat of our fathers and the care of our mothers do not still our hunger; they do not even provide the utmost necessities. Yet, even more important than the food provided us by your Worships is the spiritual sustenance that distinguishes man from beast, that spiritual sustenance which the powerful give to us so royally, depleting their own coffers, a spiritual sustenance which would always be denied to us if your Worships' benevolent hand did not take us under protection by granting us suitable instruction. Your Worships' charity is boundless, limiting itself not just to feeding and training: every year your Worships reward our diligence and knowledge with glittering prizes and in exchange ask only that we do our best to become capable and virtuous people. My Lords, we recognize the significance of the benevolence strewn over us, and we recognize the duty which rests upon us: we learn in school to behave towards our teachers as later, when we have become members of the social family, we ought to behave towards your Worships and our fellow citizens.[19]

Only twice during the period under study did the bourgeoisie of Antwerp raise significant sums of money for the relief of the labouring poor: during the Belgian Revolution and during the 'hungry forties' (1845–1847). In both cases, socio-political factors were decisive.

On 25 August 1830, in Brussels, the Belgian Revolution began, leading to a declaration of independence on 4 October. Three weeks later, on 26 October, the rebels took control of Antwerp, except for the citadel, which was not overcome until taken by French troops in 1832. During the winter of 1830–1831, the socio-economic situation at Antwerp was catastrophic. The bombardment of the town by the Dutch general David Hendrik Chassé destroyed in whole or in part 611 houses, of which 266 were situated in the fourth ward. The blockade by the Dutch brought traffic on the Scheldt to a standstill; only at the end of January 1831 could some ships enter the harbour, and it was not until the summer that a real recovery took place. In addition to destruction, hundreds of propertied burghers fled the city in fear of new military operations, so that the demand for luxury goods collapsed. The resultant crippling of trade and industry brought massive unemployment, pushing to extremes the misery and desperation of the lower classes, who met a sharp rise in the prices of food.[20] The revolutionaries understood that hunger was the best ally of the Orangists, the supporters of King William I. As the head of the *Commission provisoire de Sûreté* declared on 10 December 1830: 'The maintenance of peace in this town appears difficult, if not impossible, if someone does not soon provide for the needs of the working population'. His view was seconded by a spy of Cornelis van Maanen, the Dutch Minister of Justice: 'If one can turn the lower classes into beggars, then counterrevolution is a certainty'. He reported gloatingly that paupers had gathered near the *Bourse* and demanded work, and that the police had driven them away by force. 'Poverty', he concluded, 'becomes daily more unbearable; one cannot go out on the street without being swamped by beggars.'[21]

A large-scale programme of support was thus necessary if the revolutionaries were to secure their victory. But where could the money come from? Seeing that the town treasury was effectively empty and that the Provisional Government in Brussels was bankrupt, the bourgeoisie had to make do on their own. After long discussions and considerable delays, it was resolved to take out a voluntary loan at 5 per cent interest, redeemable within 10 years. In each section of the town a committee of 6 notables was instructed to go from house to house with a registration list. The panic among the upper classes must have been considerable for, on 20 December, 250,000 guilders, more than half a million francs, had already been collected; even avowed Orangists had volunteered.[22] And it was not too soon. According to the Chief of Police, 'symptoms of a deep dissatisfaction and an alarming agitation began to manifest themselves among the workers, with crowds in all the public places raising the spectre of trouble'.[23]

The authorities concluded that at this critical stage an employment scheme was the most appropriate means to maintain order. Distribution of alms to idle wage labourers hindered efficient control and increased the danger of spontaneous action. Besides, damage caused by the bombardment had to be restored, while the defence of the town against the Dutch garrison in the citadel and the army that would eventually try to relieve it demanded the strengthening of the walls and the gates. Hence in the first week of January 1831, more than 1,600 were put to work. Preference was given to heads of families with at least 3 children; they received somewhat more than one franc a day, *i.e.* the equivalent of 5 kg. of ryebread. By mid-February, the number had risen to 2,600 – including their families, nearly 18 per cent of Antwerp's population. At the same time the Charity Bureau provided extraordinary assistance to 2,400 needy families, excluding those who received the *secours continuel*. No wonder that the capital raised through voluntary donations rapidly disappeared. Even the gifts assembled by the *Comité provisoire de Bienfaisance* between 20 December, 1830 and 31 March 1831 – some 200,000 francs – was inadequate to support such a campaign for any length of time.[24]

At the end of February, the municipal authorities laid off 400 relief workers. Since the lower classes were quiet, the bourgeoisie once again felt optimistic.

Time and again they cursed the 'laziness' of the relief workers, who, in their opinion, were paid far too well: they received 0·50 guilders a *day*, whereas extraordinary recipients of relief received at most 0·35 guilders a *week*. As one high official indignantly complained: 'It is truly tragic and even disgusting to see the carelessness and indifference with which these people feign to earn the money given them. The habit of doing nothing, robbing as it were those who pay them, is contagious. It cannot be halted soon enough'.[25] The members of the committee entrusted with supervision of public works admitted that some workers were not altogether zealous but added that one could scarcely expect that 'craftsmen diverted from sedentary activities would be good at heavy labour and would feel no abhorrance at their reduction to digging up muck'.[26] They spoke in vain. The mayor and aldermen resolved to lower the daily wage of relief workers by 20 per cent from 14 March. The expected results came swiftly. On 12 March, the police informed the mayor that workers planned to march through the town 'with red and black flags as symbols of fire and death, massing by the *Bourse*, burning the Orange flag and slaying the 'Grands Seigniors' who are suspected of attachment to the old order and of having brought about the reduction in wages'.[27] Seized by panic, the municipal authorities made it known that wages would in due course be restored. This surrender to several hundred '*hommes sans aveu*' lay heavily upon the upper classes – all the more since, given that no financal assistance came from Brussels, they had to bear the costs themselves. They compensated for the maintenance of the 'high' wages, however, by laying off relief workers; by the end of March, their numbers had been reduced to 1,200. The dismissed workers were not, however, abandoned. They were directed to the Charity Bureau which, through lack of funds, could only provide a pittance. The relieving officers noted correctly that not much was needed to drive these embittered and desperate people to their wit's end.[28]

The bomb burst when it emerged that the military governor of Antwerp, with other officers and various prominent Orangists, had attempted to seize power. On 30 March, troops who had obstructed the counter-revolution cele-brated wildly; the next day, riots broke out across the town. Hundreds of workers stormed and sacked the homes of newspaper publishers, former offi-cials, and merchants known for their Orangist sympathies. Without a doubt, the disturbances were provoked by a small group of revolutionaries from Brus-sels, who, as they had done in their own town and elsewhere, attempted to direct popular rage along the 'proper' path in Antwerp – the country's strate-gic centre. The plunderers should not however be portrayed merely as puppets of a handful of agitators. Police reports indicate that a growing part of Antwerp's proletariat was tired of being seen as beggars to whom were thrown alms insufficient to provide the barest minimum. The municipal government was quite conscious that many workers could turn just as easily against the pro-Belgians as against the Orangists. Hence, not only was martial law proclaimed, but the authorities began actively reinstating the laid-off relief workers; in the first week of April, their number rose to 1,710, some 500 more than on the eve of the troubles. When financial reserves were exhausted several weeks later, the bourgeoisie themselves agreed to a special, monthly surtax on income to pay the relief workers. In conjunction with an efficient apparatus of repression, combining military and the burghers, this policy restrained the proletariat from further 'adventures'. Aside from two minor incidents, on 24 May and 2 June, the peace at Antwerp was not disturbed again. In the end, the misery of the labouring poor had been the vehicle by which a minority had grasped power, a minority which would soon enough institutionalize itself to the advantage of the bourgeoisie.[29]

During the famine of 1845–1847, the upper classes again succeeded in preventing unrest through organizing large-scale campaigns to benefit the needy.[30] In December 1845, when the price of potatoes reached its highest level since the crisis of 1816–1817, the Chamber of Commerce instituted a committee of businessmen to gather money for the poor. The Charity Bureau cooperated actively and provided the committee with the names of all families registered on the poor lists. Since the primary purpose of the Chamber of Commerce was the maintenance of social order, they did not limit their charitable activities to the 9,000 regular recipients of relief. The business community well understood that the numerous wage labourers who could not call upon either the *secours continuel* or the *secours casuel* now represented the greatest threat to public order. Hence it was resolved to support every family listed by the poor relief authorities (including those only considered for the *secours accidentel*), and to provide each with the same allowance. Certainly the upper classes were not planning to cope fully with the needs of the masses; the cost of that would be prohibitive. They did intend – wholly to their advantage as the future would show – to give short-term assistance to demonstrate their compassion and liberality. The effectiveness of the philanthropic gesture was determined by its spectacular character, not by its material impact. The point was to convert a little money into the maximum possible symbolic capital.

In January and February 1846, the committee gave alms to no fewer than 6,125 families, comprising 23,641 persons, or 29 per cent of the total population. It was an impressive number, but what did this assistance entail? Each family received tickets once a week for 3 kg. of ryebread, 1 litre of peas or beans, a half kg. of rice, and a half litre of coal. But the food was no outright gift: the tickets only allowed them to purchase at reduced prices. The discount amounted to 40 per cent on bread, 25 to 40 per cent on peas and beans, 20 to 25 per cent on rice, and around 30 per cent on coal. In other words, the magnanimity of the Chamber of Commerce enabled families who could not even afford to eat potatoes to purchase enough ryebread for one day a week – at a mere 60 per cent of retail prices!

The winter of 1846–1847 saw the same scenario. In December and early January, the committee once again gathered donations which were then transformed into food tickets. The reduction for ryebread was lowered to 35 per cent, but this time *every* family member had a right to 12 kg., spread over 5 weeks. Since the committee parcelled out 336,109 tickets altogether, the number of persons supported numbered 28,000, or 34 per cent of Antwerp's population. The needy could also buy peas and beans at half price – a dubious charity, since some merchants had in 1846 stockpiled gigantic quantities of peas and beans and not succeeded in selling them.

In March 1847 the Chamber of Commerce, now financially exhausted, negotiated for credit with the municipal government. The governors declared it was vitally important to continue assistance, for the price of rye had sky-rocketed higher than in the last 30 years, and the price of potatoes had also begun to rise. The misery of the lower classes was indescribable. Although the Charity Bureau had received an extraordinary subsidy of 108,000 francs, it could not even afford the minimum help to those families entitled to the *secours continuel*. From a report in March 1847, it appears that families of eight earning 7 francs a week received an allowance of 1·50 francs, *i.e.*, the equivalent of 963 grams of potatoes or 674 calories per day per person. Widows with three children hardly fared better: their average weekly income amounted to 3·72 francs and their allowance to 1·20 francs; after subtraction of rent, 3·65 francs remained, the equivalent of 1,023 grams of potatoes or 716 calories per day per person.[31] The poor relief authorities justly argued that the distribution organized by the Chamber of Commerce would be of little use and that it would be preferable to provide greater subsidies to the Charity Bureau. Nonetheless on 13 March the mayor and aldermen – among whom the business community was well represented – voted a subsidy of 3,000 francs and, some weeks later, another 15,000 francs for the Chamber of Commerce. Meanwhile the committee (augmented with representatives of the municipal government) had launched a new registration which provided 25,000 francs. Between 23 March and 3 June, 402,083 bread tickets were distributed. The largest number went to the fourth ward: 167,833, or 42 per cent of the total; the ratio there of tickets to inhabitants stood at 6:1, against 3:1 in the third ward and 4:1 in the rest of the town.

When grain and potato prices collapsed after the good harvest of 1847, the Chamber of Commerce concluded that its task was complete. Indeed, there were now other more efficient means of assisting the proletariat: the Ladies of Charity and the Gentlemen of St. Vincent demonstrated from day to day how much the bourgeoisie pitied the labouring poor. Many philanthropists, moreover, were drawn into the *comités de charité* instituted by the poor relief authorities and maintained thereby direct contact with the needy. The efficacy of such a policy was clearly revealed when February 1848 passed and, despite massive unemployment, public order remained undisturbed. On 22 and 23 March minor demonstrations occurred: the mayor was twice confronted on the street by 150 workers begging for jobs; after he had harangued them, they dispersed peacefully.[32] The next day the town government voted a sum of 17,000 francs to employ 300 men; for 1·56 frans a day they would deepen a small canal. Subsequent subsidies of 35,000 francs kept them occupied until September.[33] There was no further disturbance. In the course of 1848 the police found two hand-written pamphlets threatening plunder and murder,[34] but nothing followed.

Too little evidence exists to calculate the total monetary value of gifts collected during 1845–1847. Yet without any doubt the upper classes escaped cheaply. The third and last subscription list of the Chamber of Commerce totalled 25,000 francs. Even if each of the previous campaigns had garnished as much (which is unlikely) and that all the other private institutions together provided financial support equal to the Chamber of Commerce (which is certainly not the case), the grand total could not have exceeded 150,000 francs. Assuming that the 3,410 propertied bourgeois (*i.e.* those who paid direct taxes)[35] all contributed equally, then each set aside 15 francs a year for charity during the period 1845–1847, the equivalent of half a month's wages for an unskilled male labourer. As one contemporary said, 'they were lucky indeed to maintain order at so small a cost'.[36]

CHAPTER 12

The Struggle for Self-Preservation

If public assistance was very difficult to obtain and alms were little more than crumbs on an otherwise empty plate, how then did the labouring poor manage to survive? Chapters 3 and 10 suggested that in the first half of the nineteenth century marriage and procreation were for the lower classes increasingly the immediate source of their economic difficulties: for working-class couples children meant deprivation because of the long period during which they were unable to earn their keep. Did the proletariat adapt to new circumstances by developing new courtship and marital strategies? The present state of research does not permit a wholly adequate answer. Published materials are too limited and fragmentary to be the basis of extended interpretations. There is no lack of archival sources: masses of quantitative data and even more descriptive material collected by contemporary officials have survived. Even the most elementary analysis of these sources is however time consuming in the extreme. Nonetheless, it has been possible to throw some light on changes in proletarian attitudes and patterns of behaviour toward family formation.

Given that the economic transformation of Antwerp entailed structural unemployment for a growing number of women and nearly all young children, and that the real wages of those who could still get a job fell sharply, it seems probable that more and more male workers would have thought twice before marrying. The odds were that their prospective brides could contribute little or nothing financially, while the founding of a new family required much greater expenditure than at the end of the *ancien régime* owing to the extraordinary rise in rents. To verify this assumption, all available data on the proportion of men and women over 20 who remained single have been assembled.[1]

Percentage of unmarried citizens over 20 in Antwerp, categorized by sex, 1796–1856

	Males	Females
1796	32·3	44·4
1830	38·0	44·9
1846	41·7	41·4
1856	43·0	41·2

Within half a century, the number of bachelors rose by more than 10 per cent. For women, the pattern was completely different: between 1796 and 1830, the percentage of spinsters remained at the same high level, with a slight decline thereafter. Interpretation of these figures, however, must take into account the changes in the sex ratio: between 1796 and 1830, the number of women over 20 per 100 men over 20 diminished from 136 to 132, and by 1856 it had declined further to 111. It is clear that this drastic reduction in the relative surplus of women did not coincide with an equally large diminution in the proportion of those unmarried, which signifies that the position of women in the marriage market had in fact worsened.

It would be useful to analyse these data by socio-economic groups, but, since that is possible only for 1796, the proportion of single men and women have instead been calculated for the fourth ward on one hand and for the rest of the town on the other. In this way the shifts which took place between 1796 and 1830 can be studied.[2] In Chapter 6 it was noted that the fourth ward had in the second quarter of the nineteenth century a distinctly proletarian character. That was already the case at the end of the eighteenth century, for it appears from the census of 1796 that the proportion of those unmarried in this district closely mirrored the proportion in the urban proletariat generally. For males the figures were 24·4 per cent and 20·3 per cent respectively; for women 36·1 per cent and 32·9 per cent. The data regarding the population of the fourth ward, therefore, may be considered indicative of Antwerp's working class.

A comparison of 1796 and 1830 reveals that the number of bachelors in the fourth ward shot upwards (from 24 per cent to 39·2 per cent), while elsewhere it grew more moderately (from 35·9 per cent to 37·9 per cent). For women, the contrast was even stronger: in the fourth ward, the number of spinsters increased (from 37·3 per cent to 45·1 per cent), while it diminished in the other districts (from 47·4 per cent to 45 per cent). These contrary movements are all the more striking when one considers that the number of women over 20 per 100 men diminished from 134 to 128 in the fourth ward and only from 137 to 134 in the remainder of the town. The conclusion must be that the general trend was largely determined by the working population: the fourth ward aside, there was little change. It follows that the upward movement was a response to impoverishment. Only growing material problems explain why the proportion unmarried grew quickest in the most proletarian district and why around 1830 there were comparatively more unmarried men and women there than in any other urban area, while at the end of the *ancien régime* it had been just the opposite. Evidence on marital patterns is presented in the following table.

Percentage unmarried in the population, categorized by age and sex: ward IV compared with the rest of Antwerp, 1830

	Males		Females	
Age group	Ward IV	Other wards	Ward IV	Other wards
15–19	94·9	99·4	97·1	97·8
20–24	66·3	89·1	73·4	84·6
25–29	43·9	59·2	65·0	65·5
30–34	39·8	39·7	46·7	46·0
35–39	28·7	26·2	40·8	35·8
40–44	36·6	19·5	38·0	29·6
45 and over	36·3	14·4	34·3	26·2

Males tended to marry earlier in the proletarian district than in the remainder of Antwerp. In the age group 20–29, the number of bachelors in the fourth ward amounted to 'only' 54 per cent, against an average of 74 per cent elsewhere. That was true for females as well, but the discrepancy was smaller: 69 per cent against 75 per cent. In the age group 30–34, the proportion of those unmarried, both men and women, was similar in both parts of town. Thereafter the patterns diverged. The percentages of bachelors and spinsters fell much more slowly in the fourth ward than in the rest of the town, with the result that the differences between the neighbourhoods became even more pronounced. For men over 45, the proportion unmarried amounted to 36·3 per cent in the proletarian district, versus only 14·4 per cent elsewhere, and for women the proportions were respectively 34·3 per cent and 26·2 per cent. Wage labourers who had not married before the age of 35 were likely to remain unmarried the rest of their lives.

Which section of the working class married young, and why? Why did some marry later in life? Who chose celibacy willingly, and who had no choice? Such questions need answering if one seeks insight into the demographic behaviour of the various strata of the proletariat. That is all the more necessary since Michael Anderson had shown that the marital behaviour of the working class at Preston in the mid-nineteenth century was largely determined by their income levels and the prospects they enjoyed: young men and women with high wages and continued high expectations were favoured marriage partners, while the lower paid had to wait much longer or not in fact marry at all.[3] Much detailed investigation would be required to determine whether this pattern held for Antwerp too. There is no doubt, however, that the overwhelming majority of the labouring poor who married did so before the age of 30, as appears from evidence relating to children born to Antwerp families in receipt of regular support in 1827.[4]

Percentage distribution of children born to Antwerp families regularly supported in 1827, by age at first marriage

Age at first marriage	Males N = 299	Females N = 323
15–19	3·7	5·5
20–24	32·1	47·7
25–29	53·2	37·8
30 and over	11·1	9·0

The mean age at first marriage for the daughters of the poor was 24·6 and for their sons 25·5. These figures are markedly lower than the urban averages in 1830: 28·9 and 31·8, respectively.[5] The first marriages of working-class women thus generally took place around four years earlier than those of the female population as a whole, and around six years earlier with male labourers. Hence the differences in procreation between the proletariat and the rest of the population: in 1830 the number of children aged 0–4 was 1,204 per 1,000 married women aged 15–49 in the fourth ward, against only 1,046 in the remainder of town.[6] With the certainty that child mortality bore more heavily upon the lower classes than on the upper classes, the fertility ratio of the former was even higher. These results agree with the widespread contemporary opinion that the poor as a rule married younger and produced more children than other social groups.[7]

Most observers, however, failed to realize that many wage labourers never married at all and that celibacy among the lower classes assumed greater proportions during the first half of the nineteenth century. The growing number of bachelors and spinsters in the fourth ward indicates clearly that a family was beyond the reach of more and more proletarians. This can also be deduced from the available material concerning illegitimacy. Since the number stillborn before 1827 is not known, all calculations are made on the basis of total births.[8]

Illegitimacy ratios in Antwerp, 1779–1859

Period	Number per 100 births
1779–1800	4·4
1801–1809	11·5
1810–1819	14·8
1830–1839	16·1
1840–1849	14·5
1850–1859	13·5

Even assuming that the figure for the period 1779–1800, derived from baptismal entries in parish registers, gives a distorted picture of reality because of underregistration, the conclusion remains unambiguous: the illegitimacy ratio shot up between 1801 and 1819, and continued to rise until the late 1830s, though at a slower pace. The shortcomings of illegitimacy ratios are notorious;[9] calculation of the general illegitimate fertility rate, relating the number of illegitimate births to the total number of unmarried women in the reproductive ages (usually defined as 15 to 49), however, requires data which are available only for 1830, 1846 and 1856. In any case the rise in the ratio between 1800 and 1840 was too sharp simply to be ascribed to changes in marital fertility or similar factors.

Illegitimate births are not necessarily the product of casual promiscuity. It does seem highly probable that during the first quarter of the nineteenth century working-class girls found it increasingly difficult to force marriage on their sexual partners and even to make them acknowledge the child. The spectacular rise in the number of foundlings between 1802 and 1839 suggests that ever more pregnant women fell victim to abandonment, pointing to a greater incidence of unstable unions. According to contemporaries, there was a close connection between illegitimacy and the foundling problem. They were accurate in the sense that the overwhelming majority of abandoned children were illegitimate infants.[10] The explanation for this behaviour is obvious: since the Charity Bureau as a rule did not provide support to the mother of an illegitimate child even if she was without means of subsistence and she did not live with a man, there was often nothing else for her to do than to abandon the baby. Yet the *enfants trouvés* were merely a fraction of all illegitimate births, as appears from the following table, which also shows that major changes took place in the period under study.[11] The mean number of foundlings rose steadily during the last two decades of the *ancien régime*, but between 1820 and 1839 the upward trend accelerated. During the 1830s, there were three and a half times more recorded newborn orphans than in the late-eighteenth century; the figures for foundlings as a percentage of illegitimate births on the other hand differed little. The 1840s clearly represented a turning point. The number of foundlings began to diminish, not only compared to all births but compared

Foundlings recorded in Antwerp, 1765–1859

Period	Mean number per year	Foundlings as % of	
		total births	illegitimate births
1765–1778	4	?	?
1779–1800	12	0·7	15·7
1802–1811	24	?	?
1830–1839	59	2·5	15·3
1840–1849	55	2·0	13·8
1850–1859	63	1·8	13·5

also to the total number of illegitimate births. Socio-economic factors are scarcely an explanation, since the lowest proportions (1·7 per cent and 12·8 per cent respectively) were recorded precisely at the time when misery reached its zenith, *i.e.* during the crisis of 1845–1848. It would be tempting to ascribe the phenomenon to the moralizing campaigns of the *Dames de la Charité* and the *Messieurs de Saint-Vincent*, but the former were few in number and the latter's activities intensified only in the course of the 1850s. It is thus highly unlikely that the changing attitudes of the proletariat with respect to illegitimate children can be explained by external factors, specifically their application of the norms which their social superiors instilled in – or imposed upon – them. Nor would the supposition hold much weight that the poor in the early nineteenth century felt less affection for bastards than in the 1840s and 1850s. During the whole of the period under consideration, the police commissioners reported that the mothers of foundlings identified lived in extreme destitution and the directors of the poor relief office, who so often decried the 'misbehaviour' of the lower classes, always emphasized that extreme poverty was the heart of the foundling problem, not dissipation or heartlessness.[12] In support of their statements, these observers referred to the poignant notes and identifying marks which most foundlings had beside them. Although they are not suitable for statistical treatment, the hundreds of short letters, small pieces of cloth, bits of holy prints, and other objects which have been preserved suggest that many mothers did indeed reveal their illegitimate children in the hope of retrieving them years later – a tragic delusion, since at least one in three children died within one year of admission to the Foundling Hospital.[13]

Although the available evidence demands no single interpretation, it tends to support the notion that the poor gradually adapted to new circumstances. The explosion of bastardy in the early-nineteenth century reflected a growing disparity between customary expectations and sexual behaviour on one hand and deteriorating socio-economic opportunities on the other. From the 1840s, that disequilibrium began slowly to be resolved, not because living conditions of the proletariat improved, but as a result of diminishing prospects. Unlike their parents, working-class children born during the Dutch régime or shortly after the Belgian Revolution grew up in a town in which poverty had taken on massive proportions. They had seen innumerable cases of couples who, through lack of financial means, had to delay their marriage or were never able to marry. It does not seem unreasonable to assume that they were more conscious than the previous generation of uncertainties and that as a result different patterns of behaviour began to develop with respect to courtship and marital strategies.[14]

This reasoning would explain why the number of foundlings declined markedly after 1840, not only compared to all births but also to the total number of illegitimate births, while the illegitimacy rate remained unaltered – in 1830 as well as in 1856, the number of natural births per 1,000 unmarried, widowed and divorced women aged 15–44 amounted to 31·2.[15] The coincidence of both phenomena suggests that a growing proportion of illegitimate births was the product of stable consensual unions. Unfortunately there are no statistics about acknowledgement and legitimations of illegitimate children for that period, nor quantitative data on bridal pregnancies resolved by marriage. There is, however, some evidence to support the idea that progressively more children born out of 'concubinage' were integrated into the families of their parents.

From the 1830s on, the Charity Bureau repeatedly declared that ever more lower-class couples lived permanently in 'concubinage'. Although these assertions rested on fragmentary observations only and served to illustrate the immorality of the proletariat, they were certainly not unfounded. Two samplings suggest not only that free unions among the lower classes occurred frequently, but also that they often had a long-lasting character. Of the 407 women who in 1830 entered into a first marriage, 70 or 17·2 per cent had already borne one or more children; the average number was 1·61 and the maximum 8. No fewer than 55 of these brides were casual labourers, lace workers, or seamstresses, *i.e.*, 27 per cent of all brides who practised such trades, and nearly all had wage labourers as partners.[16] The second sampling relates to sons and daughters younger than five of parents with at least four children who received the *secours continuel* in 1827; 393 of these children married prior to 1860, mostly between 1842 and 1856. From their marriage certificates it appears that some 32 per cent of the brides already had one or more children; the average was 1·31 and the maximum 4. As to the time which had passed since the (first) illegitimate birth: in two out of ten cases, it was less than one year and in four out of ten 1 to 3 years, but 10 per cent of the children were born six years before the lawful wedlock of their parents. The fact that in 1841 a charitable society, dedicated to St. Jean-François Régis, was founded with the exclusive aim of regularizing free but stable unions likewise attests to the growing extent of the phenomenon. Between 1844 and 1862, the society enabled no fewer than 877 couples to get the necessary documents and to pay the required fees – nearly 6 per cent of all civil marriages contracted in that period.[17]

That does not explain, however, how the labouring poor were able to survive without assistance from the Charity Bureau: whether married or not, every poor person at one time or another had crises involving the loss of means of existence. How did they cope with such apparently impossible conditions? Were they driven to crime? To put it differently: did the ever harder struggle for self-preservation force growing numbers of needy people into begging, theft, or prostitution?

Since 1779, solicitation of alms had been forbidden in Antwerp. The law was repeatedly broken, of course, and broken more frequently during periods with a greater incidence of poverty. Nonetheless, begging was the exception rather than the rule. Between 1850 and 1860, an average of 145 beggars a year were arrested and dispatched to the *dépot de mendicité* at Hoogstraten. This institution was founded in 1810 to serve as an asylum for the whole of the province of Antwerp, but primarily it lodged beggars from that town. During the 1850s, its population consisted overwhelmingly of young, unmarried males, who, according to the administration, were in good physical condition. Furthermore, only one in five internees could not claim to have practised a trade; the others had worked intermittently, most as casual labourers.[18]

This evidence suggests that 'sturdy' beggars were a small minority, and consequently that most of the internees had been compelled by chronic unemployment to take recourse to 'criminal' solutions. Two facts support this supposition. In the first place, the number of recidivists was extremely small. No less than 84 per cent of the persons entering the *dépôts* of Hoogstraten, Terkameren (for Brabant), and Rekem (for Limburg) in the years 1840–1842 were first offenders. Even during the economic crisis which followed shortly thereafter, recidivists remained the minority: 61 per cent of the beggars held in the *dépôts* in the period 1843–1847 were newcomers, 22 per cent had been there once before, 10 per cent twice, and 7 per cent at least three times.[19] In the second place, until 1843 around 60 per cent of the internees at Hoogstraten were there voluntarily. Most of these unfortunates were unemployed wage labourers who could not fall back upon relatives and who were not eligible for public assistance. Their situation must have been completely hopeless before coming to the beggars' colony, for everyone knew of the iron discipline that ruled there. Any infraction against the rules was punished by solitary confinement in dark, subterranean pits: fifteen days for those who swore, chewed tobacco in the chapel, or were caught a second time playing cards; a month for those who smoked in the dormitories, the refectories, the latrines or who committed moral infractions. According to Ducpétiaux, even prison regimen was less strenuous than that of the *dépôts de mendicité*. His judgement was supported by a member of the Council of Inspection, who wrote to the Minister of Justice that the discipline at Hoogstraten rested exclusively on intimidation and cruelty.[20] Rations, moreover, were limited to the strict minimum. Adult internees received 625 grams of ryebread daily, one to one and a half litres of Rumfordsoup, a portion of stewed vegetables and water mixed with vinegar.[21] Yet still the hungry volunteers streamed in. Their number rose so high that on 25 June

1843 the municipal authorities of Antwerp refused any longer to bear the costs of the poor who went to the beggars' colony on their own initiative; henceforth they first had to petition the municipal council, which only gave approval for inclusion upon the advice of the Charity Bureau.[22]

After a thorough investigation of the social background of Belgian criminals held in the *maisons centrales*, Ducpétiaux concluded in 1855 that the overwhelming majority belonged to the lower classes: 4,796 out of 5,461 internees, nearly 88 per cent, had lived in utter destitution before their imprisonment.[23] The data from Antwerp fully indicate that there was a close correlation between poverty and criminality. Whereas in the last quarter of the eighteenth century an average of only 16 *vols simples* (thefts without additional offences) a year were recorded by the police, *i.e.*, barely 3 per 10,000 inhabitants, the number amounted to no less than 220 a year in the decennium 1850–1859, or 23 per 10,000 inhabitants. Yet it is clear that crimes against property remained a marginal phenomenon during the fifties. Even adding all cases of burglary, fraud, and fencing to the *vols simples*, the general total did not exceed 28 per 10,000.[24] To all appearances, the Charity Bureau was correct in its declaration of 1860 that, although most law-breakers were poor, only an extremely small fraction of the working population was guilty of criminal activities.[25]

Prostitution was also on the increase during this period. The census of 1796 registered no brothels, which of course does not imply an absence of prostitution: between 1775 and 1794, twenty women were found guilty of such activity and sent to the provincial house of correction at Vilvoorde.[26] With the end of the eighteenth century, however, complaints surfaced about the growing extent of the problem. In 1800, the prefect of the *département des Deux-Nèthes* asked the mayor of Antwerp to take care regarding the rising number of bawdy houses – establishments which he claimed had not existed earlier. Five years later the number of prostitutes had risen so sharply that the municipal authorities were compelled to take measures which in effect amounted to regulation and thus acceptance of the situation: brothel-keepers could no longer admit women without a *carte de sûreté*, and prostitutes henceforth had to submit to weekly medical examinations. In 1817, moreover, it was decided that they could only ply their trade in brothels whose owners kept registers of names, place of birth, age, and date of arrival.[27]

The first police reports on prostitution, in 1818, noted 19 *maisons publiques*, officially-registered brothels. By 1845 the number had doubled, and in 1857 had risen to 49. The number of *filles publiques* had grown even more: from 160 in 1845 to 276 in 1857.[28] Although these data undeniably reveal a trend, they cannot by themselves be used to calculate the real growth of the activity, even approximately. In the first place, the police regularly tracked down illegal brothels. Unfortunately enough, the surviving statistics do not provide detailed evidence of the total number of 'suspects' sheltered in 'houses of ill-repute'. In any case, there is no doubt that the phenomenon spread like wild-fire, despite the growing vigilance of the police and the steadily more rigorous enforcement of penalties. While around 1818 only 32 houses were presumed to be functioning as illegal brothels in the whole town, in 1863 the fifth ward *alone* had 33 *maisons suspectes*.[29] In the second place, there is no information regarding the number of *raccrocheuses*, streetwalkers. This lacuna is all the more regrettable because contemporaries who were concerned with the problem during the 1840s and 1850s – police officers, judges, medical commissioners – agreed that this form of clandestine prostitution had expanded remarkably.[30] Although they never neglected to blame the depravity of the poor, these observers had to admit that nearly all 'fallen women' from the lower classes had been driven by material need. They were seconded by Ducpétiaux, who declared in 1860 that nothing had contributed so much to the growth of low-class prostitution as the rapid decline of traditional employment opportunities for women.[31] Even on the assumption that many girls and women from the lower classes had to prostitute themselves either regularly or sporadically in order to survive, such activities could never have amounted to more than a transitory phase in their lives. Samples indicate that only one out of every ten prostitutes – whether they worked in a brothel or on the street – was younger than 15 or older than 30.[32]

In conclusion, although child abandonment, begging, petty theft, and prostitution were on the increase during the first half of the nineteenth century, these methods of individual survival continued to be marginal. It follows that the vast majority of proletarians had to develop other, more lasting strategies in order to overcome critical periods of their lives. What were these alternatives? Did they build patterns of reciprocity with kin and neighbours? In other words: how important was mutual aid within and among working class families?

CHAPTER 13

Proletarian Networks

Recent research suggests that the family did not disintegrate in areas where the industrialization process was rapid, notably in textile centres. Rather individual chances of survival were to a large extent determined by mutual support within the family. Some historians even go so far as to argue that, in the new manufacturing towns, 'more often than not, migration and entry to the factory employment were acts pursued within a family-oriented social context . . . which would not conflict with values brought from the sending community'.[1] By emphasizing cohesion, adaptability and continuity, these scholars suggest that the preservation of the family was not so much the *result* of a wider social process as its *purpose*. From such a perspective it seems as though family-based strategies were relatively autonomous and self-regulating, so that they could continually be adapted to changes in the capitalist division of labour.

This final chapter is intended to explore the significance of proletarian networks in Antwerp during the first half of the nineteenth century. Two closely interconnected questions arise here. First, did the lower classes in port cities develop social networks similar to those of factory workers in textile centres, or did the family disintegrate in places where casual labour became increasingly more important? Second, were family-based strategies the most adequate and rational response to growing material insecurity? In other words, was the family the most suitable 'instrument' for the construction of relations of reciprocity and solidarity, or did other forms of co-residence offer more opportunities for mutual assistance?

Michael Anderson has shown the crucial importance of family and kin as sources of help for the majority of the nineteenth-century working class as they coped with illness, unemployment, death, or old age. His thorough investigation of family structure in Preston, Lancashire, led him to conclude that in spite of migration, residential mobility, industrial employment, and high mortality rates, most people managed to maintain relationships with their family, both the current nuclear family and the family as a web of wider kinship relations. The very fact that migrants and the widowed and the old made efforts to move near kin suggests that it was a functionally important unit too.

Widows without children often lived with relatives (44 per cent of those studied); many of the elderly moved in with their married (32 per cent) or unmarried (36 per cent) children; and young couples sometimes lived for years with one set of parents. Relations with both immediate family and more distant kin were usually based on 'short-run bargains': they were maintained so long as they were mutually beneficial, often for rather a short time. Geographic mobility, high mortality, and frequent unemployment made the future uncertain and consequently limited possibilities for long-term reciprocity. Moreover, this kind of assistance would not have been available at all stages of life. Few parents with unmarried children in the home could take in other sons and daughters-in-law, and few married couples who were heads of household could share their dwelling with the parents of either spouse. Finally, mutual assistance among the poor became inoperative beyond a certain level of poverty: those who could scarcely keep themselves alive were in no state to provide assistance to others.[2]

Given that the socio-economic structures of Preston and Antwerp differed radically, comparison of family and kinship relations in the two towns would be of interest. Unfortunately such a comparison would be immensely laborious and difficult. It took Anderson some six years to assemble and process all his data: a similar investigation for Antwerp would be even more time-consuming, since its population far exceeded that of Preston. The only reasonable alternative has been to analyze the poor lists of 1827 and 1855. Although these sources make no mention of co-resident lodgers, and provide no information on the age or family structure of those who shared their dwellings with the needy, they do permit inquiry into the proportion of regular dole-drawers who found a home with kin or with other heads of household.

In 1827 as well as in 1855, most recipients of outdoor relief headed their own household. There were, however, important differences in relation to marital status and the presence of children. Widows and widowers lived more frequently with kin or as lodgers than did married couples, and those without co-residing children more frequently than others. Gender too apparently played a role: in both years there were many more households prepared to take in a woman than a man. The table also reveals that the number of supported needy who lived with kin or as lodgers was more than halved during the second quarter of the nineteenth century: from nearly 28 per cent in 1827 to barely 12 per cent in 1855. In order to explain this drastic reduction, changes in residence patterns need to be investigated for the most significant category, that of childless widows.

Proportions of families on outdoor relief living with kin or as lodgers, by marital status and children: Antwerp, 1827 and 1855

	% of all families living with kin or as lodgers		All families N (100%)	
	1827	1855	1827	1855
No children:				
widows and spinsters	60·6	32·7	487	495
widowers and bachelors	40·5	24·4	74	82
married couples	18·3	9·5	115	95
With children:				
widows	9·1	2·4	220	538
widowers	7·4	1·5	27	67
married couples	2·8	1·0	451	483
All	27·7	11·9	1,374	1,760

For working-class people growing old usually led to the most grinding poverty: they lost physical strength, so that their incomes were greatly reduced or even eliminated entirely.[3] That was particularly the case in a town like Antwerp where competition for jobs which required little physical exertion became increasingly more intense in the course of the period under study. Those who were unmarried or widowed faced the greatest difficulties. Their meagre earnings seldom met their need for food, let alone rent on a room of their own. This category deserves all the more attention because it included the overwhelming majority of old people: in 1830 as well as in 1856, no less than 60 per cent of the inhabitants aged 65 and over were unmarried or widowed.[4] It must immediately be added that the scope and the intensity of the problems posed by age differed strikingly according to sex. Spinsters and widows of 65 and over were nearly twice as numerous as males, and they had far greater trouble finding a job. Thus, the combination of being a woman, alone, and old resulted in the greatest misery, rather than old age itself.

The poor lists suggest that co-residence offered at least a partial solution. Nearly 62 per cent of widows aged 65 and over who in 1827 received permanent support from the Charity Bureau shared rooms with children or other family. Since many of them (around 3 in 10) had no income of their own, these arrangements were naturally to their advantage. But why were they taken in by people who, according to the marginal notes in the register, often themselves had difficulty making ends meet? Although many factors could have played a role, the most important was probably the ability of old women to perform services such as caring for children, washing and cooking. Nearly all elderly widows without a wage and not head of a household listed 'housekeeper' as their occupation. That only 38 per cent of the elderly widowers were accommodated by children or other kin strengthens this probability, for one can assume that older men generally were not expected to provide equally important services.[5]

During the second quarter of the nineteenth century marked transformations took place. Families still formed the foremost source of help, but their protective functions were eroded. In 1855, the number of widows aged 65 and over living with family amounted to only 48 per cent, against 62 per cent in 1827. The following table indicates that this sharp decrease must primarily be ascribed to the fact that fewer widows than previously could move in with married children.

Residence patterns of widows aged 65 and over in receipt of out-relief: Antwerp, 1827 and 1855

	1827 %	1855 %
Living:		
with married daughter	36·9	17·2
with married son	9·2	5·1
with other child	4·9	16·2
with sister or brother	3·4	1·6
with other kin	7·4	7·6
as lodger	7·4	6·7
with no other person	30·8	45·5
All living with children	51·0	38·5
All: %	100·0	99·9
N	325	314

Whereas in 1827 nearly half these widows had one married child prepared to give them room in their home, that proportion had dropped to around 22 per cent by 1855. The explanation lies in a combination of factors. In Chapter 10 it was shown that the level of unemployment shot up between 1827 and 1855: from barely 9 per cent to 45 per cent for women aged 20–54 and from 56 per cent to 89 per cent for boys and girls aged 5–14. Ever more working-class families faced a drastic reduction in their income, so that they found it increasingly difficult to take on an extra burden. In addition, they were less dependent on parents or other relatives for domestic services; certainly there was a growing number of women who had to work outside the home, but from the 1840s they could send their children to school. Considering further that few older women in mid-century Antwerp contributed anything to the family budget, it becomes clear why fewer widows than before could move in with a married daughter or son.

Unmarried sons and daughters, on the other hand, lived more frequently
with their mothers (if widowed and alone) in 1855 than in 1827. Saving on
rent appears to have been of crucial significance here. By the middle of the century, the housing shortage had assumed such proportions that even a person
with a regular income could scarcely justify renting a room on his own. Since
the *secours continuel* provided by the Charity Bureau exceeded the rent of a
single room, it became steadily more sensible for unmarried and childless adults
to share accommodation with other family members.

The poor relief authorities were alarmed by the gradual disruption of the
family life of the lower classes. In 1860 they reported 'that one finds but few
young couples who are prepared to take in their elders even if the latter receive
public support because of their age or an infirmity. In most cases, the children
require that their elders also provide them with a weekly income derived from
private charity.' Why did more and more children desert their aged parents?
The poor relief authorities had no doubt as to the answer: 'Some because of the
large family for which they must provide, others because they do not earn
enough themselves to live on, yet others because they have given themselves
over to dissipation, drink, and libertinage; all because they have forgotten their
duties to their parents'. This heartlessness had in the last instance to be seen as
evidence of a growing egoism, mirroring in turn the general immorality of the
proletariat. Nonetheless, the directors recognized that 'this egoism has in fact
become a necessity, since the incomes of most working-class families are insufficient for their own maintenance, so that they are obliged to rid themselves of
their elders'.[6]

What was left for old people without sufficient resources or charitable
family? In the first half of the nineteenth century, Antwerp had 26 civil hospices, founded in the late middle ages or the early modern period, where the
elderly could enjoy free room and board. The capacity of these institutions,
however, was limited: together they could house only two hundred women,
fifty men, and some fifty couples.[7] So long as the social costs of the economic
transformation were paid almost exclusively by the proletariat, the élites did
not burden themselves with the shortage of homes for the elderly. The 1820s
formed a watershed. It then became clear that many small shopkeepers and self-
employed artisans could not escape destitution, so that they too were hard put
to maintain themselves in old age. Since these people were presented by the
upper classes as outstanding examples of respectable poverty, they could not be
abandoned to their fate. The initiative taken by various benevolent societies in
the field of care for the elderly must be seen in that light.

In 1824, the *Société de Charité chrétienne*, founded by the dean of Our Lady's
Church and some Catholic laymen from the highest social circles, established a
home for old women; to be admitted, one had to be able to pay for one's keep.
Though the charge was not determined by the actual cost of maintenance, it was
sufficiently high to exclude the very poor. The same principle was applied in two
similar institutions founded in the second quarter of the nineteenth century, and
run by the *Soeurs de la Charité* and the *Frères de la Charité*, respectively. The old

men's home of St. Carolus, established in 1852 on the initiative of a priest, P. Hofman, and financed by the nobility and prominent commoners, was also intended for impoverished members of the lower middle class. Apart from this latter institution, which could accommodate only 50 to 60 people, the homes in mid-century admitted an average of 100 inmates.[8] Although living conditions in these homes were far from rosy,[9] in comparison with many other elderly people its inmates were highly fortunate.

Those who were wholly dependent on public support were contracted out by the Charity Bureau to families in the countryside or relegated to the *ateliers de charité*. Although the poor relief authorities were conscious that contracting out the elderly gave rise to gross abuses,[10] they increasingly had to opt for this apparent solution. The number of elderly who were in effect sold at auction rose from 20–30 a year in the early nineteenth century to more than 250 a year around 1850.[11] Six years earlier, the Charity Bureau had seen itself compelled to establish a special relief section in the *ateliers de charité* where the needy who could do only light labour or were completely unable to work received free meals: 125 grams of rye bread, a litre and a half of soup, and a cup of milk diluted with water.[12] In the period 1845–9, an average of 300 single and widowed people aged 60 and over lined up daily for this meagre diet.[13] They did not come casually. From 1847, the 'chosen people' had to remain in the institution from 7 a.m. to 7 p.m., and were subjected to an iron discipline: it was forbidden to speak, to sing, and to whistle in the workshops as well as in the halls and the refectory; it was also forbidden to make obscene or hostile gestures; nor even could they go to the toilet without the approval of an overseer. No wonder that the commission which, in 1864–1865, investigated living conditions in the workhouses, came to the conclusion that 'the needy are horrified to think that they must go into this institution: they resolve to do so only when they are in the most extreme need and when they have spent their last reserves ... Many of the poor would rather withdraw their pleas for public support than enter the *ateliers*'.[14]

It is impossible to determine the exact number, gender, and marital status of the elderly who were dependent on bureaucratized forms of assistance at mid-century. Too much information is lacking. Some sources do not mention the age of the supported needy, while others do not distinguish between men and women or between the married and the widowed. Nonetheless, the general order of magnitude can be established. The civil hospices and private homes respectively accommodated 250 and 300 boarders, either unmarried or widowed; the regulations of the institutions stipulated that no one under 60 would be accepted. Along with these groups there were around 250 single persons who were contracted out to rural families and who, according to the reports of the Charity Bureau, were 60 or older. Finally, there were the aged cared for in St. Elisabeth's hospital. In the 1850s these numbered 200,[15] but there is no information on their marital status. Supposing that the proportion of single and widowed persons among them more or less matched that of Antwerp's population over 60 as a whole, the number would be 120. In sum, then, there were more than 900 single and widowed persons over 60 housed in charitable institutions or private homes. The supported needy in this age and marital category who still headed their own households or who lived together with relatives were equally numerous: *c*. 600 recipients of out-relief and *c*. 300 frequenters of the *ateliers de charité*. The grand total thus amounted to 1,800, some 39 per cent of all single and widowed persons of 60 and older.

At first glance, these figures seem fairly impressive. They relate however, to the most vulnerable part of the populace: the unmarried or widowed elderly, many of them growing infirm. Taking into account the high levels of unemployment and rent, it is surprising that over 60 per cent of the aged in question made no claim on bureaucratized forms of support. Without doubt, the overwhelming majority lived in destitution: in 1796, nearly seven inhabitants in ten over 60 were completely without possessions,[16] and the proportion would have been much higher a half-century later as a result of massive continuing impoverishment. The only reasonable explanation seems to be that many people only turned to the Charity Bureau as a last resort.

There is considerable evidence to suggest that the poor tried any and all alternatives before applying for relief. The archives contain innumerable reports and letters in which officials, almoners, and philanthropists turned the attention of the poor relief authorities to the needy who received no public assistance, although they had a right to it and were in the greatest of misery. Subsequent investigations always revealed that the persons concerned had chosen a course which they felt was above the most extreme degradation. In January 1802, the Charity Bureau was entreated by the director of military quarters to support a childless widow of 69 whose income did not provide even the barest essentials, but who 'has such a noble heart that she would rather gnaw on a speck of black bread than beg door to door'. In the summer of 1807, the police reported that a sexagenarian, born in Antwerp and without means of subsistence, slept on the street every night; although without a roof over his head, he had not registered with the poor relief authorities. The same year the mayor informed the Charity Bureau of an old widow too ashamed to request support, though often on the verge of death.[17]

This sense of shame was clearly shared by many poor people. The correspondence of the Charity Bureau shows that even the most destitute among them found it degrading to be catalogued as dole-drawers. In March 1832 a woman whose husband had been in hospital for some two years wrote to the mayor that the landlord's resident agent threatened to evict her because she could no longer pay her rent; for the sake of her five small children she found herself compelled to call upon public support, but she petitioned the mayor to take care that her name be placed only on the list of 'quiet poor'.[18] The Charity Bureau did indeed have a special fund for the maintenance of *pauvres honteux*: families and persons who, as the directorate expressed it, 'are reluctant to turn to welfare institutions owing to their upbringing, sense of self-respect, or memories of better times'; their names were known only to a few highly-placed members of the poor relief authorities and almoners, who dispensed to them their allowances with the greatest of discretion.[19] This delicate treatment, however, was reserved for a small minority. During the first quarter of the nine-teenth century, the number of *pauvres honteux* never exceeded 300 and grew even fewer thereafter.[20] The reasons for this are obvious: extension of preferen-tial treatment would not only have presented the Charity Bureau with great practical difficulties but also would have created a flood of requests, something to be avoided at all costs. Hence the directorate almost exclusively registered as *pauvres honteux* impoverished members of the middle class who were alone, old, and ill, and applied even more selective criteria for admission.[21]

The difference between Antwerp and English textile towns is undeniable. Developments within the Antwerp labour market which allowed the elderly very little chance to contribute something to their families' incomes, coupled with the absence of permanent work for women outside the home, meant that even with household tasks and child rearing no specific role was reserved for this group. Furthermore, the Charity Bureau had to contend with an increasing lack of money, so that the institution was seldom prepared to provide for the mainte-nance of the elderly by means of a reasonable money allowance; the directorate preferred to place the elderly outside the city at the lowest possible cost. Conse-quently the charitable relationship between parent and child was undermined.

This fate was not confined to the aged. In years of crisis, many families were compelled to push members into the *ateliers de charité*, even if only to help bridge the worst months. In a town such as Antwerp, where more and more people depended directly or indirectly on shipping for a livelihood, the end of the year was always the darkest period. 'The interruption of traffic in the har-bour throws a mass of wage labourers onto the street every winter', declared the Charity Bureau in 1864.[22] We can see this in the fluctuations in the num-bers of the poor employed in the *ateliers de charité*.[23]

Monthly employment of the poor in the *ateliers de charité*, 1837–1843 (index: mean number employed during 12-month period = 100)

Month	1837	1838	1839	1840	1841	1842	1843
J	150	133	131	169	163	148	142
F	117	229	127	151	141	130	153
M	113	118	106	118	102	94	114
A	93	88	92	93	86	90	87
M	89	81	76	76	77	78	81
J	87	73	72	77	73	76	81
J	77	64	70	73	72	79	75
A	79	67	67	73	78	76	73
S	87	64	72	75	84	78	78
O	84	68	78	82	88	89	88
N	109	89	126	94	109	118	106
D	137	136	180	124	132	146	123

During December, January and February, precisely the months in which shipping stood at its lowest point, the *ateliers* housed their largest complement of poor. From March onwards, able-bodied adults were quickly pushed out of the workhouses; only young children, the aged, the lame, and some women could stay. In July, the *ateliers* generally contained half as many poor as during the winter months, but in crisis years these ratios rose to 1:4 and even 1:5.[24]

In short, family bonds in Antwerp came under increasingly greater strain. Not only did relations of reciprocity among family members barely function in a context of intensifying impoverishment and relative redundancy, but the nature of the new economic structure too was such that the vicissitudes of casual labour could best be absorbed by broader community linkages, where the risk-spreading could be more flexible. Indeed it seems reasonable to suggest that, where Antwerp is concerned, the role of the neighbourhood as the organizing principle in the construction of relations of reciprocity and solidarity ought to be accorded great importance. Although most of the supporting evidence is circumstantial, and none beyond dispute, it would seem that the neighbourhood, far more than the narrower familial context, was the most obvious circle in which the risks accompanying very insecure livelihoods and extremely irregular earnings could be absorbed. Thus one result of the economic transformation was impoverishment and class segregation in conditions of enforced overcrowding; on the other hand, the formation of dense social networks became a necessary condition for survival in the ghettos.

Although steadily more working-class people had to swallow their pride and turn to the poor relief authorities, they continued strenuously to maintain close relations with neighbours and friends to solve their problems. Some examples illustrate the general willingness among the lower classes to aid one another. In January 1804, a man whose wife (without knowing why) had been in prison for five weeks declared that their four children had been taken in by neighbours; since these people were every bit as needy as himself, they could not long continue their charitable action. In November 1828, a certain Louis Verbruecken asked the poor relief authorities to provide support to a widow who had a small grocer's shop; he and his parents had long helped her, but now their financial means were exhausted. In May 1839, a septagenarian bachelor, ill and without any source of income, was placed in the old man's home of the *Frères de la Charité*, partially at the expense of his neighbours. In June 1846, the neighbours of a very elderly widow wrote to the poor relief authorities that her allowance must be raised: after subtracting rent, she was left with only half a franc a week, wholly inadequate to feed herself; the neighbours often came to her rescue, but that was no longer possible since they themselves now had difficulty making ends meet.[25] It is impossible to determine the frequency and extent of these kinds of assistance, since they only exceptionally left written records of their existence. That the Charity Bureau during the period under study received hundreds of letters of the same tenor suggests, however, that many working-class people in critical living situations could count upon neighbours and friends.

Men of letters such as Pieter Frans Van Kerckhoven, Domien Sleeckx, and August Snieders, living in Antwerp in mid-century, viewed this neighbourhood solidarity as the most distinguishing characteristic of the proletariat. In *Volksverhalen* ('Folk Tales'), written by Van Kerckhoven in 1849, a young carpenter from the fourth ward takes in a sick man, his wife and two children, who have been evicted. He brings this Jewish family to the tiny house he shares with his mother, to whom he says simply: 'I'm enlarging the household. He's a poor fellow ... turned out like a dog. He's sick, the poor devil, give him a cup of coffee'. His mother answers: 'They can stay as long as necessary. Poor folk have to help each other, since the rich use the law to make us worse and worse off. What my son has done is right. He can provide for all of us, but we'll have to live very frugally'.[26] Similar examples of neighbourhood solidarity abound in the literature of the time. Van Kerckhoven and other contemporary authors emphasized how much could be learned from the lower classes: poor people turned to their neighbours when they were ill; proletarian families shared their food with hungry friends; working women had no difficulty in finding someone to whom they could entrust their infants during the day; adult orphans took in younger orphans; inhabitants of blind alleys cared communally for the sick and insane in their small communities; on the death of a slum-dweller, co-tenants collected funds for a couple of altar candles.[27]

The significance of these wider networks can also be observed from the position of migrants. As historians have shown for the nineteenth century and sociologists for our own time, migrants face special problems which are hard to solve without the help of others: they must find shelter; they need information on employment opportunities; they have to adapt to the new community in a hundred and one different ways.[28] Two Antwerp samples show how essential were the ties of kinship and friendship for this group.

Who took in the 544 adult migrants coming to Antwerp in 1817 has been investigated. It must be emphasized that the results of this investigation can be no more than suggestive, since only the family name and birthplace of the migrant could be used as a starting point. Marriage records were traced to learn whether these migrants married other migrants or natives of Antwerp. The following table summarizes the data up to 1830. While couples were taken in only by family members, single migrants also found fellow villagers or friends prepared to offer them shelter in Antwerp. Only a minority of the migrants, however, could enjoy the advantages of such arrangements: 111, or 20·4 per cent of the total. That does not mean that all the others had to rent a room, for servants and apprentices generally lodged with their employers. Nonetheless, on their arrival in town most migrants lacked the helping hand of kin or relatives. Marriage was for this group the obvious way to develop a social connection that would enable them to survive in urban life. Between 1817 and 1830, nearly half the male and around a quarter of the female migrants managed to find a spouse in Antwerp, usually within five years of their arrival.[29] It ought to be noted, however, that few migrants married natives of Antwerp, signifying that their chances of integration through marital ties should not be overestimated.

Proportion of adult migrants to Antwerp developing a social network in the town: Antwerp sample, 1817

Marital status when coming to Antwerp	Of all migrants,					All migrants N (100%)
	living with:		marrying	with:		
	kin %	non-kin* %	other migrant %	non-migrant %	all developing a social network %	
Married:	8·5	—	—	—	8·5	71
Single:						
Males	10·0	8·6	30·8	15·8	65·2	221
Females	12·7	12·7	15·9	10·7	52·0	252
All	11·0	9·4	19·9	11·4	51·7	544

* Excluding those in service or apprenticeship.

That conclusion is reinforced by a comparison of the migrants who took up more or less permanent residence in Antwerp and those who went elsewhere after some period of time. In 1830, all the immigrants of 1817 married to a native of Antwerp remained in the town, whereas nine male and nine female immigrants (13 per cent and 22·5 per cent, respectively) married to other immigrants had moved on. As for the unmarried: only 10 per cent of bachelors and 15·5 per cent of single women living with relatives or with friends who had previously come to Antwerp emigrated before 1830, but these proportions rose to 49 per cent and 64 per cent for men and women lacking such relationships.

Social networks thus largely determined how migrants integrated themselves into their new community. Those who did not have strong contacts in Antwerp prior to their arrival or who did not marry (preferably a native of Antwerp) had the greatest difficulty. They had to reside in Antwerp for a certain time before they could turn to the local Charity Bureau: until 1818 the minimum period was one year, between 1818 and 1844 four years, and thereafter eight years (see p.43, above). In the meanwhile they could apply to the last commune in which they had lived a sufficient number of years, but such procedure was highly time-consuming – the longer the communal authorities delayed granting relief, the less they had to pay in the long run.

An analysis of the demographics of (mainly Dutch) families in Antwerp who received, for at least one year, allowances from external charitable institutions indicates once again the crucial importance of social networks in the struggle for survival.[30] It should be noted that at the time of application for relief only 184 of the 866 foreigners concerned, or 21·2 per cent, had a spouse born in Antwerp. The overwhelming majority – whether married or not – was highly vulnerable. Hence quite different family patterns predominated among foreigners on relief than among the needy assisted by the local Charity Bureau.

Types of families receiving out-relief at Antwerp: foreigners (1845–1855) compared with long-time inhabitants (1855)

Type of family	Recent migrants from abroad	Long-time inhabitants
Married couples with		
Children present	35·6	27·4
No children present	21·1	5·4
Widowed or single persons with no children present:		
Aged 50 and over	16·3	32·8
Under 50	15·1	–
Widowed or single persons with children present	12·0	34·4
All: %	100·1	100·0
N	866	1,760

It is clear that marriage by itself offered no guarantee: the married comprised nearly 60 per cent of those seeking public assistance. The proportion of childless couples among the outsiders was nearly four times greater than among local recipients of relief: 21·1 per cent, against 5·4 per cent. This discrepancy is all the more striking given that 8 in 10 migrant household heads were younger than 60 and nearly 6 in 10 younger than 50. The same holds for widowed and single persons without co-resident children: more than half were under 50, while none from this age group was among those assisted by the Antwerp Charity Bureau. As for 'outsider' heads of household with co-resident children, it is worth noting that the mean number of children was only 3·32 for couples and 1·96 for widowed or single people, while the averages for the Antwerp group were 4·73 and 2·93, respectively. In short, the family structure of outsiders given relief was comparatively much more secure than that of local recipients: many childless, middle aged heads of household, few widowed or single persons with children, and only a few couples with large families. It seems justifiable to assume, therefore, that most of the immigrants concerned did not depend on bureaucratized forms of relief primarily as a consequence of repeated childbirth, old age, loss of primary breadwinner, or a combination of such disasters, but because they lacked family and friends to help if they were ill, unemployed, and so on. This conclusion is also suggested by the disparity in age between foreigners married to other migrants, and those who had spouses from Antwerp: when they asked for help, three in ten household heads among the former were older than 50, against five in ten among the latter. The most likely explanation lies in the fact that those married to natives of Antwerp had a greater chance of adapting themselves to urban life, helped by kin or broader social networks, and needed to turn to public assistance for the first time only later in life.

The poor relief authorities were quite conscious of the extreme difficulties with which the uprooted had to cope. Although theoretically obligated to apply equal standards to all groups of the population, they often advised communal authorities to assist their emigrants, even if these families did not meet the formal criteria. Lacking relatives and friends, the Charity Bureau testified, public relief formed the last refuge of the needy. If this last hope proved idle, then there remained nothing but starvation.[31]

Thus, although the protective functions of the family were gradually eroded, it would appear that mutual aid remained of decisive importance in the struggle for survival. The basis for this solidarity, without a doubt, is to be found in the shared experience of the proletariat. Whatever efforts the labouring poor may have expended, in the long run they faced a sharp decline in their standard of living. Every family knew that sooner or later they would be in distress and that at such moments help from kin, neighbours, and friends would be indispensible, since little was to be expected from public assistance other than the worst sorts of humiliation. Indeed it was not only growing material need from which the proletariat suffered, but also the loss of human dignity inherent in the daily search for food, in overcrowding, imposed promiscuity, absence of sanitary provisions, lack of decent clothing, and – above all – recurrent dependence upon poor relief. Innumerable letters indicate that the poor compared their lives with those of 'pigs', 'dogs', 'lice' and 'beasts'.[32] At the same time, however, that collective consciousness of permanent degradation fostered the creation of dense social networks. The very fact that a growing number of paupers were driven to particular parts of town gradually gave the inhabitants of these ghettos a communal sense, a collective identity. Beginning in the 1840s, police commissioners began to point out the dangers of ghettofication. They reported that slum-dwellers were growing more and more insolent, railing at 'honourable' citizens and even at the police, often acting in groups to hinder the arrest of their fellow workers. Even more, they organized festivities, during which the most outrageous of scenes were enacted. In particular, the carnival in the quarter of Sint-Andries, where the Boeksteegghetto was located, attracted greater crowds every year, indulging in drink and more serious abuses.[33] Without doubt these reports mirrored the norms and values of the upper classes. Yet they do suggest that the inhabitants of the ghettos were developing a community life of their own which in many respects differed from and was even opposed to that of the bourgeoisie.[34]

Conclusion

The foreword stated that current problems determine in large measure the themes of historical investigation. Past experiences attract broad interest or are radically reconsidered only when society faces a growing disparity between strongly held expectations and everyday realities. The study of poverty exemplifies this strikingly. It was long believed that economic growth was a permanent process generating ever-increasing material wealth. This euphoric belief led the so-called industrial revolution to be seen by many historians as one of the most magnificent episodes in human history, for it paved the way for the welfare state, in which poverty is only a 'residue', the result of temporary and localized backwardness. In recent years the realization has grown that such optimistic visions cannot be sustained. There is abundant evidence to show that the restructuring of the world economy entails new and massive impoverishment in the Third World as well as in the western hemisphere. Clearly linear perspectives of development must be rejected out of hand.

The historical implications of this changed perception are profound. Since the period 1750–1850 did not constitute the starting point for progressive industrialization and modernization, ending poverty in every country involved, the mechanization of production can no longer be the focus of research in and of itself. We must instead examine the transformation of the capitalist economy *as a whole*. In other words, attention should be paid not only to the new industrial centres but also to those regions and towns where the factory system remained of little importance. To view such places in terms of backwardness or retarded development is to beg the question. We should really be asking how they were affected by the reshaping of the international division of labour and what impact structural change had on the extent and the nature of poverty. The goal here has been to throw some light on this problem by studying the causes and consequences of economic transformation in one particular city.

Within less than a century Antwerp turned from a manufacturing centre of the first order into an international port where industrial production played only a minor role. Neither the boom in the production of mixed fabrics and cottons in the second half of the eighteenth century nor the growth of the harbour and its associated activities after 1800 were mere coincidences. Both resulted from the new functions assumed by the town during phases of acceleration in the development of capitalism. The commercial decline of Antwerp from the end of the sixteenth century induced merchants to invest money in the production of luxury goods. When the recession of most of these industries in the mid-eighteenth century was coupled with a rising international demand for cheap fabrics, the textile industry rapidly reoriented itself; the labour force was largely available, and businessmen went in search of new investment opportunities. The dependence on external sources of finance, however, meant that the lifespan of the industries manufacturing mixed fabrics and cottons was greatly determined by the profit margins offered to speculative money lenders. At the end of the *ancien régime* these profits declined as a result of political and economic instability. The annexation of the southern Netherlands by France created the objective conditions for an industrial recovery, but precisely at that moment overseas trade brought new opportunities for the first time in two hundred years. Although shipping and commerce did not grow uninterruptedly in the early nineteenth century, it was clear that Antwerp could again be turned into a harbour town. Antwerp's capitalists resolutely adopted a new course.

Commercial resurgence went hand in hand with massive impoverishment. Certainly poverty was not a new phenomenon. During the second half of the eighteenth century, capital had forced its way into the productive sphere at an accelerated pace, causing the proletarianization of the majority of craftsmen and the disintegration of the guild system. Pauperization on a massive scale, however, took place only upon rapid deindustrialization and the formation of a casual labour market. The collapse of the textile industry made old skills valueless, while the workforce of women, children and the elderly became largely superfluous. Increasing pressure on the wages of able-bodied men was thus coupled with growing under- and even un-employment of other members of the family. The decline of proletarian incomes can only be explained when this factor is taken into account. The daily struggle for survival obliged the young and the elderly as well as many women to any manner of odd job, characteristic of a so-called 'economy of makeshifts'.[1] Without the availability of this relative surplus population the renewed expansion of the lacemaking and embroidery trades would have been unthinkable, since these branches could only flourish in a town where a large female labour force was hunting desperately for means of subsistence.

The impoverishment of broad sections of Antwerp's population, however, cannot be understood in isolation of developments in the countryside. There too restructuring and redistribution of economic activities took place. The textile boom in the small town of Lier, which took full advantage of Antwerp's deindustrialization, is a case in point. The gradual dissolution of the traditional peasant economy was even more important. A growing number of cottars were forced to search for new resources, ranging from domestic industries to seasonal labour in agriculture and temporary moves to the cities. Uprooting and emigration were most manifest in those parts of the province where no viable alternative was available. Neither poverty itself nor underemployment uprooted people. Only when every other possibility was exhausted and no year-round working cycle could be found were people prepared to trek elsewhere. Even so, migration was hesitant. The cities did not function as centres of absolute attraction, but rather as refuges in crisis years and as centres of relative attraction during other periods; there was no causal connection between the fluctuations of the urban economy and successive waves of immigration. For many among the uprooted, Antwerp was nothing but a way-station, which they left as quickly as they came. Those who stayed were prepared to accept the most poorly-paid jobs, especially casual labour – like the unskilled foreign workers of the twentieth century. Initially they did not meet much 'competition' from the textile workers, most of whom were neither able nor eager to get a job in the harbour. During the first quarter of the nineteenth century, Antwerp's relative surplus population in fact consisted of two largely distinct groups: on the one hand a pool of déclassé textile workers and on the other a reserve army of immigrants, each of them trying to earn a living in a different way but both subject to underpayment and irregularity of employment. From the 1820s, the two groups began to merge. The vast majority of the male population now became dependent on opportunities for casual labour and had to compete for the same jobs, since alternatives were lacking – a process which went hand in hand with the sedentarization of rising numbers of immigrants and thus the further growth of Antwerp's proletariat.

In addition to greater competition on the labour market, the lower classes were confronted with a much tougher struggle for living space. The creation of harbour installations, railways, warehouses, and other commercial facilities entailed both demolition and new building. This development caused a substantial rise in land prices and house rents, since Antwerp's position as a military strongpoint inhibited expansion inland. However, without the growth *and* the impoverishment of the proletariat rents would not have skyrocketed. The declining income of the labouring masses made the construction of proper working-class houses an unprofitable business for building contractors, so that the poor were driven to miserable lodgings in zones which soon turned into true urban ghettos. Intermediate social strata were quite active and successful in exploiting this situation. They subdivided old houses to the maximum and demanded rack rents for tenements lacking the most elementary hygienic facilities. The multipliciation of slums could not be stopped as long as proletarian family incomes continued to decline. Meanwhile the poor had to queue for rotten tenements, the rental of which absorbed a steadily greater portion of their budgets. Study of the 'housing question' thus indicates that the restructuring of urban space not only reflected social polarization but also greatly accelerated the process of pauperization.

The social costs of the economic transformation were immense. All indicators point in the same direction: large sections of Antwerp's population experienced absolute impoverishment during the first half of the nineteenth century. The fact that average *per capita* diet declined drastically, both quantitatively and qualitatively, makes clear how alarmingly the fall in family incomes and the concomitant rise in house rents affected the living standard of the lower classes. The limited gains which they drew from economic growth – more potatoes and more coffee – certainly did not offset their many losses. No wonder that the proportion of the needy in the total population doubled between 1770 and 1860. Since the increase in the subsidies granted by the municipal government lagged far behind the growth in the numbers applying for relief, the poor law administration was obliged to employ increasingly stricter selection criteria. Despite this policy of retrenchment, the almoners had to support ever-swelling numbers of needy. During the second quarter of the nineteenth century one in five inhabitants received public assistance in 'normal' years and nearly twice as many in times of crisis, against one in ten at the end of the *ancien régime*.

Contrary to received opinion, the beneficiaries of outdoor relief did not constitute a 'lumpenproletariat'. That the level of employment among the supported needy was much higher than among the urban population *in toto* and that the overwhelming majority was engaged in the most labour-intensive sectors of the economy clearly indicate that they formed an integral part of the working-class – not necessarily its most impoverished members, but rather a continuously changing section of the proletariat which satisfied the formal requirements to qualify for public assistance. Many others lived in misery just as great or even worse; but, according to the standards applied by the poor-law administration, they were not among those 'eligible'. In short, the structural vulnerability of the working-class implied that nearly all its members sooner or later (and generally more than once) had to call upon bureaucratized forms of support, while an institutional 'filter-system' prevented them from remaining on the poor lists for long. As John Foster has asserted: urban poverty in the nineteenth century 'was not so much the special experience of a particular group within the labour force as a regular feature of the life of almost *all* working families at certain stages in their development'.[2]

How did the poor who were not eligible for public assistance manage to make ends meet? Although begging, prostitution, and crimes against property were on the rise during this period, it would seem that only an extremely small fraction of the needy took recourse to such activities. As to private charity: it centred almost exclusively on a limited number of 'respectable' poor, *i.e.* people whose destitution was the result of individual disability and who proved receptive to moral improvement. The misery of wage-labourers aroused the interest of benevolent societies, but generally an interest of a condescending, paternalistic variety. The philanthropy of the upper classes was prompted above all by the conviction that patronage – the new key-word – contributed to the justification of the existing social order. Hence the recipient of relief was treated as a minor whose daily life had to be inspected, recorded, and controlled. Only in times of crisis did the bourgeoisie raise significant sums of money to support the labouring poor – and even then they got off cheaply.

It follows that the majority of proletarians had to take refuge in other, more lasting means of survival. A distinction must be drawn between strategies directed toward the maintenance of the individual or the nuclear family and patterns of behaviour which can be deemed more solidaristic. Although the former are easier to trace and to measure than the latter, there is no reason to accord them greater significance. The growing proportion of those who never married and the rising number of illegitimate children and foundlings indicate that family formation was beyond the reach of ever more proletarians. It would seem, however, that stable consensual unions gained in importance during the second quarter of the nineteenth century, which suggests that the labouring poor were gradually adapting to new circumstances. Still more significant is the fact that working-class people, in spite of growing unemployment and declining incomes, continued their notable exertions to maintain close relationships with relatives and neighbours. Impoverishment sapped the protective functions of the proletarian family, but there is considerable evidence to suggest that the construction of dense social networks in the ghettos offered more opportunities for mutual aid and solidarity than the narrower familial context.

Comparison of Antwerp with other Belgian towns proves that pauperization in the first half of the nineteenth century cannot be related to the absence or presence of industrialization or modernization. To view poverty in this period as a 'residue' of the past or characteristic of one specific type of town is to beg the question. How then would the extent of destitution be comparable in cities whose economic paths diverged so markedly? In Antwerp, the growth of shipping and commerce was coupled with rapid deindustrialization; in Brussels scarcely any factories were set up, but the presence of many nobles and wealthy foreigners as well as political and administrative centralization stimulated the development of 'sweated trades'; Ghent and Liège on the other hand turned into the preeminent Belgian centres of cotton manufacturing and metallurgy, respectively. Yet in all four cities the proportion of the supported needy in the total population more than doubled during the century after 1750. Considerable though incomplete data, moreover, indicate that medium-sized and small centres fared no better. The absolute pauperization of large sections of the Belgian population was a general feature, the explanation for which must be sought in the accelerated development of capitalism, which caused widespread social dislocation both in the countryside and in the towns, irrespective of their specific economic function.

The range of quantitative evidence relating to changes in the standard of living of the urban proletariat in other western countries is still too limited and fragmentary to support an extended interpretation. Monographs concerning particular cities, however, do show that poverty was a mass phenomenon and that the economic growth of the first half of the nineteenth century did not in and of itself lead to social progress. In a major port-town like Hamburg and a large capital like Berlin, the dole-drawers represented no less than 25 per cent of the local population around 1850.[3] In all English industrial towns for which information is available, the incomes of an outright majority of working families appear still by 1850 too low to prevent these families from falling sooner or later below the poverty line of bare subsistence.[4] At Lille, a foremost textile centre in France, the total estimated wealth of the population increased by 137 per cent during the Second Empire, while the proletariat saw its portion nearly halved.[5] It is possible and even highly probable that the extent of urban poverty in some countries was greater than in others and that the average income of subgroups within the urban proletariat did rise, but that does not alter the fact that the labouring poor in all towns studied so far were losers.

Taking all this into account, the main conclusion of this study is that the so-called Industrial Revolution must be seen primarily as a phase of acceleration in the development of capitalism, entailing on one hand the restructuring and reallocation of economic activities, and on the other social dislocation on a massive scale. Clearly, instead of analysing areas in terms of advance or backwardness, they must be studied as constituent parts of an economy in the process of restructuring itself.

For some regions and towns the rise of industrial capitalism signalled a basic decline, because 'the spatial distribution of economic activities does not fluctuate around a long equilibrium norm, but tends to promote the concentration of growth in some areas at the expense of others'.[6] The process of expansion associated with rapid industrialization and commercialization certainly provided for increased employment opportunities in many centres, but three comments should be made in this connection. First, during the early phase of economic growth, mechanization directly created jobs for only a small segment of the proletariat. Indeed, by 1850, the total number of factory-hands amounted to not much more than 5 per cent of the population in England, barely 4 per cent in Belgium, only 3 per cent in France, and less than 2 per cent in Prussia and Switzerland.[7] Second, it should be remembered that the replacement of (chiefly rural) workers by machines did not automatically release a proportionate amount of capital to provide those same workers with new employment opportunities. The growth of capitalism entails a considerable gap in time and in space between the formation of a relative surplus population and the eventual reconversion of that population toward new economic activities. Large numbers of people in this period became dependent on the sectoral growth of capital. Consequently more attention must be paid to the formation of surpluses of labour and the time rates of their displacement, keeping in mind that 'the segmented nature of labour markets implied that labour shortages in particular regions or industries did not cancel out surpluses elsewhere'.[8] Finally, it should be emphasized that the Industrial Revolution signalled far more than just the rise of the factory system. In numerous regions and towns, low-paid casual workers proliferated. Handloom weavers, for example, must be put in the category of handicraftsmen who were largely the creation of capitalist industrialization in its early phase. Accelerated mechanization and the expansion of 'sweated trades' were two faces of one and the same reality. Domestic outwork was not merely an outside department of the factory, but often simply a substitute for it. The presence of a large pool of labourers prepared to accept work at whatever price was a reality in the 'new' industrial centres, where women and children constituted the bulk of the workforce, as well as in the 'old' centres where the Industrial Revolution did not produce furniture and clothing factories, but skilled artisans declining into slum-workers.[9]

In conclusion, the reshaping of the international division of labour brought about economic growth in some areas and underdevelopment in others. It was characterized equally by expanded employment and by the formation of a relative surplus population. It gave rise both to a new working class and to a host of casual labourers. In other words, it generated wealth at one pole and poverty at the other.

APPENDIX 1

Occupational classification of Antwerp's population, 1789 and 1800

The comparative list of 1789–1800, drafted by Antwerp's municipal authorities on the prefect's orders in the early nineteenth century, is the only source that permits study of the changes in occupational distribution which took place during this period.[1] Two factors, however, complicate interpretation of the figures. In the first place, some occupations were not registered by the census takers, particularly rentiers, teachers, the clergy, retailers, inn-keepers, domestic servants, and silk-throwers. To get some indication of the numbers of people in these categories, one must turn to the census of 1796 (see Appendix 2). From this source it can be seen that there were 3,360 domestic servants alone at the end of the eighteenth century. Hence it is certainly not exaggerated to suppose that the missing categories included in the aggregate some 3,000 persons. In the second place, the comparative list provides no information on the sex and age of the people employed. Taking into account the large number of people engaged in textile manufacturing, it would seem that the census takers registered only a portion of the younger workforce. It has been assumed here that children under 6 did not work and that this age group accounted for *c*. 14·5 per cent of the total population. All data in the following table thus refer to inhabitants of Antwerp over 6 years of age.

Occupation	Numbers		Per cent	
	1789	1800	1789	1800
Administration	1,677	1,795	3·92	3·89
Agriculture	1,355	1,466	3·17	3·17
Commerce, finance, etc.	1,009	1,366	2·36	2·96
Professional	456	387	1·07	0·84
Transport and distribution	165	215	0·39	0·47
Others	7	8	0·02	0·02
Total	*4,669*	*5,237*	*10·93*	*11·35*

Cont.

Occupation	Numbers		Per cent	
	1789	1800	1789	1800
Textiles	15,501	17,705	36·26	38·35
Clothing trade	4,704	4,671	11·00	10·12
Food and drink processing	1,237	1,491	2·89	3·23
Building industry	1,231	1,136	2·88	2·46
Wood and furniture	790	676	1·85	1·46
Metalworking	175	149	0·41	0·32
Miscellaneous manufacture	1,135	1,143	2·66	2·48
Total	*24,773*	*26,971*	*57·95*	*58·42*
Miscellaneous labour	3,000	3,000	7·02	6·50
No occupation	10,308	10,962	24·11	23·74
Grand total	*42,740*	*46,170*	*100·01*	*100·01*

APPENDIX 2

Occupational classification of Antwerp's population, 1796 and 1830

Two sources provide quantitative information on the transformation which took place in Antwerp's occupational structure between the end of the eighteenth century and the Belgian Revolution: the census of 1796, statistically treated by Jos De Belder, and the population registers of 1830, analysed by Jules Hannes.[1] Although changes in census nomenclature and differences in the methods of classification employed by De Belder and Hannes do not facilitate comparisons,[2] these sources do permit estimation of the proportion of people over 12/13 years of age employed and an analysis of the leading Antwerp trades. It should be underlined that all data refer to occupations, which implies that the tables presented here can suggest only rough approximations of reality. It is quite possible that some persons gave an occupation which they no longer practised, either because they were temporarily out of work or because they felt obliged to move on to another occupation without having abandoned all hope of resuming their original calling. On the other hand, the absence of occupational data does not necessarily signify that the persons concerned were not wage labourers; it only means that they practised no specific occupation and that their labour – if indeed they did work – was characterized by extreme variability and irregularity. Dockers, ship-repairers, building trades labourers, and other workers engaged in seasonal trades naturally did report a trade, even if the demand was subject to great fluctuations. The same held for those who had no professional skills whatsoever but whose physical strength enabled them to do hard labour; they portrayed themselves as 'day labourers', 'streetworkers', and the like. In contrast, men and women who did various odd jobs, providing only intermittent and minor income, apparently seldom reported an occupation. The reasons for that are obvious: their economic activities could not be reduced to a single category or were so incidental hardly to be considered real employment. This possibly explains why the population registers of 1830 mention only two rag-collectors and no street-sweepers, dung-pickers, messengers, or envelope-addressers.

A   Males over 12/13 years of age

Occupation	Numbers		Per cent		Percentage shift
	1796	1830	1796	1830	
Agriculture	678	501	4·28	2·18	− 2·10
Administration	659	1,243	4·16	5·41	+ 1·25
Rentiers	202	593	1·28	2·58	+ 1·30
Professional and teaching	349	401	2·20	1·74	− 0·46
Clerical	472	205	2·98	0·89	− 2·09
Commerce, finance, etc.	543	858	3·43	3·73	+ 0·30
Retail and distribution	827	1,680	5·22	7·31	+ 2·09
Transport, storage, etc.	414	1,261	2·62	5·49	+ 2·87
Domestic service	756	638	4·78	2·78	− 2·00
Casual labour	364	2,571	2·30	11·19	+ 8·89
Total	*5,264*	*9,951*	*33·25*	*43·30*	*+ 10·05*
Textiles	2,984	1,174	18·85	5·10	− 13·75
Clothing trade	1,617	1,189	10·21	5·17	− 5·04
Food and drink processing	762	880	4·81	3·83	− 0·98
Building industry	647	1,096	4·09	4·76	+ 0·67
Wood	686	1,897	4·33	8·26	+ 3·93
Leather	571	955	3·61	4·16	+ 0·55
Metalworking	461	822	2·91	3·58	+ 0·68
Miscellaneous manufacture	680	708	4·30	3·09	− 1·21
Total	*8,408*	*8,720*	*53·11*	*37·95*	*+ 15·16*
Miscellaneous labour	364	132	2·30	0·57	− 1·73
No occupation	1,795	4,177	11·34	18·18	+ 6·84
Grand total	*15,831*	*22,980*	*100·00*	*100·00*	

B   Females over 12/13 years of age

Occupation	Numbers		Per cent		Percentage shift
	1796	1830	1796	1830	
Agriculture	75	43	0·35	0·15	− 0·20
Rentiers	155	745	0·73	2·57	+ 1·84
Professional and teaching	262	135	1·23	0·47	− 0·76
Clerical	329	256	1·55	0·88	− 0·67
Commerce, finance, etc.	242	55	1·14	0·19	− 0·95
Retail and distribution	809	841	3·81	2·90	− 0·91
Domestic service	2,604	3,713	12·27	12·82	+ 0·55
Casual labour	116	1,858	0·55	6·41	+ 5·86
Total	*4,592*	*7,646*	*21·63*	*26·39*	*+ 4·76*

B **Females over 12/13 years of age** *(cont.)*

Occupation	Numbers		Per cent		Percentage shift
	1796	1830	1796	1830	
Lace and embroidery	4,764	2,144	22·44	7·40	− 15·04
Other textiles	1,569	179	7·39	0·62	− 6·77
Clothing trade	1,320	1,948	6·22	6·73	+ 0·51
Miscellaneous manufacture	117	45	0·55	0·16	− 0·39
Total	*7,770*	*4,316*	*36·60*	*14·91*	*− 21·69*
Miscellaneous labour	48	7	0·23	0·02	− 0·21
No occupation	8,821	16,995	41·55	58·68	+ 17·13
Grand total	*21,231*	*28,964*	*100·01*	*100·00*	

APPENDIX 3

Average daily wages of adults and children in 1780, 1827 and 1855

The sole available sources of information are the poor lists, in which, *inter alia*, are to be found the earnings of the supported needy. The reliability of this evidence is exceptionally good. Fraud on the part of the dole-drawer was impossible, because the poor law authorities received regular reports from employers. One might object that the value of these data is limited since they concern the needy, some of whom were aged, some ill, some lame. Too much weight should not be given to this criticism. First, the great majority of the poor were employed in the most labour-intensive sectors of the economy. Second, the poor lists record not only the sex and age of the beneficiaries, but also their physical ailments. The able-bodied needy in the prime of life, say from 20 to 54 years of age, can therefore be extracted from the rest. Account was taken only of those occupations for which sufficient data are available.

For the calculation of wage averages use has been made of the 'mode', *i.e.* the most common phenomenon. To facilitate comparisons, all wages have been converted to Brabant stivers. In order to calculate the price of rye bread the average has been taken of the price in the year considered and in the preceding two and subsequent two years.[1] It must be noted that 1855 was a dearth year. Use of a five-year average only partially alleviates this problem, since 1854 and 1856 were also characterized by relatively high rye prices.

A   Males and females aged 20–54

Occupations	Stivers			Kilograms of rye bread		
	1780	1827	1855	1780	1827	1855
Males						
Silk-weavers	8	11	12·80	5·440	5·375	4·833
Weavers of mixed fabrics	8	11	12·80	5·440	5·375	4·833
Shoemakers	8	11	12·80	5·440	5·375	4·833
Tailors	8	10	12·80	5·440	4·886	4·833
Masons' labourers	11	10	12·80	7·480	4·886	4·833
Painters	12	13	14·65	8·160	6·352	5·542
Casual labourers	–	10	11·02	–	4·886	4·161
Females						
Knitters	1·5	1·5	1·75	1·020	0·733	0·611
Lacemakers	2	2	2·75	1·360	0·977	1·038
Embroiderers	3	3	3·65	2·040	1·466	1·378
Laundresses	3·5	3·5	3·65	2·380	1·710	1·378
Seamstresses	3·5	3·5	3·65	2·380	1·710	1·378
Casual labourers	–	4	5·51	–	1·954	2·080

B   Children aged 6–10 and 11–15

	Stivers	Kilograms of rye bread
1780		
Children aged 6–10	0·75	0·510
Children aged 11–15	2·00	1·360
1827		
Children aged 6–10	0·75	0·366
Children aged 11–15	1·75	0·855

APPENDIX 4

Origins of migrants to Antwerp, 1817 and 1855

A Birthplaces and last residences of migrants to Antwerp recorded in 1817

	Birthplace		Last residence	
	Absolute No.	Per cent	Absolute No.	Per cent
District of Antwerp	208	30·6	214	35·4
Rest of province	136	20·0	136	22·4
Province of Brabant	121	17·8	91	15·0
Other southern provinces	77	11·3	70	11·6
Northern Netherlands	71	10·4	53	8·8
Foreign countries	67	9·9	42	6·9
Total	680	100·0	606	100·0
Not specified	9		83	

B Birthplaces and last residences of indirect migrants to Antwerp, Antwerp sample, 1817

	Last Residence						Total
Birthplace	DA	PA	PB	OP	NN	FC	(birthplaces)
District of Antwerp (DA)	67	11	4	1	2	2	87
Rest of province (PA)	20	13	0	0	3	0	36
Province of Brabant (PB)	10	9	9	3	2	2	35
Other southern provinces (OP)	4	3	2	15	1	2	27
Nothern Netherlands (NN)	6	6	3	1	8	1	25
Foreign countries (FC)	3	0	2	7	1	24	37
Total (last residences)	110	42	20	27	17	31	247

C   **Birthplaces of immigrant heads and wives receiving relief at Antwerp in 1855**

Birthplace	Absolute No.	Per cent
District of Antwerp	286	39·3
Rest of province	133	18·3
Province of Brabant	106	14·6
Other Belgian provinces	102	14·0
Netherlands	72	9·8
Other countries	29	4·0
Total	728	100·0
Not specified	48	

APPENDIX 5

Occupational classification of Antwerp-born and immigrant population, by percentages, in 1796 and 1830

A Males over 12/13 years of age

Occupation	Born in Antwerp		Percentage shift	Immigrants		Percentage shift
	1796	1830		1796	1830	
Agriculture	4·7	1·9	− 2·8	2·9	2·6	− 0·3
Administration	4·0	4·4	+ 0·2	5·2	7·1	+ 1·9
Rentiers	1·6	2·7	+ 1·1	0·9	2·4	+ 1·3
Professional, teaching, and clerical	3·4	2·0	− 1·4	9·4	3·6	− 5·8
Commerce, finance, etc.	6·4	2·7	+ 1·6	15·3	5·3	+ 0·2
Retail and distribution		5·3			10·2	
Transport	2·5	3·5	+ 1·0	3·0	8·4	+ 5·4
Domestic service	2·4	0·7	− 1·7	12·0	5·8	− 6·2
Casual labour	2·1	10·9	+ 8·8	3·0	11·6	+ 8·6
Total	*27·1*	*34·1*	*+ 7·0*	*51·7*	*57·0*	*+ 5·3*
Textiles	22·4	7·0	− 15·4	8·3	2·3	− 6·0
Clothing trade	15·2	7·0	− 8·2	8·2	2·7	− 5·5
Food and drink processing	4·2	2·1	− 2·1	9·8	6·3	− 3·5
Building industry	9·4	5·6	+ 2·6	11·4	3·6	+ 3·1
Woodworking		6·4			10·9	
Metalworking	1·1	4·2	+ 3·1	2·2	2·5	+ 0·3
Miscellaneous manufacture	6·7	9·6	+ 2·9	1·6	3·5	+ 1·9
Total	*59·0*	*40·9*	*− 18·1*	*41·5*	*31·8*	*− 9·7*
Miscellaneous labour	0·4	0·5	+ 0·1	1·8	1·9	+ 0·1
No occupation	13·5	24·5	+ 11·0	5·0	9·3	+ 4·3

Proportion of Antwerp-born men out of total male workers in each occupation, 1830*

Textiles	82	Agriculture	52
Printing	80	Administration	47
Precision industry	79	Wood working	46
Clothing trade	79	Professional & teaching	44
Leather	73	Commerce, finance, etc.	43
Metal working	70	Retail and distribution	42
Building industry	69	Transport and storage	37
Chemicals	61	Food and drink processing	32
Casual labour	53	Domestic service	14

* General average 55 per cent

B　Females over 12/13 years of age

Occupation	Born in Antwerp		Percentage shift	Immigrants		Percentage shift
	1796	1830		1796	1830	
Commerce, finance, etc	3·1	0·2	−0·3	6·6	0·2	−2·7
Retail and distribution		2·6			3·7	
Domestic service	3·9	3·6	−0·3	33·8	24·0	−9·8
Casual labour	0·7	5·7	+5·0	0·2	7·4	+7·2
Textiles	36·2	0·8	−23·7	10·6	0·4	−8·5
Lace		11·7			1·7	
Clothing trade	8·6	7·5	−1·0	8·1	7·2	−0·9
Miscellaneous labour	4·4	3·6	−0·8	3·1	3·0	−0·1
No occupation	43·1	64·2	+21·1	37·6	52·4	+14·8

Proportion of Antwerp-born women out of total female workers in each occupation, 1830*

Cottonspinners	96	Shopkeepers	48
Lacemakers	92	Laundresses	46
Laundry ironers	91	Flaxspinners	45
Embroiderers	85	Commerce	42
Tailors	72	Innkeepers	35
Seamstresses	63	Shopgirls	28
Casual labourers	51	Maidservants	17

* General average 50 per cent

APPENDIX 6

Location quotients of the Antwerp wards intra muros *by occupational groups, 1830*

The location quotient is designed to calculate the degree of concentration of a particular occupation in a particular district. If the LQ equals 1, this means that the distribution of a particular occupation is co-extensive with the distribution of the working population as a whole. Values more/less than 1 indicate higher/lower levels of concentration in particular districts than in Antwerp as a whole.[1] All figures refer to male workers, unless otherwise noted.[2]

Occupation	WARD			
	I	II	III	IV
Indicative of bourgeois habitation				
Administration	0·98	1·12	1·52	0·67
Rentiers	1·19	0·90	1·55	0·63
Professional	0·93	1·04	1·57	0·78
Commerce, finance, etc.	1·02	1·37	1·43	0·82
Domestic service				
Males	0·87	0·68	2·05	0·68
Females	1·12	0·80	1·31	0·71
Indicative of lower middle class habitation				
Retail and distribution				
Males	1·34	0·88	0·96	0·94
Females	1·32	0·88	1·11	0·80
Transport and storage	2·29	1·05	0·55	0·56
Indicative of proletarian habitation				
Casual labour				
Males	0·96	0·94	0·52	1·36
Females	1·13	0·89	0·76	1·21
Textile manufacturing	0·47	1·04	0·75	1·56
Lace working (females)	0·33	1·16	0·66	1·70

APPENDIX 7

Daily diet of the Antwerp population in 1820–1829 and 1850–1859

A   Average *per capita* daily diet

Products	Consumption per capita/day		Calories per capita/day	
	1820–1829	1850–1859	1820–1829	1850–1859
Rye flour	112 grams	45 grams	347	140
Wheat flour	228 grams	284 grams	707	880
Potatoes	600 grams	700 grams	420	490
Meat	119 grams	104 grams	268	234
Salt fish	18 grams	12 grams	48	32
Butter	47 grams	32 grams	353	240
Eggs	0·790	0·348	61	26
Total			2,204	2,042
Beer	0·687 litres	0·367 litres	313	163
Wine	0·019 litres	0·015 litres	12	10
Gin	0·020 litres	0·015 litres	54	40
Coffee	9 grams	12 grams	9	12
Grand total			2,592	2,267

Note: Tax was paid on the goods *in italics*.

B   Nutritional value of the average diet

	1820–1829			1850–1859		
	Proteins (grams)	Fats (grams)	Carbohydrates (grams)	Proteins (grams)	Fats (grams)	Carbohydrates (grams)
Rye flour	11·2	1·2	72·8	4·5	0·5	29·2
Wheat flour	22·8	5·5	141·7	28·4	6·8	176·8
Potatoes	9·9	0·5	94·0	11·5	0·6	109·0
Meat	22·1	19·8	0·0	19·2	17·2	0·0
Salted fish	8·6	1·5	0·0	5·7	1·0	0·0
Butter	0·3	39·0	0·2	0·1	26·5	0·1
Eggs	5·1	4·3	0·0	2·2	1·9	0·0
Total	80·0	71·8	308·7	71·6	54·5	315·1

APPENDIX 8

Note on Figure 13

Only two censuses – carried out in 1773 and 1789 – provide reliable information on the number of assisted needy (foundlings excepted) in Antwerp during the last decades of the Austrian regime.[1] From 1801, in contrast, an almost complete series of annual figures, assembled by the Charity Bureau and checked by the municipal government, is available; however, comparison of the available figures is not without difficulties.

In the first place, the number of the poor employed in the *ateliers de charité* is known only from 1806, although the institution was established in 1802. However, this gap influences the totals for 1801–1805[2] to a small degree only, since the workhouses never employed more than 350 persons between 1806 and 1816.

In the second place, the supported population as recorded in the accounts of the Charity Bureau were classified in a completely different manner from that of the reports to the town authorities. The annual accounts of poor relief distinguished between regular and temporary recipients of relief *intra muros* but did not record how many were considered for occasional relief (*secours accidentel*) nor how many inhabitants of the fifth ward received public support;[3] this information was noted in separate registers which have since been lost. The reports provided to the municipal authorities, on the other hand, related to all of those on relief (inhabitants of the fifth ward included), divided as follows:

1 widows and widowers;
2 married persons;
3 children of groups 1 and 2;
4 pregnant women;
5 foundlings and abandoned children;
6 recipients of occasional relief; and
7 the poor employed in the *ateliers de charité*.[4]

The question arises whether the data from the two sources cover the same categories of needy. Categories 5, 6, and 7 from the annual reports can easily be verified: foundlings and abandoned children were registered from year to year by the Charity Bureau in special detailed registers, many of which remain;[5] the amount devoted to the *secours accidentel* was included by the directors in their annual accounts and corresponds closely to the sum mentioned in the reports provided for the municipal government; and the various categories of the needy put to work in the *ateliers de charité* were recorded in separate accounts, numerous fragments of which have survived.[6] But what of the other figures? Samples based on incidental evidence show that the total number of widows, widowers, married couples, children and pregnant women given in the annual reports equalled the combined total of regular and temporary recipients of relief *intra muros* given in the annual accounts plus the regular recipients in the fifth ward.[7]

Finally, it should be noted that none of these series contain complete statistical data for the years 1846–1848, owing to the conscious policy of the authorities who feared that public knowledge of the sharply rising figures would release latent social tensions and aggravate the threat of rebellion.[8] Hence both the Charity Bureau and the town government were silent during the crisis on the number of 'extraordinary' poor; the official documents specified only the number in receipt of regular or temporary support and the number employed (or simply fed) in the *ateliers de charité*. Fortunately Edouard Ducpétiaux published in 1852 a survey of the number of families and persons dependent upon public assistance in all Belgian towns and rural communities during the period 1848–1850.[9] This is the sole source of statistical information on the extent of poverty in Antwerp in 1848. The problem remains, however, that Ducpétiaux's figures on the two subsequent years diverged significantly from those given by the Charity Bureau. According to the former, the total number of recipients in 1849 and 1850 amounted to 34,082 and 32,589 respectively, while the poor relief registered only 9,090 and 9,903. Although there can be no absolute certainty, everything points towards Ducpétiaux's being more reliable. From the books of the Charity Bureau itself it appears that Ducpétiaux's figures on the number of regular recipients of relief (5,011 in 1849 and 5,044 in 1850) corresponded closely with the truth, while those published by the poor relief (4,075 in 1849 and 2,353 in 1850) were gross underestimates.[10] Numerous reports, moreover, indicate that the Charity Bureau, despite the mild economic recovery of 1849 and 1850, had to continue supporting innumerable 'extraordinary' poor who, in the course of the preceding years, had been reduced to the status of beggars. The cholera epidemic of October 1848 to November 1849 added to requirements for the large-scale distribution of food, clothing, blankets, and medicine to the poor.

Although far from perfect, the available sources are thus sufficiently credible for general trends to be charted. To interpret Figure 13, which portrays the proportion of the supported needy in the total population during the period 1773–1860, it must be remembered that the percentages relate only to persons who received outdoor relief, including the needy employed in the *ateliers de charité*. The poor contained in the *Vondelingenhuis* (foundling hospital), the orphanages, small religious institutions, the Sint-Elisabeth hospital, and the

Zinnelozengesticht (mental hospital) were left out of consideration, because their numbers were determined by the capacity of the institutions involved; the total fluctuated around 2,500. Nor have the orphans and the aged placed with families been taken into consideration, since not all relevant data have been preserved; their numbers, in any case, appear never to have exceeded two hundred. One might suppose that this method loses sight of the needy *in toto*. This is true, but it must be considered that the sum of all of those *on support* did not correspond with the actual number of those *in need*, as two examples make clear; in 1789 only 13 per cent of Antwerp's population were considered for public support, even though the number of needy was estimated by the poor relief at 20 to 22 per cent; and in 1845 some 20,000 individuals received material aid from the Charity Bureau, although the almoners counted more than 34,000 needy, or 24·5 per cent and 42 per cent of all inhabitants respectively. Nor did the number of the *needy* correspond to the number of *poor*: according to the authorities, 39,400 people, or 56 per cent of the total population in 1829 (an exceptionally 'good' year), had to be termed actual or potential paupers.[11]

APPENDIX 9

Occupational classification of the recipients of permanent relief, by percentages in 1780, 1827 and 1855

A   Male heads of household

Occupation	1780	1827	1855
N =	239	667	771
Textiles	42·0	18·3	9·6
Clothing trades	15·0	14·0	15·3
Building industry	6·3	7·5	5·8
Wood	0·8	2·0	5·1
Metalworking	0·8	1·0	3·1
Miscellaneous manufacture	2·5	5·2	4·0
Sub-total	*67·4*	*48·0*	*42·8*
Casual labour	2·5	18·0	21·1
and one additional job	0·0	7·2	1·2
and two additional jobs	0·0	0·8	0·5
Retail and distribution	3·8	6·1	8·4
Transport, storage, etc	1·9	3·0	4·2
Miscellaneous labour	9·9	5·7	9·2
No profession	14·5	11·2	12·6
Grand total	100·0	100·0	100·0

Categorized by age

Occupation	20–54 Years			55–64 Years			65 and over		
	1780	1827	1855	1780	1827	1855	1780	1827	1855
Textiles	41·7	13·9	10·5	43·5	21·9	9·6	41·3	28·1	7·5
Clothing-trade	18·6	15·4	15·2	8·7	11·0	18·7	13·8	12·9	12·1
Building industry	8·9	10·6	7·0	8·7	5·5	4·8	1·3	0·6	4·0
Wood	0·9	1·3	6·5	0·0	6·8	3·6	1·3	1·7	2·9
Metalworking	0·9	1·0	4·7	0·0	0·0	1·2	1·3	1·7	0·6
Misc. manufacture	3·5	5·6	4·2	2·2	5·5	4·8	1·3	4·5	2·9
Sub-total	*74·5*	*47·8*	*48·1*	*63·1*	*50·7*	*42·7*	*60·3*	*49·5*	*30·0*
Casual labour	3·5	25·3	27·0	2·2	5·5	19·9	1·2	3·9	8·6
+ one add. job	0·0	11·1	1·5	0·0	5·5	1·2	0·0	0·0	0·6
+ two add. jobs	0·0	1·3	0·5	0·0	0·0	0·0	0·0	0·0	1·1
Retail & distrib.	4·4	2·8	4·0	4·4	12·3	12·1	2·5	10·7	16·1
Transport etc.	2·7	4·3	5·6	2·2	4·1	3·0	0·0	0·6	1·7
Misc. labour	11·4	3·5	7·5	10·7	8·2	9·0	7·5	9·5	12·6
No occupation	3·5	4·0	5·8	17·4	13·7	12·0	28·5	25·8	29·3
Grand total	*100·0*	*100·1*	*100·0*	*100·0*	*100·0*	*99·9*	*100·0*	*100·0*	*100·0*

B   Adult women

Occupation		1780	1827	1855
	N =	629	1,267	1,560
Lace-work		51·2	35·5	18·3
Textiles		17·3	11·7	2·7
Clothing-trade		2·7	6·5	6·3
Miscellaneous manufacture		1·4	0·6	0·3
Sub-total		*72·6*	*54·3*	*27·6*
Casual labour		0·0	4·0	13·2
Domestic service		3·5	2·7	2·7
Retail		3·2	8·4	8·7
Miscellaneous labour		1·1	2·1	1·6
Dual jobs		0·0	11·8	0·9
No occupation		19·6	16·7	45·3
Grand Total		*100·0*	*100·0*	*100·0*

Categorized by age

	20–54 Years			55–64 Years			65 and over		
	1780	1827	1855	1780	1827	1855	1780	1827	1855
Lace-work	50·4	41·5	17·5	68·8	31·9	18·8	42·5	28·8	19·3
Textiles	20·1	9·5	0·9	11·7	10·9	2·8	17·2	15·7	5·6
Clothing trade	4·8	7·4	7·2	0·8	5·8	4·8	1·3	5·3	5·4
Misc. manufacture	0·0	0·3	0·0	2·3	2·2	0·8	2·6	0·4	0·4
Sub-total	*75·3*	*58·7*	*25·6*	*83·6*	*50·8*	*27·2*	*63·6*	*50·2*	*30·7*
Casual labour	0·0	6·0	18·2	0·0	5·8	12·8	0·0	0·6	2·8
Domestic service	5·2	2·5	2·6	3·9	6·5	2·0	1·3	1·7	3·2
Retail	5·6	11·1	6·6	0·8	5·0	7·6	1·7	5·3	12·4
Misc. labour	0·8	0·8	1·0	0·8	0·7	1·6	1·7	3·5	2·5
Dual job	0·0	12·0	0·9	0·0	10·9	1·2	0·0	11·5	0·8
No profession	13·1	8·9	45·1	10·9	20·3	47·6	31·8	27·2	47·6
Grand Total	*100·0*	*100·0*	*100·0*	*100·0*	*100·0*	*100·0*	*100·1*	*100·0*	*100·0*

C   **Percentages of child paupers over 5 years of age employed out of total child paupers over 5**

	5–14 years of age		15 and over	
Year	Boys	Girls	Boys	Girls
1780	64·2	64·4	89·8	92·2
1827	46·0	43·4	88·4	85·8
1855	11·2	11·6	85·7	80·0

Abbreviations

ADH	*Annales de Démographie historique*
AESC	*Annales. Economies. Sociétés. Civilisations*
ANP	Archives Nationales
ARAB	Algemeen Rijksarchief, Brussels
ARAG NN	Algemeen Rijksarchief, The Hague, *Nationale Nijverheid*
ARAG SS	ibid., *Staatssecretarie*
BG	*Bijdragen tot de Geschiedenis*
BTFG	*Belgisch Tijdschrift voor Filologie en Geschiedenis*
BTNG	*Belgisch Tijdschrift voor Nieuwste Geschiedenis*
EcHR	*The Economic History Review*
EPA	*Exposé de la situation administrative de la province d'Anvers* (Antwerp, 1836–)
JEH	*The Journal of Economic History*
MAPA	*Mémorial administratif de la province d'Anvers* (Antwerp, 1815–)
OCMWA BW	Openbaar Centrum voor Maatschappelijk Welzijn, Antwerp, *Bureel van Weldadigheid*
OCMWA KH	ibid., *Kamer van de Huisarmen*
RAA PA	Rijksarchief, Antwerp, *Provinciaal Archief*
RI, 1846	*Recensement général de l'industrie. 15 octobre 1846* (Brussels, 1851)
RN	*Revue du Nord*
RP, 1846	*Recensement général de la population. 15 octobre 1846* (Brussels, 1849)
RP, 1856	*Recensement général de la population. 31 décembre 1856* (Brussels, 1861)
RVA	*Rapport sur l'administration et la situation des affaires de la ville d'Anvers* (Antwerp, 1837–)
SAA GA	Stadsarchief, Antwerp, *Gilden en Ambachten*
SAA KK	ibid., *Kerken en Kloosters*
SAA MA	ibid., *Modern Archief*
SAA PK	ibid., *Privilegekamer*
TG	*Tijdschrift voor Geschiedenis*
TSG	*Tijdschrift voor Sociale Geschiedenis*

Notes

Preface: The Dialogue between Yesterday and Today

1 R.M. Hartwell, *The Industrial Revolution and Economic Growth* (London, 1971).
2 Cf. *The Standard of Living in Britain in the Industrial Revolution*, ed. A. J. Taylor (London, 1975).
3 R.M. Hartwell, 'The Rising Standard of Living in England, 1800–50', *EcHR*, 2nd. ser., XII (1961), p. 399.
4 Cf. W. Abel, *Massenarmut und Hungerkrisen im vorindustriellen Deutschland* (Göttingen, 1972), p. 69.
5 W. Fischer, 'Soziale Unterschichten im Zeitalter der Frühindustrialisierung', *International Review of Social History*, 8 (1963), p. 435.
6 R.M. Hartwell, 'The Consequences of the Industrial Revolution in England for the Poor', in *The Long Debate on Poverty: Eight Essays on Industrialisation and the Conditions of England* (London, 1972), pp. 3–21.
7 E.P. Thompson, *The Making of the English Working Class* (Harmondsworth, 1968 edn.), p. 916. See also Ph. A.M. Taylor, *The Industrial Revolution in Britain: Triumph or Disaster?* (Lexington, 1970), p. viii.
8 M. Harrington, *The Other America* (New York, 1962); E.H. Keyserling, *Progress or Poverty: the U.S. at the Crossroads* (Conference on Economic Progress, Washington D.C., 1964); O. Ornati, *Poverty Amid Affluence* (New York, 1966); G. Kolko, *Wealth and Power in America* (New York, 1969).
9 B. Abel-Smith and P. Townsend, *The Poor and the Poorest* (London, 1965); A.B. Atkinson, *Poverty in Britain and the Reform of Social Security* (Cambridge, 1968); K. Coates and R. Silburn, *Poverty: The Forgotten Englishmen* (London, 1970); P.M. de La Gorce, *La France pauvre* (Paris, 1965); J. Labbens, *Le quart-monde. La pauvreté dans la société industrielle* (Paris, 1969); *Le manifeste des déshérités* (Brussels, 1969).
10 Cf. the critical comments of R. Titmuss, 'Poverty Versus Inequality', in *Poverty* edited by J.L. Roach and J.K. Roach (Harmondsworth, 1972), pp. 315–23; C. Valentine, *Culture and Poverty: Critique and Counterproposals* (Chicago, 1973); H. Rodman, 'Culture of Poverty: The Rise and Fall of a Concept', *The Sociological Review* (1977), pp. 867–76.
11 L. Thurow, *Generating Inequality* (New York, 1975); W. Beckerman, *Poverty and the Impact of Income Maintenance Programmes in Four Developed Countries* (Geneva, 1979); V. George and R. Lawson, eds., *Poverty and Inequality in Common Market Countries* (London, 1980); A.B. Atkinson, *The Economics of Inequality* (Oxford, 1975); J.C. Kincaid, 'Poverty in the Welfare State', in *Demystifying Social Statistics*, edited by J. Irvine, I. Miles and J. Evans (London, 1979), pp. 190–211; L. Fabius, *La France Inégale* (Paris, 1975); J. Roth, *Armut in der Bundesrepublik: Ueber psychische und materielle Verelendung* (Frankfurt, 1974); Werkgroep Alternatieve Economie, *Armoede in België* (Antwerp and Utrecht, 1972); H. Deleeck, *Bestaansonzekerheid en sociale zekerheid* (Brussels, 1978); J.-P. Hiernaux et al., *La face cachée. Pauvreté, politique sociale, action urbaine* (Brussels, 1981).
12 Cf. F. F. Piven and R. A. Cloward, *The New Class War: Reagan's Attack on the Welfare State and its Consequences* (New York, 1982).
13 C. Lis and H. Soly, *Poverty and Capitalism in Pre-Industrial Europe* (Atlantic Highlands, New Jersey, 1979).
14 Cf. I. Adelman and C. Taft Morris, 'Growth and Impoverishment in the Middle of the Nineteenth Century', *World Development*, 6 (1978), pp. 245–73.

Chapter 1 Antwerp as an Industrial Centre

1 W. Brulez, 'De handel', in *Antwerpen in de XVIde eeuw* (Antwerp, 1975), pp. 118–9. See also R. Baetens, *De nazomer van Antwerpens welvaart: De diaspora en het handelshuis De Groote tijdens de eerste helft der 17de eeuw*, 2 vols. (Bussels, 1976).

2 A.K.L. Thijs, *Van werkwinkel tot fabriek: De textielnijverheid te Antwerpen van het einde der vijftiende eeuw tot het begin der negentiende eeuw* (Ghent Univ. Ph.D. thesis 1978), pp. 373–4.

3 SAA GA 4202; F. Smekens, 'Schets van aard en beteekenis der Antwerpsche nijverheid onder het Oostenrijksch bewind', in *Lode Baekelmans ter Eere*, Vol. II (Antwerp, 1946), pp. 107–8.

4 Thijs, *Werkwinkel*, pp. 263–7, 371–2, 376.

5 *Ibid.*, p. 370; Smekens, 'Schets', p. 108.

6 S. Despretz-Van de Casteele, 'Het protectionisme in de Zuidelijke Nederlanden gedurende de tweede helft der 17e eeuw', TG, 78 (1965), p. 301.

7 Thijs, *Werkwinkel*, pp. 244–52.

8 E. Sabbe, *De Belgische vlasnijverheid*, Vol. II (Kortrijk, 1975 edn.), p. 157; Ph. Moureaux, *Les préoccupations statistiques du gouvernement des Pays-Bas autrichiens et le dénombrement des industries dressé en 1764* (Brussels, 1971), p. 453.

9 ANP, F 12, no. 1563; SAA PK 451, no. 55, and MA 633(2).

10 A.K.L. Thijs, 'Schets van de ontwikkeling der katoendrukkerij te Antwerpen (1753–1813)', BG, 53 (1970), pp. 157–90; S. Chassagne, 'L'Enquête dite de Champagny, sur la situation de l'industrie cotonnière française au début de l'Empire (1805–1806)', *Revue d'Histoire économique et sociale*, 54 (1976), p. 366.

11 See Appendix 1.

12 SAA PK 451, no. 55.

13 Thijs, *Werkwinkel*, pp. 251–2, 858–9; J. De Belder, *Elementen van sociale identificatie van de Antwerpse bevolking op het einde van XVIIIde eeuw. Een kwantitatieve studie*, Vol. II (Ghent Univ. Ph.D. thesis 1974), p. 154. See also SAA MA 487(7).

14 F. Prims, *Geschiedenis van Antwerpen*, Vol. XXIV (Antwerp, 1947), pp. 37–40; Moureaux, *Préoccupations*, p. 133; Thijs, *Werkwinkel*, pp. 1219–20.

15 RAA PA, J 222.

16 SAA PK 452, nos. 54–55, 64–65, PK 456 (1786). See also F. Prims, 'Fabriek tegen ambacht: P. Beirens en C° tegen de zijdestofwerkers, 1786', *Antwerpiensia*, XVII (1946), pp. 44–9.

17 SAA PK 257, f° 242, PK 438, f° 518–524, 542–557, MA 478(7); H. van Houtte, *Histoire économique de la Belgique à la fin de l'Ancien Régime* (Ghent, 1920), p. 48.

18 See J. Graeybeckx, 'De arbeiders in de XVIIe en XVIIIe eeuw', in *Flandria Nostra*, Vol. I (Antwerp, 1957), pp. 281–328.

19 SAA PK 478(7).

20 Information drawn from an unpublished paper by K. Degryse, who is presently engaged in a study of the upper classes in eighteenth-century Antwerp.

21 L. Michielsen, 'De handel', in *Antwerpen in de XVIIIde eeuw: Instellingen, Economie, Cultuur* (Antwerp, 1952), pp. 94–112.

22 *Ibid.*, pp. 100ff; Thijs, *Werkwinkel*, pp. 1142–51, 1199–1202.

23 SAA PK 451, no. 55 (1778).

24 E. Poffé, *De gilde der Antwerpsche schoolmeesters van bij haar ontstaan tot aan hare afschaffing* (Antwerp, 1895), pp. 100–102; C. Vinnis, 'Nota's over de toestand der lagere klassen te Antwerpen op het einde van het Oostenrijks regiem', BG, 21 (1930), p. 267; Prims, *Geschiedenis van Antwerpen*, Vol. XXIV, p. 82; J. Van Laerhoven, 'De kanthandel te Antwerpen in de 18e eeuw: de firma Van Lidth de Jeude', BG, 54 (1971), p. 184.

25 OCMWA KH, r. 870, no. 6.

26 ANP F 12, no. 1563; SAA PK 451, no. 54; Thijs, 'Schets', p. 171.

27 P. Bonenfant, *Le paupérisme en Belgique à la fin de l'Ancien Régime* (Brussels, 1934), pp. 374–82; E. Païs-Minne, 'Weldadigheidsinstellingen en sociale toestanden te Antwerpen in de XVIIIe eeuw', in *Antwerpen in de XVIII de eeuw*, pp. 163–7.

28 OCMWA, Library, no. 381/2 (5 and 11); L. Philippen, 'Catechismusfundaties', in *Bestuurlijk verslag over het dienstjaar 1926 van de COO* (Antwerp, 1927), p. 158; F. Prims, 'De catechismus voor bejaarden in St.-Carolus', *Antwerpiensia*, XIX (1949), pp. 247–52.

29 SAA KK 2112; OCMWA, Library, no. 381/1 (22–23); M. Dries, 'De openbare weldadigheid te Antwerpen op het einde van het oud regiem', BG, 8 (1930), pp. 237–53.

30 OCMWA, Library, no. 381/2(24); SAA PK 453 (31 March 1783).

31 C. Lis, 'Sociale politiek in Antwerpen, 1779', TSG, 2 (1976), pp. 157–60.

32 For a detailed discussion see Lis and Soly, *Poverty*, pp. 202–6.
33 See Appendix 3.
34 OCMWA, Box 'Nieuwe Bestiering' (1779); Païs-Minne, 'Weldadigheidsinstellingen', pp. 175–8. See also SAA *MA* 6199 (1805).
35 De Belder, *Elementen*, Vol. II, p. 356.
36 *Ibid.*, pp. 216, 249, 279, 313, 335.
37 A.K.L. Thijs, 'Aspecten van de opkomst der textieldrukkerij als grootbedrijf te Antwerpen in de achttiende eeuw', *Bijdragen en Mededelingen betreffende de Geschiedenis der Nederlanden*, 86 (1971), pp. 210–3.
38 OCMWA, Library, no. 283.
39 SAA *KK* 2127.
40 J. De Belder, 'Beroep of bezit als criterium voor de sociale doorsnede', *TSG*, 2 (1976), pp. 257–79.

Chapter 2   Textile Manufacturing: A Lost Chance

1 SAA *KK* 2112, *PK* 457, no. 195.
2 Lis, 'Sociale politiek', pp. 160–1.
3 SAA *MA* 633(1), no. 82; RAA *PA*, J 222; Thijs, 'Schets', p. 185. These complaints appear to contradict the census of 1800, which indicates that the number of textile workers had grown by 14 per cent since 1789; however, this census only provides data on the professional qualifications of the persons concerned, not their actual employment. Given the general economic recession, there seems to be no doubt that most labourers faced chronic underemployment during this period, many of them even unemployment. This is borne out by a letter of the poor relief authorities to the mayor, dated 20 July 1801, which stated that in two of the four wards of the town alone there were 800 adult males unemployed. OCMWA *BW*, Cop. I, 1.
4 RAA *PA*, J 222.
5 ANP, F 12, no. 1563, F 15, no. 960, F 20, no. 231. See also Thijs, 'Schets', pp. 183–5.
6 J. Dhondt, 'The Cotton Industry at Ghent during the French Régime', in *Essays in European Economic History, 1789–1914*, edited by F. Crouzet, W.H. Chaloner and W.M. Stern (London, 1969), pp. 15–52.
7 Chassagne, 'Enquête', pp. 340 n.11, 354–5; Ph. Beke, 'Aspecten van de industriële ontplooiing in het Brusselse: een overzicht van de katoenverwerkende nijverheid in de Anderlechtse deelgemeente Kuregem, 1787–1830', *BTNG*, XII (1981), pp. 741–73. See also G. Adelmann, 'Quellen zur Geschichte des belgischen Baumwollgewerbes beim Uebergang von der vorindustriellen zur industriellen Zeit, 1760–1815', in *Histoire économique de la Belgique. Traitement des sources et état des questions. Actes du Colloque de Bruxelles, 17–19 Nov. 1971* (Brussels, 1972), tables 1–2 (between pp. 140 and 141).
8 Dhondt, 'Cotton Industry', pp. 20–6; F. Leleux, *A l'aube du capitalisme et de la révolution industrielle: Liévin Bauwens, industriel gantois* (Paris, 1969).
9 ANP F 12, no. 1563; RAA *PA*, J 222 (23 February 1816).
10 ANP, F 12, no. 1616.
11 SAA *MA* 633/1, no. 3.
12 ANP, F 12, no. 1616.
13 K. Jeuninckx, 'De havenbeweging in de Franse en Hollandse periode', in *Bouwstoffen voor de geschiedenis van Antwerpen in de XIXde eeuw* (Antwerp, 1964), pp. 96–8.
14 Dhondt, 'Cotton Industry', pp. 19–20.
15 K. Veraghtert, *De havenbeweging te Antwerpen tijdens de negentiende eeuw. Een kwantitatieve benadering*, Vol. II (Leuven Univ. Ph.D. thesis 1977), pp. 1–3.
16 B. de Jouvenel, *Napoléon et l'économie dirigée: le blocus continental* (Brussels and Paris, 1942), p. 290.
17 K. Veraghtert, 'The Antwerp Port, 1790–1814', in *The Interactions of Amsterdam and Antwerp with the Baltic Region, 1400–1800* (Leyden, 1983), pp. 194–7.
18 ANP, F 14, no. 1117; G. Beetemé, *Antwerpen, moederstad van handel en kunst*, Vol. II (Antwerp, 1893), pp. 10–14; L. Bergeron, 'Problèmes économiques de la France napoléonienne', *Revue d'Histoire moderne et contemporaine*, 17 (1970), p. 486.
19 ANP, F 12, no 1563; RAA *PA*, J 222.
20 Jeuninckx, 'Havenbeweging', pp. 101–2; Veraghtert, 'Antwerp Port', pp. 195, 197–8. For the French seaports see F. Crouzet, 'Wars, Blockade, and Economic Change in Europe, 1792–1815', *JEH*, XXIV (1964), pp. 568–71.

21 Beetemé, *Antwerpen*, Vol. II, pp.40−5; de Jouvenel, *Napoléon*, pp. 351−2; Veraghtert, *Haven-beweging*, Vol. II, pp. 24−5.

22 Dhondt, 'Cotton Industry', pp. 28−39.

23 ANP, F 12, no. 1616; Stadsarchief Lier, Modern Archief, Letter from de Heyder to Cresta (22 August 1808), and 'Etat de situation des fabriques et manufactures' (30 September 1811); RAA PA, J 222. The relationship of Lier to Antwerp was very much like that of some southern German towns to Berlin. Although cotton spinning in the Prussian capital had been partially mechanized at the end of the eighteenth century, the industry gradually during the first quarter of the nine-teenth century displaced itself to the southern German centres. Even when cotton spinning expanded rapidly in Germany after 1834, Berlin remained in the doldrums. The reasons were two-fold: on the one side, the bourgeoisie of Berlin could earn higher profits on commercial and financial ventures without incurring high risks; and, on the other, factory production in Berlin required greater capital than in the southern German towns, where water power, building land, and labour was much cheaper. This last factor explains why a number of spinning mills were founded in southern Germany financed by Berlin bankers who refused to provide funds for cotton-yarn factories in the Prussian capital. L. Baar, *Die Berliner Industrie in der industriellen Revolu-tion* (Berlin, 1966), pp. 42−6.

24 Veraghtert, *Havenbeweging*, Vol. II, p. 55.

25 RAA PA, J 203 and J 222; R. Demoulin, *Guillaume Ier et la transformation économiques des provinces belges, 1815−1830* (Liège, 1938), pp. 123ff. See also ARAG NN, no. 183 (18 September 1817).

26 M. Lévy-Leboyer, *Les banques européennes et l'industrialisation internationale dans la première moitié du XIXe siècle* (Paris, 1964), pp. 60, 71 n. 24.

27 ARAG SS, no. 896/41. See also Stadsarchief Lier, Modern Archief, 'Memorie' (1819).

28 J. Dhondt and M. Bruwier, 'The Low Countries, 1700−1914', in *The Fontana Economic His-tory of Europe*, edited by C.M. Cipolla, Vol. IV, Part 1, *The Emergence of Industrial Societies* (Lon-don, 1973), pp. 349−50; J. De Visser, *De 'industrialisatie' van de Gentse katoennijverheid, 1750−1850* (Ghent Univ. thesis 1977), pp. 211−2.

29 RAA PA, J 223.

30 *Ibid.*, J 222 (23 February 1816) and J 224 (8 June 1827); J. Hannes, *Bijdrage tot de ontwikkeling van een kwantitatief-kritische methode in de sociale geschiedschrijving* (Ghent Univ. Ph.D. thesis 1969), App. I−II, p. 85.

31 ARAG NN, no. 155 (22 July 1817). See also RAA PA, J 222 (5 July, 6 August, and 28 October 1816), and SAA MA 193/1a, no. 15.

32 D. E. Varley, 'John Heathcoat, Founder of the Machine-Made Lace Industry', *Textile History*, I (1968), pp. 2−45.

33 See D. Bythell, *The Sweated Trades: Outwork in Nineteenth-Century Britain* (London, 1978), pp. 99−100.

34 Lévy-Leboyer, *Banques*, p. 72.

35 L. Truyens-Bredael, 'William Wood, baanbreker der industriële omwenteling, en zijn fabriek te Borgerhout', *Noordgouw* (1962−1963), pp. 109−130.

36 SAA MA 630(3).

37 Lévy-Leboyer, *Banques*, p. 72.

38 SAA MA 630(2). See also OCMWA, BW, Cop. I, 8 (31 June 1829).

39 SAA MA 18 (April and June 1844), MA 630(4, 6−7); RAA PA, J 225 (24 August 1844, 28 August 1848, and 19 February 1849); Hannes, *Bijdrage*, App. I−II, pp. 86 and 104.

40 J. Kruithof, 'De sociale samenstelling van de bevolking te Antwerpen, Brussel, Gent en Luik in 1846−1847', HMGOG, new ser., XI (1957), pp. 200−201, 230.

41 G. Stedman Jones, *Outcast London. A Study in the Relationship Between Classes in Victorian Society* (Oxford, 1971), pp. 19−32. Nor did Liverpool become an important centre for the manu-facture of cottons, even though between 75 and 90 per cent of the raw cotton imported into Eng-land around 1850 moved through this port: the industry remained established in inland towns such as Manchester, Bolton, Blackburn, and Oldham. J.B. Sharpless, 'The Economic Structure of Port Cities in the Mid-Nineteenth Century: Boston and Liverpool, 1840−1860', *Journal of Histori-cal Geography*, II (1976), p. 134.

42 Nantes illustrates the first case. After 1793, this port gradually lost its role as an international entrepôt. Although from the second decade of the nineteenth century there were notable signs of recovery, the town waited until 1837 before forceful expansion of overseas trade took place. Meanwhile, numerous mechanized cotton mills had been set up. In 1827 there were fifteen in operation and by 1838 their number had risen to 25, of which two-thirds were equipped with

steam engines; some factories employed nearly 500 workers. Twenty years later most had closed their doors. The explanation for their collapse is the spectacular restoration of overseas trade, evinced by the quadrupling of the tonnage between the early 1830s and 1865. Port-associated industries took the place of cotton mills; above all, the production of sugar refining rose from 7,000 tons in the early 1830s to 63,000 tons in 1863. Bergeron, 'Problèmes', pp. 480–7; J. Fiérain, 'Croissance et mutation de l'économie, 1802–1914', in *Histoire de Nantes*, edited by P. Bois (Toulouse, 1977), pp. 319–37. The second case is applicable to Rouen, which gradually lost to Le Havre its leading position as a centre of overseas trade. This shift, noticeable from the 1770s, spurred the merchants of Rouen towards the cotton industry, which during the preceding decades had expanded strongly in the surrounding countryside. By 1850, Le Havre had become the foremost importer of American cotton in France, and Rouen the heart of the cotton manufacturing in Normandy. P. Dardel, *Commerce, industrie et navigation à Rouen et au Havre au XVIIIe siècle. Rivalité croissante entre les deux ports. La conjoncture* (Rouen, 1966); Lévy-Leboyer, *Banques*, pp. 67–70, 87–90, 92–4, 270ff; C. Fohlen, *L'industrie textile au temps du second Empire* (Paris, 1956), pp. 193–205. Meanwhile, sugar refining had shifted from Rouen to Le Havre: J. Fiérain, *Les raffineries de sucre des ports en France, XIXe-début du XXe siècle* (Dissertations in European Economic History, New York, 1977), pp. 207–8.
43 See E.E. Lampard, 'The History of Cities in Economically Advanced Areas', *Economic Development and Cultural Change*, III (1955), pp. 90–93, and W. Thompson, *A Preface to Urban Economics* (Baltimore, 1965), chs. 1 and 2,

Chapter 3 Antwerp as a Port Town

1 Jeuninckx, 'Havenbeweging', p. 106.
2 Veraghtert, *Havenbeweging*, Vol. II, pp. 61–3, 67–71.
3 *Ibid.*, pp. 28–36, 82–9. The quotation comes from H. Witlox, *Schets van de ontwikkeling van welvaart en bedrijvigheid in het Verenigd Koninkrijk der Nederlanden: Benelux, 1815–1830* (Nijmegen, 1956), p. 197.
4 Demoulin, *Guillaume Ier*, pp. 139ff, 200–2; Witlox, *Schets*, pp. 133–5, 196–7; K. Jeuninckx, 'De verhouding van de haven van Antwerpen tegenover deze van Amsterdam en Rotterdam tijdens het Verenigd Koninkrijk', *Mededelingen van de Marine Academie van België*, XI (1958–1959), pp. 147–83. The storage of 3,000 cases of sugar cost four times less in Antwerp than in Amsterdam, according to the merchant-banker J. van der Hoop.
5 Veragtert, *Havenbeweging*, Vol. II, pp. 44–52.
6 C. Lis, 'Revolte en repressie: De omwentelingsjaren 1830–1831 te Antwerpen', BTNG, III (1972), pp. 333–65.
7 RAA PA, J (9 March, 1831); SAA MA 633(9); Beetemé, *Antwerpen*, Vol. II, pp. 125–6; Veraghtert, *Havenbeweging*, Vol. II, pp. 123–4, Vol. III, pp. 91–2, and App. XXV. On insurance business see E. Willemse, *Het ontstaan en de ontwikkeling van het Belgisch verzekeringswezen, 1819–1873* (Brussels Univ. thesis 1974).
8 P. Lebrun, M. Bruwier, J. Dhondt and G. Hansotte, *Essai sur la révolution industrielle en Belgique, 1770–1847* (Brussels, 1979), p. 281–5, 386–99, 433–48, 454–7; Veraghtert, *Havenbeweging*, Vol. II, pp. 124–5, and App. XXV.
9 SAA MA 830/1(1); Lévy-Leboyer, *Banques*, pp. 525–9, 570–99.
10 Veraghtert, *Havenbeweging*, App. XXV.
11 *Ibid.*, Vol. II, pp. 98, 110–5, and App. XXV.
12 A. Spiethoff, *Die wirtschaftliche Wechsellagen*, Vol. I (Tübingen and Zürich, 1955), pp. 115–7; W. Abel, *Massenarmut und Hungerkrisen im vorindustriellen Europa. Versuch einer Synopsis* (Hamburg and Berlin, 1974), pp. 358–88. For Belgium see G. Jacquemyns, *Histoire de la crise économique des Flandres de 1845 à 1850* (Brussels, 1929), and J. Mokyr, *Industrialization in the Low Countries, 1795–1850* (New Haven and London, 1976).
13 Veraghtert, *Havenbeweging*, App. XXV.
14 SAA MA 191/4 and 830/1, no. 1. See also RAA PA, J 225 (18 September 1848).
15 P. Bairoch, 'Geographical Structure and Trade Balance of European Foreign Trade from 1800 to 1970', *Journal of European Economic History*, III (1974), p. 584. See also E.J. Hobsbawm, *The Age of Capital, 1848–1875* (London, 1977 edn), pp. 43–63.
16 P. Lebrun, 'L'industrialisation en Belgique au XIXe siècle', in *L'industrialisation en Europe au XIXe siècle*, edited by P. Léon, F. Crouzet and R. Gascon (Paris, 1972), pp. 150–1; J. Gadisseur, 'La production industrielle au XIXe siècle en Belgique: construction de l'indice', in *Histoire économique de la Belgique*, p. 93

17 Veraghtert, *Havenbeweging*, App. xxv and xlvi.
18 De Belder, *Elementen*, Vol. II, pp. 339–361; Hannes, *Bijdrage*, App. i–ii, pp. 73–91.
19 See Appendix 2, p. 172.
20 *RP*, 1846, pp. 386, 391, 403, 414, 438–45, 450–3, 458–61.
21 This is confirmed by the occupational figures given by François Bédarida for London: 84·6 per cent of the male population over ten and 41·4 per cent of the female population over ten in 1851. F. Bédarida, 'Londres au milieu du XIXe siècle: une analyse de structure sociale', *AESC*, 23 (1968), pp. 275–6. It must be remembered that London, unlike Antwerp, was also a centre of luxury and consumer goods industries. Unfortunately, the data published by Henk van Dijk, *Rotterdam, 1810–1880. Aspecten van een stedelijke samenleving* (Rotterdam, 1976), p. 396, concerning the occupational structure of Rotterdam in 1849 do not distinguish between men and women nor between young children and other age groups. In any case, the level of employment in the foremost harbour town of Holland was extremely low at the mid-nineteenth century: scarcely 36 per cent of all inhabitants versus *c.* 42 per cent in Antwerp and *c.* 47 per cent in London.
22 See Appendix 2.
23 Some descriptive material does indicate that these and other women's occupations were underrepresented in the population registers of 1830. Although the gutting and curing of herring sharply declined in the early nineteenth century and the *per capita* consumption of fish gradually diminished between 1815 and 1830, the public health commission continued to lodge complaints against the (overwhelming female) hawkers who tried to market spoiled fish; in 1832 the commission declared that such malpractices in the poorest quarters remained common currency. RAA *PA*, J 223 (July 1820); SAA *MA* 483/8, no. 3. There is further evidence to suggest that a quantitative analysis based on the population registers would underestimate the level of female employment. Under the Dutch regime the Frenchman, L. Constant, who had lived a number of years in England, introduced to Antwerp a new process for refining raw sugar, requiring collection of bones in large quantity, which were collected and sorted by women and children for one franc per quintal. Nonetheless, the population registers of 1830 do not mention any 'bone grubbers'.
24 *RP*, 1846, pp. 438–41. The census of 1846 cannot be used to draw detailed comparisons with the material from 1830 because of important differences in terminology and classificatory methods.
25 Veraghtert, *Havenbeweging*, Vol. III, pp. 91–2.
26 *RP*, 1846, pp. 438, 440–1.
27 Veraghtert, *Havenbeweging*, Vol. III, pp. 277–81, 471–5.
28 This is borne out by an analysis of licence fees, an annual tax which varied according to the industrial task and the volume of business; criteria for the latter were, among others, proceeds of sales, quantity of raw materials used, machinery, and number of employees. Although some entrepreneurs gave fraudulent information (see RAA *PA*, J 224), the license fees do give a rough indication of the major changes in economic activity at Antwerp between 1830 and 1842. If all occupations which wholly or partially depended on shipping – shipwrights, ropemakers, sailmakers, and smiths – are added together, then the total number of workers engaged in these trades was more than halved. The license fees also indicate that total industrial activity between 1830 and 1842 declined noticeably: the number of workers diminished by 33 per cent, and the average firm size declined from four to three men. Hannes, *Bijdrage*, App. iii pp. 271–81, 454–62, 471–5.
29 *Ibid.*, pp. 278, 472.
30 RAA *PA*, J 225 (22 November 1849); Prims, *Geschiedenis van Antwerpen*, xvii, pp. 32–3; A. De Lattin, *Evoluties van het Antwerpse stadsbeeld*, Vol. vi (Antwerp, 1950), pp. 42–5.
31 F. Donnet, *Notice historique sur le raffinage et les raffineurs de sucre à Anvers* (Antwerp, 1892), pp. 28–30.
32 ARAG *SS*, no. 1091/97 (30 October 1820); RAA *PA*, J 224.
33 RAA *PA*, L 216–224.
34 *Ibid.*, J 224 (16 December 1837) and J 225 (27 June 1842, and 22 November 1849); Donnet, *Notice*, pp. 33–8; Lévy-Leboier, *Banques*, pp. 254–68. See also A.K.L. Thijs, 'De geschiedenis van de suikernijverheid te Antwerpen (16de–19de eeuw): een terreinverkenning', *BG*, 62 (1979), pp. 44–8.
35 De Belder, *Elementen*, Vol. ii, pp. 339–61; Hannes, *Bijdrage*, App. i–ii, pp. 73–91.
36 SAA *MA* 187.
37 For some examples of seasonal fluctuations in the shipping-traffic, see Veraghtert, *Havenbeweging*, App. cxxvii.
38 Although there is no eye-witness account available, the port of Antwerp must have looked

like the London Dock described by Henry Mayhew in 1849. See his *London Labour and the London Poor*, Vol. III (New York, 1968), p. 304. See also the perceptive remarks of Stedman Jones, *Outcast London*, pp. 118–24, and J.H. Treble, *Urban Poverty in Britain, 1830–1914* (London, 1979), pp. 56–62.
39 See Appendix 3A.
40 SAA *MA* 633, no. 9.
41 OCMWA, Poor lists, 1840.
42 See Appendix 3B.
43 SAA *MA* 187.

Chapter 4   The Uprooted

1 C. Bruneel, 'La population du duché de Brabant en 1755', *BG*, 58 (1975), p. 283.
2 F. Blockmans, 'De bevolkingscijfers', in *Antwerpen in de XVIIIde eeuw*, pp. 399–400.
3 RAA PA, J 175a. See also A. Quetelet, 'Sur les anciens recensements de la population belge', *Bulletin de la Commission centrale de Statistique*, III (1847), pp. 4–8.
4 L.H.J. Vrancken, *La Cinquantaine. Notice historique et statistique sur la vaccine depuis son introduction à Anvers en 1810* (Antwerp, 1851), p. 139.
5 Hannes, *Bijdrage*, p. 58; *Stad Antwerpen: Gezondheidsdienst, jaarboek over 1914* (Antwerp, 1916), pp. 2–3. In 1860, Brussels had some 175,000 inhabitants. The next largest town was Ghent with about 118,000 people. Liège numbered 96,000. There were six towns (Bruges, Mechelen, Tournai, Leuven, Mons, and Namur) with 25,000 to 50,000 people.
6 J. Kruithof, 'De demografische ontwikkeling in de XIXde eeuw', in *Bouwstoffen*, p. 521.
7 SAA *PK* 261 and Vierschaar 1803; OCMWA, Library, nos. 381/1–2, and 'Collection factice', nos. 12, 15, 27, and 34.
8 De Belder, *Elementen*, Vol. I, p. 55; Hannes, *Bijdrage*, p. 67; *RP*, 1846, pp. 252–3.
9 Van Dijk, *Rotterdam*, p. 14; Bédarida, 'Londres', pp. 283–4.
10 See A. Cosemans, *De bevolking van Brabant in de XVIIde en XVIIIde eeuw* (Brussels, 1939).
11 ANP, F 20, no. 435 (18 November 1811); SAA *MA* 810, no. 1; F. H. Mertens and K.L. Torfs, *Geschiedenis van Antwerpen*, Vol. VI (Antwerp, 1851), pp. 79, 82, 85; H. Wauwermans, *Napoléon et Carnot, épisode de l'histoire militaire d'Anvers, 1803–1815* (Brussels, 1888), p. 36; P. Lombaerde, 'De militaire werken van Louis-Charles Boistard en Simon Bernard te Antwerpen tijdens het eerste keizerrijk', *Belgisch Tijdschrift voor Militaire Geschiedenis*, 25 (1983), pp. 285–328. See also J. Lucassen, *Naar de kusten van de Noordzee. Trekarbeid in Europees perspectief, 1600–1900* (Gouda, 1984), p. 294.
12 Kruithof, 'Demografische ontwikkeling', p. 510; *RP*, 1846, pp. 252–3, 260–1, 290–1, 326–7.
13 SAA, Vierschaar 177.
14 OCMWA *BW*, Cop. I, 4.
15 SAA *MA* 6844 (28 February 1843). See also *MA* 189/1 (30 October 1839).
16 O.F.J. De Grave, *Commentaire des lois sur le domicile de secours* (Ghent, 1855).
17 Several studies on the demographic development of French towns between 1750 and 1850 show that Antwerp was not an exceptional case: neither in Lyon or Marseille in the second half of the eighteenth century nor in Bordeaux, Dijon, or Paris during the first half of the nineteenth century was there a connection between fluctuations in the urban economy and waves of immigration. A. Armengaud, 'Industrialisation et démographie dans la France du XIXe siècle', in Léon, Crouzet and Gascon, *Industrialisation*, p. 189; M. Vovelle, 'Prolétariat flottant à Marseille sous la Révolution française', *ADH* (1968), p. 123; P. Giullaume, *La population de Bordeaux au XIXe siècle* (Paris, 1972), p. 62; J.-P. Viennot, 'Dijon au XIXe siècle', *ADH* (1969), pp. 241ff; L. Chevalier, *Classes laborieuses et classes dangereuses à Paris pendant la première moitié du XIXe siècle* (Paris, 1969), p. 191.
18 RAA PA, J 158–9.
19 J. Verbeemen, 'Mechelen gedurende de eerste helft der XIXe eeuw', *Handelingen van de Koninklijke Kring voor Oudheidkunde, Letteren en Kunst van Mechelen* (1959), p. 112.
20 C. Tilly, 'Migration in Modern European History', in *Human Migration: Patterns and Policies*, edited by W.H. McNeill and R.S. Adams (Bloomington, 1978), pp. 175–97 (on p. 189).
21 SAA *MA* 6844 (28 February 1843). See also OCMWA *BW*, Cop. I, 13 (5 December 1843).
22 See Appendix 4A (based on SAA *MA* 2668/1–6). Although too little attention has been devoted to migration from the countryside to urban centres during the nineteenth century, the

available evidence indicates that migration by stages was a frequent phenomenon in western Europe. The studies of M. Anderson, 'Urban Migration in Nineteenth-Century Lancashire', ADH (1971), p. 22, and Van Dijk, *Rotterdam*, p. 208, suggest that the Antwerp figures were even on the low side: indirect migration presumably accounted for half of the total migration to Preston, Lancashire, in 1851 and 60 per cent to Rotterdam during the 1850s.
23 OCMWA, 'Liste des étrangers secourus', 1846–1855.
24 Few migrants who came to Antwerp during the first half of the nineteenth century originated from families with a mobile past. Data concerning the parents of foreigners show that around 55 per cent of these families had never left their homes. Only a minority of 6 per cent had moved more than once. The remaining families can be divided according to whether migration preceeded or followed marriage: 25·5 per cent and 13·8 per cent of the total, respectively. The 'sedentary' life of most of these parents thus sharply contrasted with the rootless existence of their children.
25 W. Kula, 'Recherches comparatives sur la formation de la classe ouvrière', in *Second International Conference of Economic History* (Paris and The Hague, 1960), p. 515.
26 Only four migrants were natives of the nearby province of East-Flanders.
27 See for example M. Garden, 'L'attraction de Lyon à la fin de l'Ancien Régime', ADH (1970), p. 212; Anderson, 'Urban Migration', pp. 16–8; A. Armstrong, *Stability and Change in an English County Town. A Social Study of York, 1801–51* (London, 1974), pp. 88–91; Van Dijk, *Rotterdam*, p. 209; P. Borscheid, *Textilarbeiterschaft in der Industrialisierung. Soziale Lage und Mobilität in Württemberg im 19. Jahrhundert* (Stuttgart, 1978), Chapter III.
28 See Appendix 4C.
29 MAPA (28 February 1817); RAA PA, H 130 and H 179.
30 RAA PA, H 112, H 142–144, J 158, J 170, and J 179.
31 MAPA (1817), p. 100.
32 RAA PA, J 222 (1816–1817), and J 225 (1843); L. Coveliers, *Arendonk* (Arendonk, 1937), pp. 117–21, 259–66; E. Sneyers, *Bijdrage tot de geschiedenis van Retie* (Retie, 1949), pp. 262ff., 276; J. Goots, *Geschiedenis van Dessel* (Dessel, 1971), pp. 251ff.
33 S.C. Delacroix, *Défrichement des terrains incultes dans la Campine belge et les autres contrées de la Belgique* (Paris, 1860), p. 15; E. Vliebergh, *De Kempen in de 19e eeuw en in het begin der 20e eeuw* (Ieper, 1908), and *De landelijke bevolking der Kempen gedurende de 19e eeuw* (Brussels, 1906). See also E. Van Looveren, 'De privatisering van de gemeentegronden in de provincie Antwerpen: vier case-studies', BG, 66 (1983), pp. 189–216, and M. Goossens, 'Een negentiende-eeuws heidedorp in transformatie: Kalmthout, 1835–1910', BG, 67 (1985), pp. 222–6.
34 RAA PA, J 170; F. De Wever, 'Pachtprijzen in Vlaanderen en Brabant in de achttiende eeuw', TG, 85 (1972), pp. 182 and 197.
35 RAA PA, J 170; M.A. Nauwelaerts, *Putte in het Land van Mechelen* (Putte, 1966), pp. 108–10.
36 RAA PA, H 143, J 170, and J 222.
37 RAA PA, J 170.
38 P.M.M. Klep, *Groeidynamiek en stagnatie in een agrarisch grensgebied. De economische ontwikkeling in de Noordantwerpse Kempen en de Baronie van Breda, 1850–1850* (Tilburg, 1973), p. 159, and *Bevolking en arbeid in transformatie. Een onderzoek in Brabant, 1700–1900* (Nijmegen, 1981), p. 100.
39 RAA PA, J 158.
40 For data concerning migration from and to the Rupelregion, see RAA PA, J 158–159.
41 An analysis of migration to Brussels likewise suggests that paupers generally left their traditional milieu only if their situation became utterly desperate. See P. Van den Eeckhout, 'De recrutering van de Brusselse armenbevolking in relatie met de afstotingsmechanismen in het gebied van herkomst', in *Taal en sociale integratie*, Vol. IV (Brussels, 1981), pp. 225–34.

Chapter 5　　Patterns of Settlement

1 SAA MA 2668/1–6.
2 De Belder, *Elementen*, Vol. II, p. 77; Hannes, *Bijdrage*, App. I–II, p. 16; RP, 1846, pp. 252–3. The data published by De Belder and Hannes do not permit the calculation of dependency ratios, where groups of young people and of the elderly are compared with the number of individuals in the occupationally active age groups (15–64 years of age).
3 De Belder, *Elementen*, Vol. II, pp. 77 and 132; A. Smits, *Demografische toestanden van de stad Antwerpen in de jaren 1810–1820* (Leuven Univ. thesis, 1962), pp. 47 and 77; Hannes, *Bijdrage*, p. 66; RP, 1846, pp. 252–3.
4 J. Verbeemen, 'De werking van economische factoren op de stedelijke demografie der XVIIe

en der XVIIIe eeuw in de Zuidelijke Nederlanden', BTFG, 34 (1956), pp. 688–90; Bruneel, 'Population', pp. 240–53.
5 De Belder, *Elementen*, Vol. I, pp. 94–5.
6 A. Thys, *Négociants et industriels anversois au siècle dernier* (Antwerp, 1906).
7 De Belder, *Elementen*, Vol. II, p. 132.
8 See Appendix 5A (calculated from De Belder, *Elementen*, Vol. II, pp. 126–33, and Hannes, *Bijdrage*, App. I–II, pp. 74–91).
9 Numerous examples in OCMWA *BW*, Cop. I, 4 and 5.
10 *Enquête sur la condition des classes ouvrières et sur le travail des enfants*, Vol. II, *Réponses, mémoires et rapports des Chambres de Commerce, des ingénieurs des mines et des collèges médicaux* (Brussels, 1846), p. 205.
11 The Medical Commission had no complaint against child labour in this trade. See *Enquête*, Vol. III, *Réponses, lettres, mémoires et rapports médicaux* (Brussels, 1846), pp. 184, 205, 209–210.
12 Hannes, *Bijdrage*, App. III, pp. 270–1.
13 *Ibid.*, App. I–II, pp. 81–2.
14 *Enquête*, Vol. III, p. 203.
15 L. Lees, 'Mid-Victorian Migration and the Irish Economy', *Victorian Studies*, XV (1976), p. 30.
16 See Appendix 5B (sources: see note 8 above).
17 Cf. D. Bythell, *The Handloom Weavers* (Cambridge, 1969), p. 136, and M. Garden, *Lyon et les Lyonnais au XVIIIe siècle* (Paris, 1970), pp. 58–9.
18 See the perceptive remarks in Léon, Crouzet and Gascon, *Industrialisation*, pp. 198–9. See also L. Chevalier, *La formation de la population parisienne au XIXe siècle* (Paris, 1960), p. 88; M. Lachiver, *La Population de Meulan du XVIIe au XIXe siècle, 1600–1870* (Paris, 1969), p. 211; Garden, 'Attraction de Lyon', p. 215; Anderson, 'Urban Migration', pp. 19ff.
19 S. Thernstrom, *Poverty and Progress. Social Mobility in a Nineteenth-Century City* (Cambridge, Mass., 1964), p. 85.
20 Cf. Th. M. McBride, *The Domestic Revolution. The Modernization of Household Service in England and France, 1820–1920* (London, 1976), pp. 82 and 98; S.C. Crawford, *Domestic Service in Eighteenth-Century France* (London, 1980), pp. 91–3; J.-P. Gutton, *Domestiques et serviteurs dans la France de l'ancien régime* (Paris, 1981), pp. 78–81.
21 During the French régime the *naties* of Antwerp lost their charter dating back to the fifteenth and sixteenth centuries. The *naties* repeatedly petitioned the municipal authorities to restore their former monopolies in carrying traffic, but this was firmly refused in order to keep wage levels as low as possible. Nonetheless, these 'unions' continued to play a major role, because for organizational purposes most merchants and shippers preferred to contract with a *natie* than to recruit dockers themselves. See F. Prims, 'De namen onzer natiën', *Antwerpiensia*, XVIII (1947), pp. 206–7; A. Haeck, *De kerbinders van het Hessenhuis en de Hessenatie* (Antwerp, 1960), pp. 114–5, 124; K. Van Isaker, *De Antwerpse dokwerker, 1830–1940* (Antwerp, 1966), pp. 17–8.
22 SAA *MA* 754/2, no. 4.
23 OCMWA *BW*, Cop. I, 8 (27 March 1829).

Chapter 6   The Struggle for Living Space

1 De Belder, *Elementen*, Vol. II, pp. 400–403; *RP*, 1856, p. 354.
2 Chevalier, *Classes laborieuses*, p. 217; H.F.J.M. van den Eerenbeemt, 'Woontoestanden van de volksklasse in de 19e eeuw', *Spiegel Historiael*, IX (1976), p. 494; H.J. Dyos and D.A. Reeder, 'Slums and Suburbs', in *The Victorian City. Images and Realities*, edited by H.J. Dyos and M. Wolff (London, 1973), pp. 359ff; J. Thienel, *Städtewachstum im Industrialisierungsprozess des 19. Jahrhunderts* (Berlin and New York, 1973).
3 Jones, *Outcast London*, p. 160; Chevalier, *Classes laborieuses*, pp. 230–1.
4 J. van den Nieuwenhuizen, 'De stadsuitbreiding van Antwerpen tussen 1860 en 1914', *Antwerpen*, VI (1960), pp. 110–2.
5 *RP*, 1846, p. 184.
6 In 1568 Antwerp contained *intra muros* around 12,000 houses. Although that number had been reduced to around 10,000 by 1591, no new space was opened for construction, since the decline resulted primarily from connection of two or three units into single dwellings after the dramatic drop in population which followed Parma's taking of the town. H. Soly, 'De megalopolis Antwerpen', in *De Stad Antwerpen van de Romeinse tijd tot de 17de eeuw* (Brussels, 1978), pp. 95–9.

7 Hannes, *Bijdrage*, p. 109.
8 R. Vande Weghe, *Geschiedenis van de Antwerpse straatnamen* (Antwerp, 1977), pp. 166–7, 192, 357, 452.
9 Between 1796 and 1861, Antwerp was divided into five administrative units or wards: four within and one outside the town. The fifth ward *extra muros* included the hamlets of Kattendijk, Dambrugge, Sint-Willebrords, Haringrode, Lei, and Kiel.
10 SAA *MA* 189/1 (24 August and 30 October 1839); OCMWA *BW*, Cop. I (29 August 1845). See also *RVA*, 1843, p. 29.
11 SAA *MA* 187 (28 September 1860), and *MA* 439 (18 November 1858).
12 Jones, *Outcast London*, pp. 171ff.
13 Calculations based on Hannes, *Bijdrage*, App. I–II, pp. 20–91.
14 SAA *MA* 16/6.
15 Cf. D.J. Olsen, 'Victorian London: Specialization, Segregation and Privacy', *Victorian Studies*, XVII (1974), p. 268, and D.A. Reeder, 'A Theatre of Suburbs: Some Patterns of Development in West London, 1801–1911', in *The Study of Urban History*, edited by H.J. Dyos (London, 1976 edn.), p. 255.
16 Population figures taken from RAA *PA*, J 182A (1796); Vrancken, *Cinquantaine*, p. 140 (1815); Hannes, *Bijdrage*, p. 109 (1829); *RVA*, 1847, p. 12 (1845). Information on total built-up area drawn from Hannes, *Bijdrage*, p. 143.
17 Hannes, *Bijdrage*, App. I–II, pp. 144–6, 162–4.
18 Calculations based on De Belder, *Elementen*, Vol. II, pp. 400–3, and Hannes, *Bijdrage*, pp. 109 and 147.
19 Similar contrasts were notable in many other nineteenth-century towns. London counted nearly 8 per cent empty dwellings in 1883–1884 – exactly the period in which the housing crisis reached its peak. Jones, *Outcast London*, pp. 206–8. Between 1817 and 1826, living accommodation was created for 15,000 people in the tenth *arrondissement* of Paris, while the actual number of occupiers amounted to only 9,500. Contemporaries ascribed this short-term building mania, which resulted in a serious crisis at the end of the Restoration, chiefly to the rising bourgeoisie's incessant search for status. Construction of superfluous *appartements de luxe* went hand in hand with a growing shortage of housing, aggravated by the razing of hundreds of slums. The population of the fourth *arrondissement* grew by 5,169 individuals during the decade after 1817; only 1,720 of them, some 33 per cent, could move into new buildings. Chevalier, *Classes laborieuses*, pp. 217–8. Adeline Daumard, 'Quelques remarques sur le logement des Parisiens au XIXe siècle', *ADH* (1975), p. 54, has concluded: 'Taking into consideration the number of empty houses, it seems as if Parisians had no difficulty finding lodgings during the nineteenth century' – all very true if 'Parisians' means the Parisian bourgeoisie.
20 OCMWA *BW*, Cop. I (16 April 1850).
21 The same held for other nineteenth-century towns. In 1884, *The Builder* wrote that the English poor 'cannot afford to pay more than a rental of from 1s to 2s per week for their dwellings, of whatever size and construction, and wheresoever situated . . . but no practical plan has yet been devised by which dwellings can be built . . . which can be let at these low rentals *and prove remunerative to builders*'. Quoted in E. Gauldie, *Cruel Habitations. A History of Working-Class Housing, 1780–1918* (London, 1974), p. 161. In 1896, Professor D.J. Jitta testified that it was practically impossible to build proper working-class houses in Amsterdam, because the incomes of most families were much too small. In support of his assertion, he pointed to the plan of a philanthropic building-society to erect 21 workers' dwellings. The price of the land and the cost of construction amounted to some 30,000 guilders, or 1,429 guilders per dwelling, each consisting of two rooms and an attic. Since their weekly rental had to be no more than 1·20 to 1·50 guilders if they were to be available to wage labourers, gross returns varied between 4·4 and 5·5 per cent *per annum*. Taking running expenses into account, the society made 3·3 to 4·1 per cent. Needless to say, private entrepreneurs were not interested in returns this low. L.M. Hermans, *Krotten en sloppen: Een onderzoek naar den woningtoestand te Amsterdam, ingesteld in opdracht van den Amsterdamschen Bestuursraad* (Amsterdam, 1975), pp. 88, 95–6.
22 Hannes, *Bijdrage*, App. III, pp. 269–70, 276.
23 See Appendix 6.
24 Calculations based on Hannes, *Bijdrage*, App. III, pp. 47–8, 51, 133–4, 139, 390–1, 393, 465–6, 470.
25 J. De Belder, 'De behuizing te Antwerpen op het einde van de XVIIIe eeuw', *BING*, VIII (1977), pp. 367–443.
26 Each ghetto was occupied by some 80 per cent of the supported families living in the Zone concerned.

27 SAA *MA* 748/68.
28 SAA *MA* 2642/2.
29 SAA *MA* 15/35 (4 January 1850). See also G.H. Guerrand, *Les origines du logement social en France* (Paris, 1969), p. 283; W. Treue, 'Haus und Wohnung im 19. Jahrhundert', in *Städte-, Wohnungs- und Kleidungshygiene des 19. Jahrhunderts in Deutschland* (Stuttgart, 1969), p. 38; Jones, *Outcast London*, pp. 224–5.
30 H. Fassbinder, *Berliner Arbeiterviertel, 1800–1918* (Berlin, 1875), pp. 70–1.
31 Jones, *Outcast London*, pp. 179–207. See also H.J. Dyos, 'Railways and Housing in Victorian London', *Journal of Transport History*, II (1950), pp. 14–8.
32 L. Houdeville, *Pour une civilisation de l'habitat* (Paris, 1969), pp. 40–1.
33 Hermans, *Krotten*, pp. 84–7.
34 See the pertinent remarks of H. Kaelble, *Industrialisierung und soziale Ungleichheit* (Göttingen, 1983), pp. 119–43.
35 E. Ducpétiaux, *De la mortalité à Bruxelles comparée à celle des autres grandes villes* (Brussels, 1844), p. 62

Chapter 7   Living Like Pigs

1 SAA *MA* 937, no. 1; De Belder, *Elementen*, Vol. I, p. 300.
2 SAA *MA* 439 (18 November 1858).
3 OCMWA *BW* Cop. I (1 February 1837).
4 C. Lis and J. Hannes 'De sociale hiërarchie in de woningbouw. Antwerpen omstreeks 1834', *BTNG*, I (1969), pp. 88–91.
5 Calculations based on De Belder, *Elementen*, Vol. II, pp. 395–400, and Hannes, *Bijdrage*, App. I–II, pp. 141–65.
6 For a detailed analysis, see C. Lis, 'Woontoestanden en gangensaneringen te Antwerpen in het midden der 19e eeuw', *BTNG*, I (1969), pp. 108–27.
7 SAA *MA* 439 (25 November 1854).
8 *Ibid.*, 'Commission médicale locale'.
9 *Rapport sur le travail des enfants et la condition des ouvriers dans la province d'Anvers par Berchem, C. Broeckx, J. Jacques, J. Koyen et F.J. Matthysens, rapporteurs, addressé à M. le Gouverneur de la province d'Anvers* (Antwerp, 1844), pp. 17–8.
10 SAA *MA* 439, 'Hygiène publique: Enquête'.
11 Lis, 'Woontoestanden', p. 128.
12 *Commission du travail*, Vol. IV (Brussels, 1888), p. 61. See also A.-C. Content, 'L'habitat ouvrier à Bruxelles au XIXe siècle', *BTNG*, VIII (1977), pp. 501–16.
13 W. Steensels, 'De tussenkomst van de overheid in de arbeidershuisvesting: Gent, 1850–1904', *ibid.*, pp. 468–9.
14 L. Niethammer, 'Wie wohnten Arbeiter im Kaiserreich?', *Archiv für Sozialgeschichte*, XVI (1976), pp. 69–71; Fassbinder, *Berliner Arbeiterviertel*, p. 74.
15 F. Sheppard, *London, 1808–1870: The Infernal Wen* (London, 1971), p. 289; Jones, *Outcast London*, pp. 219–20.
16 Guerrand, *Origines*, pp. 95, 212–4; Houdeville, *Civilisation*, pp. 75–6.
17 Van den Eerenbeemt, 'Woontoestanden', pp. 498–9.
18 This was true for other western European towns as well. In London, for example, hundreds of small tradesmen, retired builders, and vestrymen each owned or leased a few small houses during the 1880s. It was the same for French towns such as Lille and Paris. Only in exceptional cases were members of the working class in the strict sense to be found among slumlords; perhaps this minority considered such investments as the most adequate means to protect themselves against old age, sickness, and other forms of unemployability. Jones, *Outcast London*, pp. 212–3; F.-P. Codaccioni, *De l'inégalité sociale dans une grande ville industrielle. Le drame de Lille de 1850 à 1914* (Lille, 1976), pp. 64–5, 74, 332–3, 360; *Les fortunes françaises au XIXe siècle*, edited by A. Daumard (Paris and The Hague, 1973).
19 SAA *MA* 439 (July 1853) and *MA* 937, no. 1.
20 Information on the profitability of slum dwellings in nineteenth-century towns is scarce, but the few available data indicate that exploitation of such lodgings was lucrative in the extreme. In 1841, a member of Brussels' Public Health Committee testified that 'the most insalubrious dwellings yield the greatest profits for their owners. The income from decent houses seldom exceeds 12 per cent per year, but that from hovels often amounts to more than 20 per cent'. Quoted in P.

Van den Eeckhout, *Determinanten van het 19de-eeuws sociaal-economisch leven te Brussel. Hun betekenis voor de laagste bevolkingsklassen* (Brussels Univ. Ph.D. thesis 1980), Vol. II, p. 230. Forty years later, the noted Dutch physician and philanthropist Samuel Coronel wrote: 'It is shameful usury to provide workers with such rotten tenements in exchange for their hard-earned money. Or is it right to make 7 or 8 per cent profit from the good burghers on a proper house and 16 to 20 per cent from the poor on a slum out of repair?' Quoted in van den Eerenbeemt, 'Woontoestanden', pp. 500–1. At about the same time, Lord Compton's agent reported to the Royal Commission on Housing that slumlords in London could make an annual return of 150 per cent on their funds if the dwellings were subdivided to the maximum. Jones, *Outcast London*, pp. 211–2. In the German towns, things were no different. In Berlin at the end of the nineteenth century, profits from the rental of three or more separate rooms were four to six times greater than from a medium-sized house with the same number of apartments. Niethammer, 'Wie wohnten Arbeiter', p. 80.

21 Lis, 'Woontoestanden', pp. 108–27.
22 SAA *MA* 439 (20 April 1849).
23 *Ibid.* (30 October 1850).
24 *Ibid.*, 'Comité de Salubrité publique', 1850.
25 *RVA*, 1850, p. 108.
26 OCMWA *BW*, Cop. I (24 July 1855); SAA *MA* 439 (4 September 1855).
27 For detailed figures, see E. Scholliers, 'Un indice du loyer: les loyers anversois de 1500 à 1873', in *Studi in Onore di Amintore Fanfani*, Vol. v (Milan, 1962), pp. 604, 607, 616–7. All available evidence suggests that the boom in urban rents was a general western European phenomenon: in Ghent they rose by 160 per cent between 1800 and 1860; in Brussels they doubled during the same period; in Paris they were one and a half times higher in 1870 than in 1835; in Berlin they trebled during the nineteenth century. G. Avondts and P. Scholliers, *Gentse prijzen, huishuren en budgetonderzoeken in de 19e en 20e eeuw* (Brussels, 1977), pp. 148–9; P. Van den Eeckhout and P. Scholliers, *De Brusselse huishuren, 1800–1940* (Brussels, 1979), pp. 104–5; Daumard, 'Quelques remarques', p. 56; Niethammer, 'Wie wohnten Arbeiter', p. 78.
28 Hannes, *Bijdrage*, App. III, p. 113 (1827); SAA *MA* 748/68 (1874). .
29 That was also the case in Paris: Chevalier, *Classes laborieuses*, pp. 271ff.
30 *Rapport de la Commission médicale de la ville d'Anvers. L'épidémie de choléra, 1866* (Antwerp, 1867), p. 28.
31 The following method has been used. The wages of all members of a family were added together and supplemented with the financial aid provided by the Charity Bureau. The families and their total incomes were then divided according to the number of members, after which the average income (relief included) was converted into kilograms of rye bread..
32 Hannes, *Bijdrage*, pp. 99–100.
33 33 OCMWA *BW*, Rep. I, 1 (1 June 1832).

Chapter 8   Food Consumption

1 *Pour une histoire de l'alimentation*, edited by J.-J. Hémardinquer (Paris, 1970); H.J. Teuteberg and G. Wiegelmann, *Der Wandel der Nahrungsgewohnheiten unter dem Einfluss der Industrialisierung* (Göttingen, 1972); 'Histoire de la consommation', *AESC*, XXX (1975), pp. 402–632 (special issue); Taylor, *Standard of Living*, pp. xxix–xxxiv; *The Making of the Modern British Diet*, edited by D.J. Oddy and D. Miller (London, 1976); W. Abel, *Stufen der Ernährung. Eine historische Skizze* (Göttingen, 1981); *Consumer Behaviour and Economic Growth in the Modern Economy*, edited by H. Baudet and H. J. van der Meulen (London and Canberra, 1982).
2 Originally intended to provide supplementary funds for the poor relief, these new taxes were soon largely diverted to cover deficiencies in local government resources. R. Laurent, 'Une source: les archives d'octroi', *AESC* XI (1956), pp. 197–204; *Abolition des octrois communaux en Belgique: Documents et discussions parlementaires*, 2 vols. (Brussels, 1860).
3 R. Boumans, *Het Antwerps stadsbestuur voor en tijdens de Franse overheersing* (Bruges, 1965), pp. 429–37. See also SAA *MA* 766/1.
4 SAA *MA* 811–816, *MA* 817/1–2, *MA* 818/1–2.
5 The only important evasion which took place related to the amounts collected, not the quantities taxed: J.-C. and M. Mattheesens, 'Un procès sous le premier Empire: l'octroi d'Anvers, 1811–13', *RN*, XXXVII (1955), pp. 135–42.
6 C. Lis and H. Soly, 'Food Consumption in Antwerp between 1807 and 1859: A Contribution to the Standard of Living Debate', *EcHR*, 2nd ser., XXX (1977), pp. 460–82.

7 SAA *MA* 163/2, *MA* 9081–9082.
8 Quoted in Lis and Soly, 'Food Consumption', p. 475. Charitable institutions in other towns saw similar reductions in *per capita* food consumption. Whereas adult internees in the *dépot de mendicité* of Terkameren, near Brussels, had around 1810 an average daily intake of 3,000 calories, by 1850 this quantity had been reduced to merely 2,400; moreover, in the latter year, meat, butter, and beer provided only 3 per cent of calories, versus 15 per cent in the former year. Van den Eeckhout, *Determinanten*, Vol. III, p. 95.
9 SAA *MA* 830/1; E. Ducpétiaux, *Budgets économiques des classes ouvrières en Belgique. Subsistance, salaires, population* (Brussels, 1855), p. 148.
10 Calculations based on *Rapport sur les octrois communaux de Belgique présenté à la Chambre des Représentants le 28 janvier 1845 par le Ministre de l'Intérieur*, Vol. I (Brussels, 1845), Tables 10, 25 and 26.
11 SAA *MA* 438/D, no. 4.
12 SAA *MA* 438/B, no. 3.
13 *Rapport sur le travail des enfants*, p. 15.
14 SAA *MA* 493, nos 7–8.
15 Both quotations come from Lis and Soly, 'Food Consumption', p. 472.
16 *Enquête sur la condition des classes ouvrières*, Vol. I, p. lxii, and Vol. III, p. 216.
17 Lis and Soly, 'Food Consumption', p. 472.
18 SAA *MA* 438/B, no. 3; OCMWA, Library, no 224/12.
19 F. De Wachter, 'Du lard et ses auxiliaires', *Annales de la Société de Médicine d'Anvers*, XX (1859), p. 185.
20 See SAA *MA* 828/2 (10 December 1817), and RAA *PA*, J 224 (9 March 1831).
21 Calculations based on C. Vandenbroeke, *Agriculture et alimentation dans les Pays-Bas autrichiens* (Ghent and Leuven, 1975), p. 569; *Octrois communaux. Rapport adressé au Ministre de l'Intérieur par la Commission de révision institué en vertu de l'arrêté royal du 9 novembre 1847* (Brussels, 1848), p. 53; *Abolition des octrois communaux*, Vol. I, p. 33. See also P. Van den Eeckhout and P. Scholliers, 'De hoofdelijke voedselconsumptie in België, 1831–1939', *TSG*, 9 (1983), pp. 284–5, 293–4. Conversely, the average consumption of beer in all Belgian towns subject to *octrois* dropped from 254 litres per head and per day in the 1820s to scarcely 140 litres in the years 1851–1857, a diminution of 45 per cent. *Octrois communaux. Rapport adressé au Ministre de l'Intérieur*, p. 52; E. Cauderlier, *Les boissons alcooliques et leurs effets sociaux en Belgique d'après les documents officiels* (Brussels, 1883), p. 24.
22 Since Antwerp was one of the most important importers of coffee on the Continent, the quantity consumed there was possibly even higher. It was certainly no accident that in 1842 the town had no fewer than 24 chicory roasting enterprises when there had been none at the beginning of the century. Hannes, *Bijdrage*, App. III, p. 454.
23 *Abolition des octrois communaux*, Vol. I, pp. 90–1. See also Van den Eeckhout and Scholliers, 'Hoofdelijke voedselconsumptie', pp. 284, 293–4. In Britain *per capita* sugar consumption amounted to 40 grams per day in the 1850s. G.N. Johnstone, 'The Growth of the Sugar Trade and Refining Industry', in Oddy and Miller, eds., *Making of the Modern British Diet*, p. 60.
24 This interpretation is supported by a pronouncement of the director of the communal revenue service, who wrote to the town government in 1841: 'Receipts have diminished with respect to all produce which make up the food and drink of the lower middle class and the little folk, but they have increased with respect to the things which grace the tables of the well-to-do'. It is also reinforced by the stabilization between 1845 and 1859 of the (small) *per capita* consumption of luxuries such as meat and fish pies, truffels, fowl, and small game. SAA *MA* 830/1, no. 1 (30 June 1841), *MA* 830/3, *MA* 830/4, no. 3.
25 SAA *MA* 830/1, no. 1 (3 July 1850).
26 SAA *MA* 478, no. 7, and *MA* 805/2, no. 6.
27 SAA *MA* 830/1, no. 1 (21 July 1838).
28 *Rapport sur le travail des enfants*, p. 17.
29 Van Isacker, *Antwerpse dokwerker*, pp. 48–53.
30 A. De Weerdt, *Oude en nieuwe liedjes* (Antwerp, 1858), pp. 161–6 (on p. 163). Antwerp had more than a thousand pubs in the 1850s, one for every 95 inhabitants. SAA *MA* 805/2, nos 2 and 6.
31 SAA *MA* 438/D, no. 16 (24 August 1855).
32 *Commission du Travail*, Vol. I, pp. 1095, 1151–3.
33 Unless otherwise stated, the following exposé is based on Lis and Soly, 'Food Consumption', pp. 474–7.

34 For the period 1820–1829 a ratio of 6 litres of gin per hectolitre of raw material has been taken as a basis, and for the period 1850–1859 a ratio of 1:7.

35 See Appendix 7A.

36 A very young child needs between 1,200 and 1,600 calories per day; a boy from seven to ten about 2,200 calories, a girl from seven to nine about 2,000 calories; a boy between 11 and 19 an average of 3,000 calories, a girl between 10 and 19 an average of 2,300 calories; a man from 20 to 54 with moderately strenuous work about 2,800 calories; an adult woman in the same circumstances about 2,200 calories; older active men and women respectively 2,500 and 2,000 calories. C. Den Hartog, *Nieuwe voedingsleer* (Utrecht and Antwerp, 1972), pp. 78–80, 308–35.

37 See Appendix 7B.

38 ANP, F 20, no. 145; *Enquête sur la condition des classes ouvrières*, Vol. III, p. 216.

39 Ducpétiaux, *Budgets, passim*. His material was statistically treated by E. Engel, *Die Lebenskosten belgischer Arbeiterfamilien früher und jetzt* (Dresden, 1895). See the critical comments by M. Neirynck, *De lonen in België sedert 1846* (Antwerp, Brussels, and Ghent, 1944), pp. 210–21, and D. De Weerdt, 'Arbeiderstoestanden van 1850 tot 1876', in *Geschiedenis van de socialistische arbeidersbeweging in België*, edited by J. Dhondt (Antwerp, 1968), pp. 216–22.

40 F. Digand, *Abolition complète des droits d'octroi* (Antwerp, 1847), pp. 39–40.

41 Quoted by Lis and Soly, 'Food Consumption', p. 471.

42 *Rapport de la Commission médicale locale de la ville d'Anvers* (Antwerp, 1867), p. 30.

43 *De Werker*, 2 May 1869.

44 *RVA*, 1853, p. 48.

45 *MAPA*, 1855, p. 201 (no. 6793).

46 *RVA*, 1854–1874, *passim*.

47 OCMWA *BW*, PV (13 February 1841).

48 For some comparisons, see esp. A. Kraus, *Die Unterschichten Hamburgs in der ersten Hälfte des 19. Jahrhunderts* (Stuttgart, 1965), pp. 51–67; W. Köllmann, *Sozialgeschichte der Stadt Barmen im 19. Jahrhundert* (Tübingen, 1960), pp. 138–40; R. Engelsing, 'Hanseatische Lebenshaltungen und Lebenshaltungskosten im 18. und 19. Jahrhundert', in *Zur Sozialgeschichte deutschen Mittel- und Unterschichten* (Göttingen, 1973), pp. 30–1.

49 A. De Weerdt, *Al de liederen*, Vol. I (Antwerp, 1886), p. 64 (1854).

50 For salted fish: SAA *MA* 831/1. For meat and beer: C. Vandenbroeke, 'Voedingstoestanden te Gent tijdens de eerste helft van de 19de eeuw', *BTNG*, IV (1973), pp. 118, 122–3.

51 Calculations based on M.-L. Verheydt, *De voedingstoestanden te Brussel op basis van de octrooien en accijnzen, 1840–1860* (Brussels Univ. thesis, 1976).

52 E. Stevens, 'Notice sur les octrois communaux de Belgique', *Bulletin de la Commission centrale de Statistique*, III (1947), p. 409.

53 Ducpétiaux, *Budgets*, p. 147. In 1839, one author declared that the wage-labourers of Verviers ate little besides rye bread and potatoes, and sometimes (but seldom) a bit of bacon. N.M. Briavoine, *De l'industrie en Belgique, causes de décadence et de prospérité, sa situation actuelle*, Vol. II (Brussels, 1839), p. 62.

54 J. Mareska and J. Heyman, *Enquête sur le travail et la condition physique et morale des ouvriers employés dans les manufactures de coton à Gand* (Ghent, 1846).

55 Ducpétiaux, *Budgets*, p. 150. See also the conclusions of P. Scholliers and C. Vandenbroeke, 'The Transition from Traditional to Modern Patterns of Demand in Belgium', in Baudet and van der Meulen, eds., *Consumer Behaviour*, pp. 25–71.

Chapter 9   On Relief: Numbers

1 The crude death rate remained virtually unchanged between 1827 and 1860; it averaged 23·5 per 1,000, if the terrible years 1832, 1849 and 1859, when mortality bounded up to 35·1, 45·0 and 43·1 respectively as a result of epidemic diseases, are left aside. Calculated from Hannes, *Bijdrage*, p. 53, and Kruithof, 'Demografische ontwikkeling', pp. 541–2.

2 S. Janssens-Even, 'De openbare liefdadigheidsinstellingen van 1794 tot 1830', in *Bouwstoffen*, pp. 214–8, 224–6. See also ANP, F 15, no. 956 (June 1804); RAA *PA*, H 13 (1806); OCMWA *BW*, Bestuursraad, Box 'Verordeningen' (1810).

3 Boumans, *Antwerps stadsbestuur*, p. 432.

4 SAA *MA* 182/7, no. 4, *MA* 3532 (1806), *MA* 6844, no. 1.

5 SAA *MA* 3533/9–54.

6 OCMWA *BW*, Cop. I, 2.

7 RAA *PA*, H 13 (September 1804).
8 OCMWA, Library 381/1, no. 24; SAA *MA* 6199/1.
9 OCMWA *KH* 870, no. 6; 'Collection factice', nos 22 and 27; Library 381/1, nos 22–24; SAA *KK* 2112 (19 February 1780).
10 OCMWA *BW*, Bestuursraad, Box 'Verordeningen' (1799).
11 RAA *PA*, H 143 (22 May 1823); SAA *MA* 193/1a.
12 OCMWA *BW*, PV (25 January 1837); SAA *MA* 193/1a, no. 15.
13 OCMWA, Library 381/2, no. 22 (1779); 'Collection factice', no. 27 (1781); *BW*, Bestuursraad, Box 'Verordeningen' (1799); SAA *MA* 189/1 (1805 and 1826); OCMWA *BW*, PV (25 January 1837, 8 February 1841, and 14 November 1850).
14 OCMWA *BW*, Cop. I, 1 (17 December 1800, 20 July 1801, and 27 September 1802), PV (18 October 1802); SAA *MA* 6199/1 (1805); RAA *PA*, H 13.
15 SAA *MA* 3532 (31 March and 24 July 1812); OCMWA *BW*, Cop. I, 3 (April 1812 and October 1815).
16 OCMWA *BW*, Cop. I, 4–5.
17 SAA *MA* 189/1 (21 November 1839); OCMWA *BW*, PV (13 February 1841). The quotation comes from SAA *MA* 187. See also OCMWA, *Rapport décennal, 1864 à 1855*, p. 33.
18 SAA *MA* 3533, *passim*.
19 To interpret these data, it must be remembered that the *Nieuwe Bestiering* still functioned in 1780 and that the primary goal of that institution was to limit poor relief as much as possible. Further, 1804 was a year of dearth, in which the demand for support skyrocketed; 1850 was a year of very low grain prices.
20 SAA *MA* 189/1 (13 March 1832).
21 OCMWA *BW*, Cop. I (16 December 1845).
22 SAA *MA* 189/1 (29 June 1846).
23 OCMWA *BW*, Cop. I (1 March 1850).
24 See Appendix 8.
25 SAA *MA* 3532, nos 12–18. See also OCMWA *BW*, Cop. I, 6 (29 August 1821, 11 February 1822, and 30 January 1823).
26 OCMWA *BW*, Cop. I, 8 (1829).
27 Inter alia: OCMWA *BW*, Cop. I, 9 (3 May 1832), and Rep. I, 3 (7 February 1836).
28 OCMWA *BW*, Rep. II, 1 (18 July 1843).
29 It ought to be noted that the number of supported needy could vary strongly from month to month and even week to week. In February 1817, for example, it shot up to 33 per cent, while the annual average amounted to only 23·5 per cent. *MAPA*, 28 February 1817. See also OCMWA *BW*, Cop. I, 4 (27 January 1817), and RAA *PA*, H 112, 8 February 1817).
30 The example of the English county of Durham shows how carefully one must treat data based on institutional accounts. In 1844, the pitmen struck in the Houghton-le-Spring Union for 22 weeks. Although around 1,000 men and their families endured bitter poverty, the number of beneficiaries of outdoor relief barely rose, while the workhouses lodged only half again as many indigents as before; both increases accounted for less than 10 per cent of the strikers. It was not an isolated instance. Throughout Durham during the slump of the 1840s, a considerable body of needy were completely divorced from the formal mechanisms of support and were forced to rely upon other means of subsistence, particularly public work programmes. In 1847, a guardian testified for the Settlement and Poor Removal Committee 'that very many who were got rid of as applicants under the poor-rate were merely transferred to the list of the surveyor of the highways'. P. Dunkley, 'The Hungry Forties and the New Poor Law: A Case Study', *HJ* XVII (1974), pp. 339–40. See also J. Walvin, *English Urban Life, 1776–1851* (London, 1984), p. 88.
31 M. Kin, 'Economische transformaties en verarming te Gent in de achttiende eeuw', *TSG*, VIII (1982), pp. 34–53; Lebrun, Bruwier, Dhondt and Hansotte, *Essai*, pp. 118–38, 148–50, 155–7; E. Ducpétiaux, *Institutions de bienfaisance de la Belgique. Résumé statistique* (Brussels, 1852), pp. 4–5; Steensels, 'Tussenkomst', p. 450.
32 N. Haesenne-Peremans, *La pauvreté dans la région liégeoise à l'aube de la révolution industrielle. Un siècle de tension sociale, 1730–1830* (Paris, 1981), pp. 125–45, 228, 234; Lebrun, Bruwier, Dhondt and Hansotte, *Essai*, pp. 299–301, 335–6; Ducpétiaux, *Institutions*, pp. 8–9.
33 G. Kurgan-Van Hentenryck, 'Economie et transports', and J. De Belder, 'Structures socio-professionnelles', in *Bruxelles. Croissance d'une capitale*, edited by J. Stengers (Antwerp, 1979), pp. 216–34; M.-R. Thielemans, 'De aanzet van de industrie in het Brusselse voor 1830', *Drie-maandelijks Tijdschrift van het Gemeentekrediet van België*, 38 (1984), pp. 151–84. Data taken from A. Cosemans, *Bijdrage tot de demografische en sociale geschiedenis van de stad Brussel,*

1796–1846 (Brussels, 1967), pp. 118–22, and Van den Eeckhout, *Determinanten*, Vol. II, pp. 151–60.

34 M. Van der Auwera, 'Armoede en sociale politiek te Mechelen in de 16e en de 18e eeuw', *BG*, 59 (1976), p. 235; J. Van Borm, 'Aspecten van het vroege industriële pauperisme. Mechelen, 1822', *L'Hôpital belge*, XII (1968), p. 42; RAA *PA*, H 130; *EPA*, 1850, p. 76.

35 Bonenfant, *Problème*, p. 15; E. Darquenne, 'Les profils sociaux du département de Jemappes', *Anciens Pays et Assemblées d'Etats*, LVI (1972), p. 293; A. Lacroix, *Recherches sur le paupérisme et la bienfaisance publique en Hainaut, XVIIIe–XIXe siècles* (Mons, 1850), pp. 58–9.

36 J. Lothe, *Paupérisme et bienfaisance à Namur au XIXe siècle, 1815–1914* (Brussels, 1978), pp. 61–4, 385.

37 A. Quetelet, *Recherches statistiques sur le royaume des Pays-Bas* (Brussels, 1829); Ducpétiaux, *Institutions*, pp. 12–3. See also Demoulin, *Guillaume Ier*, p. 224.

38 RAA *PA*, H 130;

Chapter 10   On Relief: Occupations

1 J. Giele and G.J. van Oenen, 'De sociale structuur van de Nederlandse samenleving rond 1850', *Mededelingenblad. Orgaan van de Nederlandse Vereniging tot beoefening van de Sociale Geschiedenis*, no. 45 (1974), p. 25, and 'Theorie en praktijk van het onderzoek naar de sociale structuren', *TSG*, II (1976), pp. 173–5.

2 SAA *MA* 3532/0–32.

3 Hannes, *Bijdrage*, App. I–II, pp. 114–9.

4 See Appendix 9A.

5 Cf. Chevalier, *Classes laborieuses*, p. 426, who characterizes the clothing-trade in this period as 'the last refuge for the very weak'. See also E. Tardieu, 'L'industrie du vêtement pour hommes à Bruxelles', in *Les industries à domicile en Belgique* (Brussels, 1899).

6 See Appendix 9A.

7 See Appendix 9B.

8 See the comments of the poor-law administration in SAA *MA* 187.

9 SAA *MA* 182; *Notice sur les écoles gardiennes à Anvers, 1839–1857* (Leuven, 1857); H. Van Daele, *150 jaar stedelijk onderwijs te Antwerpen, 1819–1969* (Antwerp, 1969), pp. 87–8. The quotation comes from *Enquête sur la condition des classes ouvrières*, Vol. III, pp. 214–5.

10 See Appendix 9C.

11 *Enquête sur la condition des classes ouvrières*, Vol. II, pp. 194, 197–198, and Vol. III, p. 227. See also OCMWA *BW*, Bestuursraad, Box 'Verordeningen', 1841.

12 Calculations based on *RP*, 1846, p. 386, and H. Van Daele, *Geschiedenis van het stedelijk lager onderwijs te Antwerpen van 1830 tot 1872* (Brussels, 1972), pp. 251ff.

13 SAA *MA* 18 (April and June 1844); RAA *PA*, J 225 (28 August 1844, and 4 October 1848).

14 Data taken from H. Van Daele, 'Het ontstaan van de eerste stedelijke meisjesschool', *Antwerpen*, XIII (1967), pp. 84–91.

15 Cf. De Belder, *Elementen*, Vol. I, p. 70, and G. Vandenven, *Bijdrage tot een sociaal-demografische studie van de behoeftigen in de 19e eeuw* (Leuven Univ. thesis, 1966), p. 128.

16 Unfortunately, the Charity Bureau kept the register of 1860 totally differently from the preceding one: it mentioned the names of the heads of household but not the number and age of family members nor their occupation, income, or physical condition; such data were henceforth recorded in separate dossiers, all of which have been lost. The sole usable information in relation to the period 1860–1865 are the dates on which families were eventually struck off the poor list. Although only names of the heads of household were noted by the Charity Bureau, there is no danger of confusing two families: the administrators drew up concordances which allow the identification number of a family registered in the list of 1855–1859 to be traced in that of 1860–1865.

17 Cf. SAA *MA* 187. See also OCMWA *BW*, Cop. I, 1 (6 April 1802), and Rep. I, 1 (23 October 1811, and 9 May 1821).

18 Cf. J. Foster, *Class Struggle and the Industrial Revolution: Early Industrial Capitalism in Three English Towns* (London, 1974), pp. 98–9.

19 *Commission du Travail*, Vol. III, pp. 523–5.

20 C. Tindemans, *Mens, gemeenschap en maatschappij in de toneelletterkunde van Zuid-Nederland, 1815–1914* (Ghent, 1973), *passim* (esp. pp. 163ff.)

Chapter 11   Philanthropy, Respectability and Social Control

1 Calculated from O. Vorlat-Raeymaeckers, 'De sociale toestand in Antwerpen, 1845—1850', *Noordgouw*, x (1970), p. 68 n. 84. See also J. Jacobs, *Rapport sur les oeuvres de charité existant à Anvers, présenté à l'assemblée générale des catholiques à Malines, dans la session de 1864* (Brussels, 1865).
2 J.B. Duroselle, *Les débuts du catholicisme social en France, 1822—1870* (Paris, 1957), pp. 154—97.
3 *Bulletin de la Société Saint-Vincent de Paul*, no. 1 (Paris, 1848), p. 159.
4 SAA *MA* 193/6bis; *Rapport sur les oeuvres de la Société de Saint-Vincent de Paul* (Antwerp, 1855—1856).
5 Quoted by P.F. Broeckaert, *Predicatie en arbeidersprobleem: Onderzoek naar de sociale opvattingen van de seculiere en reguliere clerus in Vlaanderen, 1800—1914* (Mechelen, 1963), p. 105.
6 Charles Périn quoted by A. Simon, 'De houding van het episcopaat', in *150 jaar katholieke arbeidersbeweging in België, 1789—1939*, edited by S.H. Scholl, Vol. I (Brussels, 1963), p. 137.
7 J. Art, *Kerkelijke structuur en pastorale werking in het bisdom Gent tussen 1830 en 1914* (Kortrijk and Heule, 1977), pp. 272—83.
8 P. Joye and R. Lewin, *L'Eglise et le movement ouvrier en Belgique* (Brussels, 1967), pp. 46—9. See also Broeckaert, *Predicatie*, pp. 100—22.
9 *Instruction sur les devoirs des présidents de la Société Saint-Vincent de Paul* (Paris, 1849 edn.); *Manuel abrégé de la Société de Saint-Vincent de Paul* (Brussels, 1855); Jacobs, *Rapport*, pp. 13—4.
10 *Rapports sur les oeuvres de la Société de Saint-Vincent de Paul* (Antwerp, 1847—1860).
11 Ducpétiaux, *Budgets*, pp. 54—6. See also Engel, *Lebenskosten*, App. I, p. 25.
12 RAA *PA*, J 225; M.J.C. Kramp, *L'école dominicale, considérée comme base fondamentale du bonheur de la classe ouvrière* (Antwerp, 1838); P. Visschers, *De zondagsscholen te Antwerpen van in de vroegste jaren tot op den huidigen dag* (Antwerp, 1847).
13 SAA *MA*, Stadsplakkaten, Grote Reeks (26 April 1850); EPA, 1850—1857; *Société d'Epargne pour l'achat de provisions d'hiver* (Antwerp, 1855—1861).
14 P. De Decker, *Mission sociale de la charité* (Brussels, 1854), pp. 8, 34—5.
15 SAA *MA* 187.
16 Ph. H. De Pillecyn, *Sociaal probleem en verhalend proza, 1830—1886. Een sociografische literatuurstudie* (Antwerp, 1967), p. 138.
17 OCMWA *BW*, PV, I (March 1847).
18 OCMWA *BW*, Bestuursraad, Box 'Verordeningen'.
19 OCMWA, Ateliers de Charité, Box 1.
20 F. Prims, *Antwerpen in 1830*, Vol. II (Antwerp, 1930), pp. 46—52; Lis, 'Revolte', pp. 344—7.
21 The quotation comes from Lis, 'Revolte', pp. 347—8. See also SAA *MA* 191/6, *MA* 462/1, no. 4, *MA* 1062/1, no. 3.
22 SAA *MA* 754/1—2; Prims, *Antwerpen in 1830*, Vol. II, pp. 77—80.
23 SAA *MA* 1073, no. 2 (23 December 1830).
24 Lis, 'Revolte', pp. 349—50.
25 SAA *MA* 191/4, no. 1 (2 March 1831).
26 SAA *MA* 1073, no. 2 (7 March 1831).
27 SAA *MA* 2682/20.
28 RAA *PA*, F 11; SAA *MA* 1065.
29 Lis, 'Revolte', pp. 355—65.
30 Information drawn from SAA *MA* 191/3 and Vorlat-Raeymaeckers, 'Sociale toestand', pp. 64—7.
31 SAA *MA* 189/1.
32 ARAB, Administration de la Sûreté publique, no. 124.
33 SAA *MA* 191/4, nos 8—17; RAA *PA*, J 225.
34 SAA *MA* 466/2, no. 4.
35 Kruithof, 'De sociale samenstelling', p. 218.
36 SAA *MA* 191/4, no. 5

Chapter 12   The Struggle for Self-Preservation

1 Calculated from De Belder, *Elementen*, Vol. II, pp. 14, 59, 68; Hannes, *Bijdrage*, App. I—II, pp. 11—15; *RP*, 1846, p. 386; *RP*, 1856, p. 162.
2 Calculated from De Belder, *Elementen*, Vol. II, pp. 8, 14, 50, 59, 68, and Hannes, *Bijdrage*, App. II—II, pp. 11—5.

3 M. Anderson, *Family Structure in Nineteenth-Century Lancashire* (Cambridge, 1971), pp. 133–4. See also Armstrong, *Stability*, pp. 165–6.
4 Around 75 per cent of them married in the late 1830s or in the course of the 1840s.
5 Recalculated from Hannes, *Bijdrage*, pp. 87–8.
6 Calculated from *ibid.*, App. I–II, pp. 11–5.
7 See, for example, SAA *MA* 187.
8 Data taken from Vrancken, *Cinquantaine*, pp. 142–143; Smits, *Demografische toestanden*, p. 121; *Stad Antwerpen. Gezondheidsdienst. Volksbeschrijvende en geneeskundige statistiek* (Antwerp, 1915), p. 2.
9 Cf. E. van de Walle, 'Illegitimacy in France during the Nineteenth Century', in *Bastardy and its Comparative History*, edited by P. Laslett (London, 1980), p. 270.
10 E. Geudens, *Recherches historiques sur l'origine des hospices des aliénés et des enfants trouvés à Anvers* (Antwerp, 1896), p. 54.
11 Data taken from L. Van Damme, *Misdadigheid te Antwerpen, 1765–1794* (Ghent Univ. thesis, 1973), p. 61; Vrancken, *Cinquantaine*, p. 142; M. Blom-Verlinden, 'Vondelingen en bestede kinderen te Gent en te Antwerpen, 1850–1815', *Annalen van de Belgische Vereniging voor Hospitaalgeschiedenis*, X (1972), pp. 77–129; H. Verheyen, *De schuif. Onderzoek naar het vondelingenvraagstuk te Antwerpen in de 19de eeuw, 1830–1870* (Ghent Univ. thesis, 1978), p. 246; Vorlat-Raeymaeckers, 'Sociale toestand', p. 173.
12 SAA *MA* 482, no. 4; OCMWA, *Rapport décennal, 1846 à 1855*.
13 Verheyen, *De schuif*, pp. 86–92.
14 See the perceptive remarks of P. Laslett, D. Levine and K. Wrightson in Laslett, ed., *Bastardy*, pp. 57, 184–5, 190–1.
15 Calculated from Hannes, *Bijdrage*, App. I–II, pp. 11–5; RP, 1856, p. 162; *Stad Antwerpen: Gezondheidsdienst*, p. 2.
16 Recalculated from Hannes, *Bijdrage*, p. 95.
17 Jacobs, *Rapport*, p. 17. See the perceptive remarks of L.A. Tilly and J.W. Scott, *Women, Work, and Family* (New Yor, 1978), pp. 97–8.
18 RAA *PA*, J 46 SAA *MA* 140/9; *Recueil des lois… concernant les établissements de bienfaisance*, Vol. I (Brussels, 1871), p. 103; *RVA*, 1850–1859; *EPA*, 1856, p. 224; *Exposé de la situation du royaume, 1851–1860*, Vol. I, pp. 99–107.
19 Ducpétiaux, *Institutions*, p. 63.
20 RAA *PA*, J 55; SAA *MA* 144/1–2; ARAB, Section IV, no. 163; E. Ducpétiaux, *Des moyens de soulager et de prévenir l'indigence et d'éteindre la mendicité* (Brussels, 1832), pp. 41–5.
21 ARAB, Section IV, no. 162 (1826); RAA *PA*, J 83/C1 (21 August 1840); R. de La Sagra, *Voyage en Hollande et en Belgique sous le rapport de l'instruction primaire, des établissements de bienfaisance et des prisons, dans les deux pays*, Vol. II (Paris, 1839), p. 159.
22 ARAB, Section IV, no. 163; *Exposé de la situation du royaume, 1851–1860*, Vol. I, p. 100^c.
23 E. Ducpétiaux, *De l'association dans les rapports avec l'amélioration du sort de la classe ouvrière* (Brussels, 1860), p. 272. See also H. Denis, *Les 'index numbers' des phénomènes moraux* (Brussels, 1911).
24 Calculated from Van Damme, *Misdadigheid*, pp. 75–82, and *RVA*, 1850–1859, *passim*.
25 SAA *MA* 187.
26 Van Damme, *Misdadigheid*, p. 114.
27 RAA *PA*, F 86; SAA *MA* 524(2), nos 1–3, and *MA* 525/1(1).
28 SAA *MA* 526/1(1), *MA* 2642/2; *RVA*, 1857.
29 SAA *MA* 527/1(5) and *MA* 2642/2.
30 SAA *MA* 526/1(4); *EPA*, 1857, p. 86.
31 Ducpétiaux, *Association*, p. 5.
32 SAA *MA* 450/81, *MA* 524(2), no. 7/2, and *MA* 525/2.

Chapter 13   Proletarian Networks

1 M. Anderson, *Approaches to the History of the Western Family, 1400–1914* (London, 1980), p. 79.
2 Anderson, *Family Structure*, *passim*.
3 See J. Quadagno, *Aging in Early Industrial Society* (New York, 1982), and *Old Age in Pre-Industrial Society*, edited by P.N. Stearns (New York, 1983).
4 Calculated from Hannes, *Bijdrage*, App. I–II, pp. 11–15, and RP, 1856, p. 156.
5 Perhaps this also suggests a sex differential in the strength of networks of obligations. See

J. Modell and T.K. Hareven, 'Transitions: Patterns of Timing', in *Transitions, the Family and the Life Course in Historical Perspective* (New York, 1978), p. 252.
6 SAA *MA* 187.
7 E. Geudens, *Le compte moral de l'An XII des hospices civils d'Anvers* (Antwerp, 1898), pp. 20–85, 160–7; *Gemeentebulletijn der stad Antwerpen* (1863), p. 166; *Compte moral et administratif de l'administration des hospices civils d'Anvers* (Antwerp, 1870), p. 5.
8 Jacobs, *Rapport*, pp. 23–5; P.J. Loos, *Geschiedenis der gasthuiszusters van Antwerpen sedert hun ontstaan tot op onze dagen* (Antwerp, 1912); Prims, *Antwerpen in 1830*, Vol. I, pp. 94–103, and *Sint-Carolusgesticht, 1852–1952* (Antwerp, 1952).
9 The cost of board varied between 200 and 300 francs *per annum*. The allowance which some boarders received from the Charity Bureau always fell short of these expenses. A certain P.J. Janssens, for example, an inmate of the old men's home run by the Brothers of Charity, had to find 300 francs a year, of which only one-fifth was provided by the Charity Bureau. By 1866, his income had fallen to such an extent that he repeatedly had to seek delays in payment. Although he wrote pitiously to the director of poor relief that 'death is far preferable to such a life of degradation', he failed to gain an extra allowance. SAA *MA* 191/4.
10 See, for example, *Gemeentebulletijn der stad Antwerpen* (1864), pp. 315–316. See also de Pillecyn, *Sociaal probleem*, pp. 143–144.
11 SAA *MA* 6199/2; Ducpétiaux, *Institutions*, p. 23.
12 Vorlat-Raeymaeckers, 'Sociale toestand', p. 177.
13 SAA *MA* 18; OCMWA, *Rapport décennal, 1846 à 1855*, p. 33.
14 OCMWA, Ateliers de charité, Boxes 2 and 4.
15 SAA *MA* 163/2.
16 Calculated from De Belder, *Elementen*, Vol. II, pp. 58–9, 67–8.
17 OCMWA *BW*, Rep. I, 1.
18 SAA *MA* 189/1.
19 OCMWA *BW*, Box 'Reglementen'.
20 SAA *MA* 3533.
21 OCMWA *BW*, Rep. I, 2 (8 May 1839).
22 OCMWA, Ateliers de Charité, Box 4, no. 2.
23 SAA *MA* 190/3b.
24 OCMWA, Ateliers de Charité, Box 1 (1817), and *Rapport décennal, 1846 à 1855*.
25 OCMWA *BW*, Rep. I, 1–2; SAA *MA* 189/1.
26 P.F. Van Kerckhoven, *Volksverhalen* (Antwerp, 1870 edn.), pp. 150–151.
27 P.F. Van Kerckhoven, *Jaek of een arm huisgezin* (Antwerp, 1842), and *Jan Reim* (Antwerp, 1852); D. Sleeckx, *In alle standen* (Brussels, 1851), and *In 't Schipperskwartier* (Brussels, 1861); A. Snieders, *De gasthuisnon* (Antwerp, 1855), and *Het zusterken der armen* (Antwerp, 1867). See also E. Van Bergen, *Antwerpen omstreeks 1850* (Antwerp, 1927), pp. 57–8, and de Pillecyn, *Sociaal probleem*, pp. 120–1. On the complexity, and significance to survival, of neighbourhood-based 'charitable' exchanges in nineteenth-century England, see the perceptive remarks of E. Ross, '"Fierce Questions and Taunts": Married Life in Working-Class London, 1870–1914', *Feminist Studies*, 8 (1982), pp. 575–602.
28 Anderson, *Family Structure*, pp. 152–60; B. Roberts, *Cities of Peasants. The Political Economy of Urbanization in the Third World* (London, 1978), pp. 136–52.
29 Without doubt, the discrepancy between the sexes must be ascribed to the fact that many women were domestic servants; the question remains, however, whether the reason they did not marry in Antwerp was because marriage would have terminated their employment, or whether during the term of their service they saved up for a trousseau with a view towards a wedding in their birthplace.
30 OCMWA *BW*, 'Liste des étrangers secourus', 1845–1855.
31 SAA *MA* 187.
32 *Inter alia*: OCMWA *BW*, Rep. I (28 April 1817, 9 May 1821, 13 March 1832, and 5 March 1842); SAA *MA* 439, *passim*. See also de Pillecyn, *Sociaal probleem*, pp. 57, 140, 161.
33 SAA *MA* 450/150–162. See also A. de Lattin, *De politie waakt* (Antwerp, 1946), pp. 101–3.
34 See J. Wilms, *Onder Sint-Andriestoren* (Antwerp, 1944), pp. 47–91, and *De parochie van miserie* (Antwerp, 1953), *passim*.

Conclusion

1 See O. Hufton, *The Poor of Eighteenth-Century France, 1750–1789* (Oxford, 1974), p. 69.
2 Foster, *Class Struggle*, p. 96.
3 G. Liebchen, 'Zu den Lebensbedingungen der unteren Schichten im Berlin des Vormärz', in *Untersuchungen zur Geschichte der frühen Industrialisierung vornehmlich im Wirtschaftsraum Berlin/Brandenburg*, edited by O. Büch (Berlin, 1971), pp. 294 and 311; F.D. Marquardt, 'Sozialer Aufstieg, sozialer Abstieg und die Entstehung der Berliner Arbeiterklasse, 1806–1848', *Geschichte und Gesellschaft*, I (1975), pp. 65–7; Kraus, *Unterschichten*, pp. 49–51, 67, 76.
4 Foster, *Class Struggle*, p. 95; Armstrong, *Stability*, pp. 59–60. See also N.F.R. Crafts, 'National Income Estimates and the British Standard of Living Debate: A Reappraisal of 1801–31', *Explorations in Economic History*, 17 (1980), pp. 176–188.
5 Codaccioni, *Inégalité*, pp. 86 and 141.
6 S. Holland, *Capital Versus the Regions* (London, 1976), p. 49.
7 J.-F. Bergier, 'The Industrial Bourgeoisie and the Rise of the Working Class, 1700–1914', in *The Fontana Economic History of Europe*, edited by C.M. Cipolla, Vol. III, *The Industrial Revolution* (London, 1973), p. 426.
8 Adelmann and Morris, 'Growth', p. 257.
9 Thompson, *The Making*, pp. 266–88, 309–34; R. Samuel, 'Workshop of the World: Steam Power and Hand Technology in Mid-Victorian Britain', *History Workshop Journal*, 3 (1977), pp. 6–72; Bythell, *Sweated Trades*, *passim*; J.A. Schmiechen, *Sweated Industries and Sweated Labour. The London Clothing Trades, 1860–1914* (Beckenham, 1984).

Appendix 1

1 SAA *MA* 478(7). See also ANP, F 20, no. 231. This source was statistically treated by De Belder, *Elementen*, Vol. II, pp. 134–8. The occupational data presented here slightly differ from those published by De Belder, who employed other methods of classification.

Appendix 2

1 De Belder, *Elementen*, Vol. II, pp. 339–61; Hannes, *Bijdrage*, App. I–II, pp. 73–91.
2 The data published by De Belder have been regrouped in order to make them correspond to the categories employed by Hannes

Appendix 3

1 For 1780: J. Craeybeckx, 'De prijzen van graan en brood te Antwerpen, 1608–1817', in *Documenten voor de geschiedenis van prijzen en lonen in Vlaanderen en Brabant*, edited by C. Verlinden, Vol. I (Bruges, 1959), p. 514. For 1827 and 1855: SAA *MA* 830/2, no. 2, and *MA* 5213, nos. 4–8; E. Scholliers, 'Prijzen en lonen te Antwerpen en in het Antwerpse, 16e–19e eeuw', in Verlinden, ed., *Dokumenten*, Vol. II (Bruges, 1965), pp. 948–9.

Appendix 6

1 For use of this method, see Jones, *Outcast London*, p. 371.
2 Calculations based on Hannes, *Bijdrage*, App. I–II, pp. 20–91.

Appendix 8

1 SAA *KK* 2112, *MA* 166/1; OCMWA *KH*, r. 870, no. 6.
2 SAA *MA* 166/1, *MA* 6199/1.
3 SAA *MA* 3533.
4 SAA *MA* 3532.
5 RAA *PA*, H 101–105; SAA *MA* 177/1–4; OCMWA, 'Proces-verbaalboeken', KBP-KBV.

6 ocmwa, Ateliers de Charité.
7 Compare, for example, saa *MA* 3532/10 with *MA* 3533/19 and *MA* 6199/2 (1821), or saa *MA* 3532/13 with *MA* 3533/22 and ocmwa *BW*, Cop. i, 7 (1824).
8 *RPA*, 1846, p. 95. Cf. A. Vermeersch, 'Pers en pauperisme in Vlaanderen', *Bijdragen voor de Geschiedenis der Nederlanden,* xiii (1959), p. 85.
9 Ducpétiaux, *Institutions,* pp. 4–5.
10 ocmwa *BW*, Cop. i (18 July 1850, and 25 July 1851); *Rapport décennal, 1846 à 1855.*
11 raa *PA*, j 170.

Bibliography

I MANUSCRIPT SOURCES

1 Archives Nationales, Paris

Series F 12: Commerce et industrie

606–607	Commerce et industrie de la Belgique (an IV–1810)
1563	Circulaire du 30 janvier 1806 sur le coton, dép. des Deux-Nèthes
1602	Relevés généraux des renseignements recueillis sur le chanvre et le lin (1810–1815), le coton (1810–1815), le drap (an XI–1815), la soie (1789–1812), les papeteries (1813) et les tanneries (1812–1813)
1616	Documents sur l'industrie, le commerce et l'agriculture des départements étrangers (an III–1814), dép. des Deux-Nèthes

Series F 14: Travaux publics

973	Comptabilité du Service des Ponts et Chaussées et de la Navigation (1792–1813), dép. des Deux-Nèthes
1117	Ports maritimes. Adjudications de travaux, devis, rapports, mémoires et plans (1790–1814), dép. des Deux-Nèthes

Series F 15: Hospices et secours

955–961	Hospices, Bureaux de Bienfaisance, Enfants Trouvés (an VI–1809), dép. des Deux-Nèthes

Series F 20: Statistiques

145	Statistiques départementales (an VIII–1812), dép. des Deux-Nèthes
231	Mémoires et tableaux statistiques (1793–1813), dép. des Deux-Nèthes

2 Algemeen Rijksarchief, The Hague

Ministerie van Binnenlandse Zaken

    Armwezen (1817–1829)
    Nationale Nijverheid (1818–1829)

Staatssecretarie (1815–1829)

3 Algemeen Rijksarchief, Brussels

Section IV: Ministère de la Justice

124	Administration de la Sûreté publique
163–164	Dossiers concernant l'administration de la colonie d'Hoogstraten (1831–1906)

Papiers Charles Rogier

316–322	Documents se rapportant au gouvernement de la province d'Anvers (1831–1839)
430–432	Affaires financières, économiques et sociales (1848–1860)

4 Rijksarchief, Antwerp

Series F: Police

5	Police (an IV–1854)
86	Prostitution (an VII–1849)
90	Police (an XI–1858)

Series H: Public Assistance

13	Charity Bureaux (an VI–1856)
112–124	Pauperism (1806–1860)
130–149	Charitable institutions (an III–1860)

Series J: Statistics

45–56	Dépôts de Mendicité, regulations and accounts (an IV–1868)
82–83	Dépôts de Mendicité, miscellaneous (1816–1859)
158–159	Civil registration (1779–1861)
168–171	Statistics (an IV–1856)
172–179	Population (an IV–1848)
203	Customs (an V–1857)
222–225	Industry (an IV–1858)
233	Workmen (an IV–1859)

5   Stadsarchief, Antwerp

Gilden en Ambachten

| 4202 | Linen-weavers |
| 4582 | Cotton-printing works |

Kerken en Kloosters

2110–2112	Almoners (1500–1790)
2127	Poor-law administration (1635–1789)
2207	Almoners (1685–1781)

Privilegekamer

255–261	Collection P.J. Van Setter
427–443	Minutes of F.M. De Baltin (1840–1773)
449–467	Minutes of P.J. Van Setter (1774–1794)
2857–2859	'Stadsplakkaten' (1785–1793)

Vierschaar

| 177 | 'Domicilieboeck' (1780–1795) |
| 1803 | 'Naemboeck der vremdelingen' (1780–1795) |

Modern Archief

15/1–45	Municipal corporation, minutes (an IV–1860)
16/1–6	Public works (1816–1858)
17–18	Public administration (an VI–1850)
161–163	Public assistance (1793–1863)
166	Civil Hospices (1789–1857)
182	Charity Bureau (an III–1824)
187–193	Charity Bureau and Workhouses (an IX–1860)
438–439	Public health (an IV–1859)
450/150–162	Police, Ward IV (1823–1853)
478	Statistics (an IV–1846)
482–483	Abandoned children (1796–1848)
493	Markets (1821–1859)
524–527	Prostitution (1798–1865)
630–633	Industry (1794–1840)
748/68	Cholera (1866–1867)
759–763	*Octrois*, miscellaneous (1794–1859)
766–769	*Octrois*, regulations (1798–1858)
805–806	*Octrois*, breweries and distilleries (1814–1860)
809–818	*Octrois*, food-stuffs (1816–1860)
826–831	*Octrois*, statistics (1796–1860)
868/1–3	Public works (an XI–1819)

937	Street-names (1779–1876)
1037–1038	Commerce (an XII–1880)
1055	Agriculture (an II–1849)
1065	Revolution of 1830
1073	Commission provisoire de Sûreté publique (1830–1833)
2634	Political events (1831)
2642	Etat nominatif des hôtels, auberges, cabarets et maisons publiques (1813)
2668/1–6	Police, foreigners (1803–1820)
2682	Police, correspondence (1830–1832)
3523/8–66	Town-accounts (1808–1860)
3532/0–52	Town-budget (1807–1860)
3533/9–54	Accounts of the Charity Bureau (1811–1860)
6197	Dock-workers in receipt of relief (1829–1830)
6199/1	Compte moral explicatif et justificatif du Bureau de Bienfaisance de la ville d'Anvers de l'an XIII
6199/2	Compte moral du secours à domicile pour l'an 1818
6844	Public administration (1833–1839)
9081–9089	Public assistance (1815–1822)
26906–26910	*Octrois*, receipts (1806–1810)

6 Openbaar Centrum voor Maatschappelijk Welzijn, Antwerp

Kamer van de Huisarmen

866	'Memorieboek' (1652–1783)
870	'Nieuwe Bestiering' (1779–1791)

Collection factice

Pièces écrites et imprimées relatives à la gestion des biens de l'administration des pauvres (1779–1790)

Library

381/1–4	'Nieuwe Bestiering', miscellaneous (1779–1790)

Box 'Nieuwe Bestiering' (1779–1780)

Bureel van Weldadigheid

Bestuursraad, Box 'Verordeningen' (1790–1865)
Box 'Reglementen' (1791–1867)
'Proces-verbaalboeken' (1802–1850)
Liste des étrangers secourus (1845–1855)
Cop. I–II: Livres des copies des lettres (1799–1857)
Rep. I–III: Analyses des lettres reçues (1798–1859)

Ateliers de Charité

Boxes 1–4 (1802–1867)

Rapport décennal, 1846 à 1855

Poor lists: 1780, 1804, 1827, 1840, 1850, and 1855–1865

II PRINTED SOURCES

Abolition des octrois communaux en Belgique. Documents et discussions parlementaires, 2 vols. (Brussels, 1860).

Avondts, G., and Scholliers, P., *Gentse prijzen, huishuren en budgetonderzoeken in de 19e en 20e eeuw* (Brussels, 1977).

Commission du Travail, 4 vols. (Brussels, 1887).

Compte moral et administratif de l'administration des hospices civils d'Anvers (Antwerp, 1870).

Craeybeckx, J., 'De prijzen van granen en brood te Antwerpen, 1608–1817', in *Dokumenten voor de geschiedenis van prijzen en lonen in Vlaanderen en Brabant*, edited by C. Verlinden, Vol. I (Bruges, 1959), pp. 504–22.

De Decker, P., *Mission sociale de la charité* (Brussels, 1854).

De Gérando, J.M., *De la bienfaisance publique*, 2 vols (Brussels, 1839).

De Grave, O.F.J., *Commentaire des lois sur le domicile de secours* (Ghent, 1855).

De La Sagra, R., *Voyage en Hollande et en Belgique sous le rapport de l'instruction primaire, des établissements de bienfaisance et des prisons, dans les deux pays*, 2 vols. (Paris, 1839).

Digand, F., *Abolition complète des droits d'octroi* (Antwerp, 1847).

Ducpétiaux, E., *Budgets économiques des classes ouvrières en Belgique. Subsistance, salaires, population* (Brussels, 1855).

Ducpétiaux, E., *De l'association dans les rapports avec l'amélioration du sort de la classe ouvrière* (Brussels, 1860).

Ducpétiaux, E., *Des moyens de soulager et de prévenir l'indigence et d'éteindre la mendicité* (Brussels, 1832).

Ducpétiaux, E., *Institutions de bienfaisance. Résume statistique* (Brussels, 1852).

Ducpétiaux, E., *Le paupérisme en Belgique. Causes et remèdes* (Brussels, 1844).

Enquête sur la condition des classes ouvrières et sur le travail des enfants, 3 vols (Brussels, 1846–1848).

Geudens, E., *Le Compte Moral de l'an XIII des Hospices civils d'Anvers* (Antwerp, 1898).

Hermans, L.M., *Krotten en sloppen. Een onderzoek naar den woningtoestand te Amsterdam, ingesteld in opdracht van den Amsterdamschen Bestuursraad* (Amsterdam, 1975 edn.).

Instructiën voor de Nieuwe Bestiering van den Algemeynen Aermen binnen de stad Antwerpen (Antwerp, 1779).

Instruction sur les devoirs des Présidents de la Société Saint-Vincent de Paul (Paris, 1849 edn.).

Jacobs, J., *Rapport sur les oeuvres de charité existant à Anvers, présenté à l'assemblée générale des catholiques à Malines, dans la session de 1864* (Brussels, 1865).

Kramp, M.J.C., *L'école dominicale considérée comme base fondamentale du bonheur de la classe ouvrière* (Antwerp, 1838).

Lacroix, A., *Recherches sur le paupérisme et la bienfaisance publique en Hainaut, XVIIIe–XIXe siècles* (Mons, 1850).

Manuel abrégé de la Société Saint-Vincent de Paul (Brussels, 1855).

Mareska, J., and Heyman, J., *Enquête sur le travail et la condition physique et morale des ouvriers employés dans les manufactures de coton à Gand* (Ghent, 1846).

Mayhew, H., *London Labour and the London Poor*, 4 vols. (New York, 1968 edn.).

Mémorial administratif de la province d'Anvers (Antwerp, 1815–).

Notice sur les écoles gardiennes à Anvers, 1839–1857 (Leuven, 1857).

Octrois communaux. Rapport addressé au Ministre de l'Intérieur par la commission de révision instituée en vertu de l'arrêté royal du 9 novembre 1847 (Brussels, 1848).

Pasinomie ou collection complète des lois, décrets, arrêtés et règlements généraux qui peuvent être invoqués en Belgique, 1st ser., *1789–1814* (Brussels, 1833–1836).

Quetelet, A., *Recherches statistiques sur le royaume des Pays-Bas* (Brussels, 1829).

Quetelet, A., 'Sur les anciens recensements de la population belge', *Bulletin de la Commission centrale de Statisque*, III (1847).

Rapport de la Commission médicale de la ville d'Anvers: L'épidémie de choléra, 1866 (Antwerp, 1867).

Rapport sur l'administration et la situation des affaires de la ville d'Anvers (Antwerp, 1837–).

Rapport sur les octrois communaux de Belgique présenté à la Chambre des Représentants le 28 janvier 1845 par le Ministre de l'Intérieur, 2 vols. (Brussels, 1845).

Rapport sur les oeuvres de la Société de Saint-Vincent de Paul. Conférences d'Anvers (Antwerp, 1846).

Rapport sur le travail des enfants et la condition des ouvriers dans la province d'Anvers, par Berchem, C. Broeckx, J. Jacques, J. Koyen et F.J. Matthysens, rapporteurs, addressé à M. le Gouverneur de la province d'Anvers (Antwerp, 1844).

Recensement général de l'industrie. 15 octobre 1846 (Brussels, 1851).

Recensement général de la population. 15 octobre 1846 (Brussels, 1849).

Recensement général de la population. 31 décembre 1856 (Brussels, 1861).

Recueil des lois concernant les établissements de beinfaisance, 2 vols. (Brussels, 1871).

Scholliers, E., 'Antwerpse merkuriale van granen, brood, ardappelen, boter en vlees in de 19e eeuw', in *Documenten voor de geschiedenis van prijzen en lonen in Vlaanderen en Brabant*, ed. C. Verlinden, Vol. II (Bruges, 1965), pp. 941–61.

Scholliers, E., 'Prijzen en lonen te Antwerpen en in het Antwerpse, 16e–19e eeuw', *ibid.*, pp. 641–940.

Sleeckx, D., *In alle standen* (Brussels, 1851).

Sleeckx, D., *In 't Schipperskwartier* (Brussels, 1861).

Snieders, A., *De gasthuisnon* (Antwerp, 1855).

Snieders, A., *Het zusterken der armen* (Antwerp, 1867).

Société d'Epargne pour l'achat de provisions d'hiver (Antwerp, 1855–).

Stad Antwerpen. Gezondheidsdienst. Volksbeschrijvende en geneeskundige statistiek (Antwerp, 1915).

Stevens, E., 'Notice sur les octrois communaux de Belgique', *Bulletin de la Commission centrale de statistique*, III (1847).

Traité touchant la suppression de la mendicité et l'administration des pauvres dans la ville d'Anvers (Antwerp, 1780).

Van Bergen, E., *Antwerpen omstreeks 1850* (Antwerp, 1927).

Van den Eeckhout, P., and Scholliers, P., *De Brusselse huishuren, 1800–1940* (Brussels, 1940).

Van Kerckhoven, P.F., *Jaek of een arm huisgezin* (Antwerp, 1842).
Van Kerckhoven, P.F., *Jan Reim* (Antwerp, 1892).
Van Kerckhoven, P.F., *Volksverhalen* (Antwerp, 1870 edn.).
Visschers, P., *De zondagsscholen te Antwerpen van in de vroegste jaren tot op den huidigen dag* (Antwerp, 1847).
Vranckcken, L.H.J., *La Cinquantaine. Notice historique et statistique sur la vaccine depuis son introduction à Anvers en 1810* (Antwerp, 1851).
Wilms, J., *De parochie van miserie* (Antwerp, 1953 edn.).
Wilms, J., *Onder Sint-Andriestoren* (Antwerp, 1944 edn.).

III UNPUBLISHED THESES

De Belder, J., *Elementen van sociale identificatie van de Antwerpse bevolking op het einde van de XVIIIde eeuw. Een kwantitatieve studie*, 2 vols. (Ghent Univ. Ph.D. thesis, 1974).
De Visser, J., *De 'industrialisatie' van de Gentse katoennijverheid, 1750–1850* (Ghent Univ. thesis, 1977).
Hannes, J., *Bijdrage tot de ontwikkeling van een kwatitatief-kritische methode in de sociale geschiedschrijving* (Ghent Univ. Ph.D. thesis, 1969).
Smits, A., *Demografische toestanden van de stad Antwerpen in de jaren 1810–1820* (Leuven Univ. thesis, 1962).
Thijs, A.K.L., *Van werkwinkel tot fabriek. De textielnijverheid te Antwerpen van het einde der vijftiende tot het begin der negentiende eeuw* (Ghent Univ. Ph.D. thesis, 1978).
Van Damme, L., *Misdadigheid te Antwerpen, 1765–1794* (Ghent Univ. thesis, 1973).
Van den Eeckhout, P., *Determinanten van het 19de-eeuws sociaal-economisch leven te Brussel. Hun betekenis voor de laagste bevolkingsklassen* (Brussels, Univ. Ph.D. thesis, 1980).
Vandenven, G., *Bijdrage tot een sociaal-demografische studie van de behoeftigen in de 19e eeuw* (Leuven Univ. thesis, 1966).
Veraghtert, K., *De havenbeweging te Antwerpen tijdens de negentiende eeuw. Een kwantitatieve benadering*, 4 vols. (Leuven Univ. Ph.D. thesis, 1977).
Verheydt, M.-L., *De voedingstoestanden te Brussel op basis van de octrooien en accijnzen, 1740–1860* (Brussels Univ. thesis, 1976).
Verheyen, H., *De schuif. Onderzoek naar het vondelingenvraagstuk te Antwerpen in de 19de eeuw, 1830–1870* (Ghent Univ. thesis, 1978).
Willemse, E., *Het ontstaan en de ontwikkeling van het Belgisch verzekeringswezen, 1819–1873* (Brussels Univ. thesis, 1974).

IV SECONDARY WORKS

Abel, W., *Massenarmut und Hungerkrisen im vorindustriellen Deutschland* (Göttingen, 1972).
Abel, W., *Massenarmut und Hungerkrisen im vorindustriellen Europa. Versuch einer synopsis* (Hamburg-Berlin, 1974).
Abel, W., *Stufen der Ernährung. Eine historische Skizze* Göttingen, 1981).

Abel-Smith, B., and Townsend, P., *The Poor and the Poorest* (London, 1965).

Adelman, I., and Morris, C. Taft, 'Growth and Impoverishment in the Middle of the Nineteenth Century', *World Development*, 6 (1978), pp. 245–73.

Adelmann, G., 'Quellen zur Geschichte des belgischen Baumwollgewerbes beim Ueber-gang von der vorindustriellen zur industriellen Zeit, 1760–1815', in *Histoire économique de la Belgique. Traitement des sources et état des questions. Actes du Colloque de Bruxelles, 17–19 Nov. 1971* (Brussels, 1972), pp. 127–44.

Anderson, M., *Approaches to the History of the Western Family* (London, 1980).

Anderson, M., *Family Structure in Nineteenth-Century Lancashire* (Cambridge, 1971).

Anderson, M., 'Urban Migration in Nineteenth-Century Lancashire. Some Insights into Two Competing Hypotheses', *Annales de Démographie historique* (1971), pp. 13–26.

Antwerpen in de XVIIIde eeuw. Instellingen. Economie. Cultuur (Antwerp, 1952).

Armstrong, A., *Stability and Change in an English Town: A Social Study of York, 1701–51* (Cambridge, 1974).

Art, J., *Kerkelijke struktuur en pastorale werking in het bisdom Gent tussen 1830 en 1914* (Kortrijk-Heule, 1977).

Atkinson, A.B., *The Economics of Inequality* (Oxford, 1975).

Atkinson, A.B., *Poverty in Britain and the Reform of Social Security* (Cambridge, 1968).

Baar, L., *Die Berliner Industrie in der industriellen Revolution* (Berlin, 1966).

Baetens, R., *De nazomer van Antwerpens welvaart. De diaspora en het handelshuis De Groote tijdens de eerste helft der 17de eeuw*, 2 vols. (Brussels, 1976).

Bairoch, P., 'Geographical Structure and Trade Balance of European Foreign Trade from 1800 to 1970', *Journal of European Economic History*, III (1974), pp. 557–608.

Baudet, H., and van der Meulen, H. (eds.), *Consumer Behaviour and Economic Growth in the Modern Economy* (London and Canberra, 1982).

Beckerman, W., *Poverty and the Impact of Income Maintenance Programmes in Four Developed Countries* (Geneva, 1979).

Bédarida, F., 'Londres au milieu du XIXe siècle: une analyse de structure sociale', *Annales. E.S.C.*, XXIII (1968), pp. 268–95.

Beetemé, G., *Antwerpen, moederstad van handel en kunst*, 2 vols. (Antwerp, 1893).

Beke, Ph., 'Aspecten van de industriële ontplooiing in het Brusselse: een overzicht van de katoenverwerkende nijverheid in de Anderlechtse deelgemeente Kuregem, 1787–1830', *Belgisch Tijdschrift voor Nieuwste Geschiedenis*, XII (1981), pp. 741–73.

Bergeron, L., 'Problèmes économiques de la France napoléonienne', *Revue d'Histoire moderne et contemporaine*, 17 (1970), pp. 469–505.

Bergier, J.-F., 'The Industrial Bourgeoisie and the Rise of the Working Class', in *The Fontana Economic History of Europe*, ed. C.M. Cipolla, Vol. III, *The Industrial Revolution* (London, 1973), pp. 397–451.

Blockmans, F., 'De bevolkingscijfers', in *Antwerpen in de XVIIIde eeuw*, pp. 395–412.

Blom-Verlinden, M., 'Vondelingen en bestede kinderen te Gent en te Antwerpen, 1750–1815', *Annalen van de Belgische Vereniging voor Hospitaalgeschiedenis*, X (1972), pp. 77–129.

Bonenfant, P., *Le problème du paupérisme en Belgique à la fin de l'Ancien Régime* (Brussels, 1934).

Borscheid, P., *Textilarbeiterschaft in der Industrialisierung. Soziale Lage und Mobilität in Württemberg im 19. Jahrhundert* (Stuttgart, 1978).

Boumans, R., *Het Antwerps stadsbestuur voor en tijdens de Franse overheersing* (Bruges, 1965).

Bouwstoffen voor de geschiedenis van Antwerpen in de XIXde eeuw. Instellingen. Economie. Cultuur (Antwerp, 1964).

Briavoine, N.M., *De l'industrie en Belgique. Causes de décadence et de prospérité*, 2 vols. (Brussels, 1839).

Broeckaert, P.F., *Predicatie en arbeidersprobleem. Onderzoek naar de sociale opvattingen van de seculiere en reguliere clerus in Vlaanderen, 1800–1914* (Mechelen, 1963).

Brulez, W., 'De handel', in *Antwerpen in de XVIde eeuw* (Antwerp, 1975), pp. 109–42.

Bruneel, Cl., 'La population du duché de Brabant en 1755', *Bijdragen tot de Geschiedenis*, 58 (1975), pp. 220–83.

Bythell, D., *The Handloom Weavers: A Study of the English Cotton Industry during the Industrial Revolution* (Cambridge, 1969).

Bythell, D., *The Sweated Trades: Outwork in Nineteenth-Century Britain* (London, 1978).

Cauderlier, E., *Les boissons alcooliques et leurs effets sociaux en Belgique d'après les documents officiels* (Brussels, 1883).

Chassagne, S., 'L'enquête dite de Champagny, sur la situation de l'industrie cotonnière française au début de l'Empire, 1805–1806', *Revue d'Histoire économique et sociale*, 54 (1976), pp. 336–70.

Chevalier, L., *Classes laborieuses et classes dangereuses à Paris pendant la première moitié du XIXe siècle* (Paris, 1969 edn.).

Chevalier, L., *La formation de la population parisienne au XIXe siècle* (Paris, 1960).

Coates, K., and Silburn, R., *Poverty: The Forgotten Englishmen* (London, 1970).

Codaccioni, F.-P., *De l'inégalité sociale dans une grande ville industrielle. Le drame de Lille de 1850 à 1914* (Lille, 1976).

Content, A.-C., 'L'habitat ouvrier à Bruxelles au XIXe siècle', *Belgisch Tijdschrift voor Nieuwste Geschiedenis*, VIII (1977), pp. 501–16.

Cosemans, A., *De bevolking van Brabant in de XVIIe en XVIIIe eeuw* (Brussels, 1939).

Cosemans, A., *Bijdrage tot de demografische en sociale geschiedenis van de stad Brussel, 1796–1846* (Brussels, 1967).

Coveliers, L., *Arendonk* (Arendonk, 1937).

Craeybeckx, J., 'De handarbeiders. De 17de en de 18de eeuw', in *Flandria Nostra*, I (Antwerp, 1957), pp. 281–330.

Crafts, N.F.R., 'National Income Estimates and the British Standard of Living Debate: A Reappraisal of 1801–1831', *Explorations in Economic History*, 17 (1980), pp. 176–88.

Crawford, S.C., *Domestic Service in Eighteenth-Century France* (London, 1980).

Crouzet, F., 'Wars, Blockade, and Economic Change in Europe, 1792–1815', *Journal of Economic History*, XXIV (1964), pp. 567–88.

Dardel, P., *Commerce, industrie et navigation à Rouen et au Havre au XVIIIe siècle. Rivalité croissante entre les deux ports: La conjoncture* (Rouen, 1966).

Darquenne, R., 'Les profils sociaux du département de Jemappes', *Anciens Pays et Assemblées d'Etats*, LVI (1972), pp. 279–306.

Daumard, A. (ed.), *Les fortunes françaises au XIXe siècle* (Paris-The Hague, 1973).

Daumard, A., *Maisons de Paris et propriétaires parisiens au XIXe siècle* (Paris, 1965).

Daumard, A., 'Quelques remarques sur le logement des Parisiens au XIXe siècle', *Annales de Démographie historique* (1975), pp. 49–64.

De Belder, J., 'Beroep of bezit als criterium voor de sociale doorsnede', *Tijdschrift voor Sociale Geschiedenis*, II (1976), pp. 257–79.

De Belder, J., 'De behuizing te Antwerpen op het einde van de XVIIIe eeuw', *Belgisch Tijdschrift voor Nieuwste Geschiedenis*, VIII (1977), pp. 367–446.

De Belder, J., 'De gehiërarchiseerde statische doorsnede als vertrekpunt voor de studie van demografische gedragspatronen. Casus: de Antwerpse bevolking op het einde van de XVIIIde eeuw', in *Demografische evoluties en gedragspatronen van de 9de tot de 20ste eeuw in de Nederlanden* (Ghent, 1977), pp. 1–81.

De Jouvenel, B., *Napoléon et l'économie dirigée: Le blocus continental* (Brussels-Paris, 1942).

Delacroix, S.C., *Défrichement des terrains incultes dans la Campine belge et les autres contrées de la Belgique* (Paris, 1860).

De La Gorce, P.M., *La France pauvre* (Paris, 1965).

Deleeck, H., *Bestaansonzekerheid en sociale zekerheid* (Brussels, 1978).

De Metsenaere, M., 'Migraties in de gemeente Sint-Joost-ten-Node in het midden van de negentiende eeuw', *Taal en Sociale Integratie*, Vol. IV (Brussels, 1978), pp. 81–152.

Demoulin, R., *Guillaume Ier et la transformation économique des provinces belges, 1815–1830* (Liège, 1938).

Denis, H., *Les 'index numbers' des phénomènes moraux* (Brussels, 1911).

De Pillecyn, Ph. H., *Sociaal probleem en verhalend proza, 1830–1886. Een sociografische literatuurstudie* (Antwerp, 1967).

Despretz-Van de Casteele, S., 'Het protectionisme in de Zuidelijke Nederlanden gedurende de tweede helft der 17e eeuw', *Tijdschrift voor Geschiedenis*, 78 (1965), pp. 294–317.

De Wever, F., 'Pachtprijzen in Vlaanderen en Brabant in de achttiende eeuw. Bijdrage tot de konjunktuurstudie', *Tijdschrift voor Geschiedenis*, 85 (1972), pp. 180–204.

Dhondt, J., 'The Cotton Industry at Ghent during the French Régime', in *Essays in European Economic History*. Edited by F. Crouzet, W.H. Chaloner and W.M. Stern (London, 1969), pp. 15–52.

Dhondt, J. (ed.), *Geschiedenis van de socialistische arbeidersbeweging in België* (Antwerp, 1960).

Dhondt, J., and Bruwier, M., 'The Industrial Revolution in the Low Countries, 1700–1914', in *The Fontana Economic History of Europe*, ed. C.M. Cipolla, Vol. V, *The Emergence of Industrial Societies*, Part 1 (London, 1973), pp. 329–66.

Donnet, F., *Notice historique et statistique sur le raffinage et les raffineurs de sucre à Anvers* (Antwerp, 1892).

Dries, M., 'De openbare weldadigheid te Antwerpen op het einde van het Oud Regiem', *Bijdragen tot de Geschiedenis*, 8 (1930), pp. 237–54.

Dunkley, P., The Hungry Forties and the New Poor Law: A Case Study', *Historical Journal*, XVII (1974), pp. 329–46.

Duroselle, J.B., *Les débuts du catholicisme social en France, 1822–1870* (Paris, 1957).

Dyos, H.J., 'Railways and Housing in Victorian London', *Journal of Transport History*, II (1955), pp. 11–21, 90–100.

Dyos, H.J., and Wolff, M. (eds.), *The Victorian City: Images and Realities*, 2 vols (London-Boston, 1973).

Engel, E., *Die Lebenskosten belgischer Arbeiterfamilien früher und jetzt* (Dresden, 1895).

Engelsing, R., 'Hanseatische Lebenshaltungen und Lebenshaltungskosten im 18. und 19. Jahrhundert', in *Zur Sozialgeschichte deutschen Mittel- und Unterschichten* (Göttingen, 1973), pp. 26–50.

Fabius, L., *La France inégale* (Paris, 1975).

Fassbinder, H., *Berliner Arbeiterviertel, 1800–1918* (Berlin, 1975).

Fiérain, J., 'Croissance et mutation de l'économie, 1802–1914', in *Histoire de Nantes*, ed. P. Bois (Toulouse, 1977), pp. 319–37.

Fiérain, J., *Les raffineries de sucre des ports en France, XIXe-début du XXe siècle* (Dissertations in European Economic History, New York, 1977).

Fischer, W., 'Soziale Unterschichten im Zeitalter der Frühindustrialisierung', *International Review of Social History*, 8 (1963), pp. 115–35.

Fohlen, Cl., *L'industrie textile au temps du second Empire* (Paris, 1956).

Foster, J., *Class Struggle and the Industrial Revolution. Early Industrial Capitalism in Three English Towns* (London, 1974).

Gadisseur, J., 'La production industrielle au XIXe siècle en Belgique: construction de l'indice', in *Histoire économique de la Belgique. Traitement des sources et état des questions: Actes du Colloque de Bruxelles, 17–19 Nov. 1971, Ve et VIe sections* (Brussels, 1973), pp. 79–96.

Garden, M., 'L'attraction de Lyon à la fin de l'Ancien Régime', *Annales de Démographie historique* (1970), pp. 205–22.

Garden, M., *Lyon et les Lyonnais au XVIIIe siècle* (Paris, 1970).

Gauldie, E., *Cruel Habitations: A History of Working-Class Housing, 1780–1918* (London, 1974).

George, V., and Lawson, R. (eds.), *Poverty and Inequality in Common Market Countries* (London, 1980).

Geudens, E., *Recherches historiques sur l'origine des hospices des aliénés et des enfants trouvés à Anvers* (Antwerp, 1896).

Giele, J., and Van Oenen, G.J., 'De sociale structuur van de Nederlandse samenleving rond 1850', *Mededelingenblad van de Nederlandse Vereniging tot beoefening van de sociale geschiedenis*, no. 45 (1974), pp. 2–33.

Giele, J., and Van Oenen, G.J., 'Theorie en praktijk van het onderzoek naar de sociale structuren', *Tijdschrift voor Sociale Geschiedenis*, II (1976), pp. 67–86.

Goossens, M., 'Een negentiende-eeuws heidedorp in transformatie: Kalmthout, 1835–1910', *Bijdragen tot de Geschiedenis*, 67 (1984), pp. 197–261.

Kin, M., 'Economische transformaties en verarming te Gent in de achttiende eeuw', *Tijdschrift voor Sociale Geschiedenis*, VIII (1982), pp. 34–53.

Kincaid, J.C., 'Poverty in the Welfare State', in *Demystifying Social Statistics*, ed. J. Irvine, I. Miles and J. Evans (London, 1979), pp. 190–211.

Klep, P.M.M., *Bevolking en arbeid in transformatie: Een onderzoek in Brabant, 1700–1900* (Nijmegen, 1981).

Klep, P.M.M., *Groeidynamiek en stagnatie in een agrarisch grensgebied: De economische ontwikkeling in de Noordantwerpse Kempen en de Baronie van Breda, 1750–1850* (Tilburg, 1973).

Köllmann, W., *Sozialgeschichte der Stadt Barmen im 19. Jahrhundert* (Tübingen, 1960).

Kolko, G., *Wealth and Power in the United States* (New York, 1962).

Kraus, A., *Die Unterschichten Hamburgs in der ersten Hälfte des 19. Jahrhunderts* (Stuttgart, 1965).

Kruithof, J., 'De demografische ontwikkeling in de XIXe eeuw', in *Bouwstoffen*, pp. 508–43.

Kruithof, J., 'De sociale samenstelling van de bevolking te Antwerpen, Brussel, Gent en Luik in 1846–7', *Handelingen der Maatschappij voor Geschiedenis en Oudheidkunde te Gent*, new ser., XI (1957), pp. 197–235.

Kula, W., 'Recherches comparatives sur la formation de la classe ouvrière', in *Première Conférence internationale d'Histoire économique* (Paris-The Hague, 1960), pp. 510–23.

Labbens, J., *Le quart-monde: La pauvreté dans la société industrielle* (Paris, 1969).

Lachiver, M., *La population de Meulan du XVIIe au XIXe siècle, 1600–1870* (Paris, 1969).

Lampard, E.E., 'The History of Cities in Economically Advanced Areas', *Economic Development and Cultural Change*, III (1965), pp. 81–136.

Laslett, P. (ed.), *Bastardy and its Comparative History* (London, 1980).

Laurent, R., 'Une source: les archives d'octroi', *Annales. E.S.C.*, XI (1956), pp. 197–204.

Lebrun, P., Bruwier, M., Dhondt, J., and Hansotte, G., *Essai sur la révolution industrielle en Belgique, 1770–1847* (Brussels, 1979).

Lees, L., 'Mid-Victorian Migration and the Irish Economy', *Victorian Studies*, XV (1976), pp. 25–43.

Leleux, F., *A l'aube du capitalisme et de la révolution industrielle: Liévin Bauwens, industriel gantois* (Paris, 1969).

Léon, P., Crouzet, F., and Gascon, R. (eds.), *L'industrialisation en Europe au XIXe siècle: Cartographie et typologie* (Paris, 1972).

Lévy-Leboyer, M., *Les banques européennes et l'industralisation internationale dans la première moitié du XIXe siècle* (Paris, 1964).

Lewinski, J., *L'évolution industrielle de la Belgique* (Brussels, 1911).

Liebchen, G., 'Zu den Lebensbedingungen der unteren Schichten im Berlin des Vormärz', in *Untersuchungen zur Geschichte der frühen Industrialisierung vornehmlich im Wirtschaftsraum Berlin/Brandenburg*. Edited by O. Büch (Berlin, 1971), pp. 275–314.

Lis, C., 'Peilingen naar het belang van de steun verleend door het Bureel van Weldadigheid te Antwerpen, 1836–75', *Annalen van de Belgische Vereniging voor Hospitaalgeschiedenis*, VI (1968), pp. 81–120.

Lis, C., 'Revolte en Repressie: De omwentelingsjaren 1830–1831 te Antwerpen', *Belgisch Tijdschrift voor Nieuwste Geschiedenis*, III (1972), pp. 333–65.

Lis, C., 'Sociale politiek in Antwerpen (1779)', *Tijdschrift voor Sociale Geschiedenis*, II (1976), pp. 146–66.

Lis, C., 'Woontoestanden en gangensaneringen te Antwerpen in het midden der 19e eeuw', *Belgisch Tijdschrift voor Nieuwste Geschiedenis*, I (1969), pp. 93–131.

Lis, C., and Hannes, J., 'De sociale hiërarchie in de woningbouw: Antwerpen omstreeks 1834', *Belgisch Tijdschrift voor Nieuwste Geschiedenis*, I (1969), pp. 86–92.

Lis, C., and Soly, H., 'Food Consumption in Antwerp between 1807 and 1859: A Contribution to the Standard of Living Debate', *Economic History Review*, 2nd ser., XXX (1977), pp. 460–86.

Lis, C., and Soly, H., *Poverty and Capitalism in Pre-Industrial Europe* (Atlantic Highlands, New Jersey, 1979).

Lombaerde, P., 'De militaire werken van Louis-Charles Boistard en Simon Bernard te Antwerpen tijdens het eerste keizerrijk', *Belgisch Tijdschrift voor Militaire Geschiedenis*, 25 (1983), pp. 285–328.

Loos, P.J., *Geschiedenis der gasthuiszusters van Antwerpen sedert hun ontstaan tot op onze dagen* (Antwerp, 1912).

Lothe, J., *Paupérisme et bienfaisance à Namur au XIXe siècle, 1815–1914* (Brussels, 1978).

Lucassen, J., *Naar de kusten van de Noordzee. Trekarbeid in Europees perspectief, 1600–1900* (Gouda, 1984).

Manifeste des déshérités (Brussels, 1969).

Marquardt, F.D., 'Sozialer Aufstieg, sozialer Abstieg und die Entstehung der Berliner Arbeiterklasse, 1806–1848', *Geschichte und Gesellschaft*, I (1975), pp. 43–77.

Mattheessens, J.-C. and M., 'Un procès sous le premier Empire: l'octroi d'Anvers, 1811–1813', *Revue du Nord*, 37 (1955), pp. 135–42.

McBride, Th. M., *The Domestic Revolution: The Modernization of Household Service in England and France, 1820–1920* (London, 1976).

Mertens, F.H., and Torfs, K.L., *Geschiedenis van Antwerpen*, 7 vols. (Antwerp, 1843–1853).

Michielsen, L., 'De handel', in *Antwerpen in de XVIIIde eeuw*, pp. 94–122.

Mokyr, J., *Industrialization in the Low Countries, 1795–1850* (New Haven and London, 1976).

Moureaux, Ph., *Les préoccupations statistiques du gouvernement des Pays-Bas autrichiens et le dénombrement des industries dressé en 1764* (Brussels, 1971).

Nauwelaerts, M.A., *Putte en het Land van Mechelen* (Putte, 1966).

Neyrinck, M., *De lonen in België sedert 1846* (Brussels, 1944).

Niethammer, L., 'Wie wohnten Arbeiter im Kaiserreich?', *Archiv für Sozialgeschichte*, XVI (1976), pp. 61–134.

Oddy, D.J., and Miller, D. (eds.), *The Making of the Modern British Diet* (London, 1976).

Olsen, D.J., 'Victorian London: Specialization, Segregation and Privacy', *Victorian Studies*, XVII (1974), pp. 265–78.

Ornati, O., *Poverty Amid Affluence* (New York, 1966).

Pais-Minne, E., 'Weldadigheidsinstellingen en sociale toestanden te Antwerpen in de XVIIIde eeuw', in *Antwerpen in de XVIIIde eeuw*, pp. 156–86.

Perrin, G., 'L'entassement de la population dans le Paris de la Révolution. La section des Lombards', *Contributions à l'histoire démographique de la Révolution française*, 2nd ser. (1965).

Pierrard, P., *La vie ouvrière à Lille sous le second Empire* (Paris, 1965).

Piven, F.F., and Cloward, R.A., *The New Class War: Reagan's Attack on the Welfare State and Its Consequences* (New York, 1982).

Poffé, E., *De gilde der Antwerpsche schoolmeesters van bij haar ontstaan tot aan hare afschaffing* (Antwerp, 1895).

Prims, F., *Antwerpen in 1830*, 2 vols. (Antwerp, 1930).

Prims, F., 'De catechismus voor bejaarden in St.-Carolus', *Antwerpiensia*, XIX (1949), pp. 247–52.

Prims, F., 'Fabriek tegen ambacht: P. Beirens en Co. tegen de zijdestofwerkers, 1786', *Antwerpiensia*, XVII (1946), pp. 44–9.

Prims, F., *Geschiedenis van Antwerpen*, vols. XXIII–XXVIII (Antwerp, 1957–1958).

Prims, F., 'De namen onzer natiën', *Antwerpiensia*, XVIII (1947), pp. 206–9.

Prims, F., *Sint-Carolusgesticht, 1852–1952* (Antwerp, 1952).

Quadagno, J., *Aging in Early Industrial Society* (New York, 1982).

Reeder, D.A., 'A Theatre of Suburbs: Some Patterns of Development in West London, 1801–1911', in *The Study of Urban History*, ed. H.J. Dyos (London, 1976 edn.), pp. 253–71.

Reinhard, M., 'Connaissance de la population de la France pendant la Révolution', *Contributions à l'histoire démographique de la Révolution française*, 2nd ser. (1965).

Roberts, B., *Cities of Peasants: The Political Economy of Urbanization in the Third World* (London, 1978).

Rodman, H., 'Culture of Poverty: The Rise and Fall of a Concept', *The Sociological Review* (1977), pp. 867–76.

Ross, E., '"Fierce Questions and Taunts"': Married Life in Working-Class London, 1870–1914', *Feminist Studies*, 8 (1982), pp. 575–602.

Sabbe, E., *De Belgische vlasnijverheid*, 2 vols. (Kortrijk, 1975).

Samuel, R., 'Workshop of the World: Steam Power and Hand Technology in Mid-Victorian Britain', *History Workshop Journal*, 3 (1977), pp. 6–72.

Schmiechen, J.A., *Sweated Industries and Sweated Labour: The London Clothing Trades, 1860–1914* (Beckenham, 1984).

Scholliers, E., 'Un indice du loyer: les loyers anversois de 1500 à 1873', in *Studi in Onore di Amintore Fanfani*, Vol. v (Milan, 1962), pp. 595–617.

Scholliers, P., and Vandenbroeke, C., 'The Transition from Traditional to Modern Patterns of Demand in Belgium', in *Consumer Behaviour and Economic Growth in the Modern Economy*, ed. H. Baudet and H. van der Meulen (London and Canberra, 1982), pp. 25–71.

Sharpless, J.B., 'The Economic Structure of Port Cities in the Mid-Nineteenth Century: Boston and Liverpool, 1840–1860', *Journal of Historical Geography*, II (1976), pp. 131–43.

Sheppard, F., *London, 1808–1870: The Infernal Wen* (London, 1971).

Smekens, F., 'Schets van aard en beteekenis der Antwerpsche nijverheid onder het Oostenrijksch bewind', in *Lode Baekelmans ter Eere*, Vol. II (Antwerp, 1946), pp. 77–108.

Sneyers, E., *Bijdrage tot de geschiedenis van Retie* (Retie, 1949).

Soly, H., 'De megalopolis Antwerpen', in *De stad Antwerpen van de Romeinse tijd tot de 17de eeuw* (Brussels, 1978), pp. 95–120.

Spiethoff, A., *Die wirtschaftliche Wechsellagen*, 2 vols. (Tübingen and Zürich, 1955).

Stearns, P.N. (ed.), *Old Age in Pre-Industrial Society* (New York, 1983).

Steensels, W., 'De tussenkomst van de overheid in de arbeidershuisvesting: Gent, 1850–1904', *Belgisch Tijdschrift voor Nieuwste Geschiedenis*, VIII (1977), pp. 447–500.

Stengers, J. (ed.), *Bruxelles: Croissance d'une capitale* (Antwerp, 1979).

Taylor, A.J. (ed.), *The Standard of Living in Britain in the Industrial Revolution* (London, 1975).

Taylor, Ph.A.M., *The Industrial Revolution in Britain: Triumph or Disaster?* (Lexington, 1970).

Teuteberg, H.J., and Wiegelmann, G., *Der Wandel der Nahrungsgewohnheiten unter dem Einfluss der Industrialisierung* (Göttingen, 1972).

Thernstrom, S., *Poverty and Progress: Social Mobility in a Nineteenth-Century City* (Cambridge, Mass., 1964).

Thielemans, M.-R., 'De aanzet van de industrie in het Brusselse voor 1830', *Driemaandelijks Tijdschrift van het Gemeentekrediet van België*, 38 (1984), pp. 151–85.

Thienel, J., *Städtewachstum im Industrialisierungsprozess des 19. Jahrhunderts* (Berlin-New York, 1973).

Thijs, A.K.L., 'Aspecten van de opkomst der textieldrukkerij als grootbedrijf te Antwerpen in de achttiende eeuw', *Bijdragen en Mededelingen betreffende de Geschiedenis der Nederlanden*, 86 (1971), pp. 200–17.

Thijs, A.K.L., 'De geschiedenis van de suikernijverheid te Antwerpen (16de-19de eeuw): een terreinverkenning', *Bijdragen tot de Geschiedenis*, 62 (1979), pp. 313–46.

Thijs, A.K.L., 'Schets van de Ontwikkeling der katoendrukkerij te Antwerpen, 1753–1813', *Bijdragen tot de Geschiedenis*, 53 (1970), pp. 157–90.

Thijs, A.K.L., 'De textielnijverheid', in *Industriële revoluties in de provincie Antwerpen* ed. R. Baetens (Antwerp, 1984), pp. 121–36.

Thompson, E.P., *The Making of the English Working Class* (Harmondsworth, 1968).

Thompson, W., *A Preface to Urban Economics* (Baltimore, 1965).

Thurow, L., *Generating Inequality* (New York, 1975).

Thys, A., *Négociants et industriels anversois au siècle dernier* (Antwerp, 1906).

Tilly, Ch., 'Migration in Modern European History', in *Human Migration: Patterns and Policies*, ed. W.H. McNeill and R.S. Adams (Bloomington, 1978), pp. 175–97.

Tilly, L.A., and Scott, J.W., *Women, Work, and Family* (New York, 1978).

Tindemans, C., *Mens, gemeenschap en maatschappij in de toneelletterkunde van Zuid-Nederland, 1815–1914* (Ghent, 1973).

Titmuss, R., 'Poverty Versus Inequality', in J.L. Roach and J.K. Roach (eds.), *Poverty* (Harmondsworth, 1972), pp. 315–23.

Treble, J.H., *Urban Poverty in Britain, 1830–1914* (London, 1979).

Treue, W., 'Haus und Wohnung im 19. Jahrhundert', in *Städte-, Wohnungs- und Kleidungshygiene des 19. Jahrhunderts in Deutschland* (Stuttgart, 1969), pp. 34–51.

Truyens-Bredael, L., 'William Wood, baanbreker der industriële omwenteling, en zijn fabriek te Borgerhout', *Noordgouw*, II (1962–1963), pp. 109–30.

Valentine, Ch., *Culture and Poverty: Critique and Counterproposals* (Chicago, 1973).

Van Borm, J., 'Aspecten van het vroege industriële pauperisme: Mechelen, 1822', *L'Hôpital belge*, XII (1968), pp. 37–53.

Van Daele, H., *Geschiedenis van het stedelijk lager onderwijs te Antwerpen van 1830 tot 1872* (Brussels, 1972).

Van Daele, H., 'Het ontstaan van de eerste stedelijke meisjesschool', *Antwerpen*, XIII (1967), pp. 84–91.

Van Daele, H., *150 jaar stedelijk onderwijs te Antwerpen, 1819–1969* (Antwerp, 1969).

Vandenbroeke, C., *Agriculture et alimentation dans les Pays-Bas autrichiens* (Ghent-Leuven, 1975).

Vandenbroeke, C., 'Het seksueel gedrag der jongeren in Vlaanderen sinds de late 16e eeuw', *Bijdragen tot de Geschiedenis*, 62 (1979), pp. 193–229.

Vandenbroeke, C., 'Voedingstoestanden te Gent tijdens de eerste helft van de 19e eeuw', *Belgisch Tijdschrift voor Nieuwste Geschiedenis*, IV (1973), pp. 106–69.

Van den Eeckhout, P., 'De rekrutering van de Brusselse armenbevolking in relatie met de afstotingsmechanismen in het gebied van herkomst', *Taal en Sociale Integratie*, Vol. IV (Brussels, 1981), pp. 219–46.

Van den Eeckhout, P., and Scholliers, P., 'De hoofdelijke voedselconsumptie in België, 1831–1939', *Tijdschrift voor Sociale Geschiedenis*, IX (1983), pp. 273–301.

Van den Eerenbeemt, H.J.F.M., 'Woontoestanden van de volksklasse in de 19e eeuw', *Spiegel Historiael*, IX (1976), pp. 494–501, 516–25.

Van den Nieuwenhuizen, J., 'De stadsuitbreiding van Antwerpen tussen 1860 en 1914', *Antwerpen*, VI (1960), pp. 110–21.

Van der Auwera, 'Armoede en sociale politiek te Mechelen in de 16e en de 18e eeuw', *Bijdragen tot de Geschiedenis*, 59 (1976), pp. 227–48.

Vande Weghe, R., *Geschiedenis van de Antwerpse straatnamen* (Antwerp, 1977).

Van Dijk, H., *Rotterdam, 1810–1880: Aspecten van een stedelijke samenleving* (Rotterdam, 1976).

Van Houtte, H., *Histoire économique de la Belgique à la fin de l'Ancien Régime* (Ghent, 1920).

Van Isacker, K., *De Antwerpse dokwerker, 1830–1940* (Antwerp, 1966).

Van Laerhoven, 'De kanthandel te Antwerpen in de 18de eeuw: de firma van Lidth de Jeude', *Bijdragen tot de Geschiedenis*, 54 (1971), pp. 173–90.

Van Looveren, E., 'De privatisering van de gemeentegronden in de provincie Antwerpen: vier case-studies', *Bijdragen tot de Geschiedenis*, 66 (1983), pp. 189–216.

Varley, D.E., 'John Heathcoat, Founder of the Machine-Made Lace Industry', *Textile History*, I (1968), pp. 2–45.

Veraghtert, K., 'The Antwerp Port, 1790–1814', in *The Interactions of Amsterdam and Antwerp with the Baltic Region, 1400–1800* (Leyden, 1983), pp. 193–9.

Verbeemen, J., 'Mechelen gedurende de eerste helft der XIXe eeuw: Demografische en economische studie', *Handelingen van de Koninklijke Kring van Oudheidkunde, Letteren en Kunst van Mechelen* (1955), pp. 70–127.

Verbeemen, J., 'De werking van economische factoren op de stedelijke demografie der XVIIe en der XVIIIe eeuw in de Zuidelijke Nederlanden', *Belgisch Tijdschrift voor Filologie en Geschiedenis*, 34 (1956), pp. 680–700, 1021–55.

Vermeersch, A., 'Pers en pauperisme in Vlaanderen', *Bijdragen voor de Geschiedenis der Nederlanden*, XIII (1959), pp. 81–100.

Viennot, J.F., 'Dijon au XIXe siècle', *Annales de Démographie historique* (1969), pp. 241–60.

Vinnis, C., 'Nota's over den toestand der lagere klassen te Antwerpen op het einde van het Oosten rijks regiem', *Bijdragen tot de Geschiedenis*, 21 (1930), pp. 255–69.

Vliebergh, E., *De Kempen in de 19e eeuw en in het begin der 20e eeuw* (Ieper, 1908).

Vliebergh, E., *De landelijke bevolking der Kempen gedurende de 19e eeuw* (Brussels, 1906).

Vorlat-Raeymaeckers, O., 'De sociale toestanden in Antwerpen, 1845–1850', *Noordgouw*, III (1963), pp. 173–211, IX (1969), pp. 169–90, X (1970), pp. 55–85.

Vovelle, M., 'Prolétariat flottant à Marseille sous la Révolution française', *Annales de Démographie historique* (1968), pp. 111–38.

Walvin, J., *English Urban Life, 1776–1851* (London, 1984).

Wauwermans, H., *Napoléon et Carnot: Episode de l'histoire militaire d'Anvers, 1803–1815* (Brussels, 1888).

Werkgroep Alternatieve Economie, *Armoede in België* (Antwerp-Utrecht, 1972).

Witlox, H., *Schets van de ontwikkeling van welvaart en bedrijvigheid in het Verenigd Koninkrijk der Nederlanden. Benelux, 1815–1830* (Nijmegen, 1956).

Wrightson, K., and Levine, D., *Poverty and Piety in an English Village: Terling, 1525–1700* (New York, 1979).

Index

Index 231

Domestic servants: and migration to Antwerp, 45, 46, 56, 57, 58, 59–60; number of, 33, 56, 59, 173–4, 179–80, 188–9; residence patterns of, 69, 181

Douai, 25

Drink, *see* beer; coffee; gin; wine

Drongen, spinning mill at, 19, 22

Drunkenness, 95; *see also* adulteration; alcohol consumption

Ducpétiaux, Edouard, 131, 147; and crime, 148; estimates of supported needy given by, 112, 114, 185; family budgets compiled by, 97; and food consumption, 100–1; and housing conditions, 73; and prostitution, 149

Dunkirk, 42

Durham, poor relief in county of, 205 n. 30

Dutch Republic, *see* Holland; Netherlands, northern

East Indies, exports to, 23, 30

Education, *see* schools

Eighty Years War, 7

Embroiderers: number of, 25; wages of, 37, 176

Embroidery on tulle, 25

Emigration, 56, 60–1; and kinship, 160; and marital status, 61

Employment: levels of, in Antwerp, 31–2, 56, 59, in other Belgian towns, 32, in foreign towns, 196 n. 21; structure of, *see* occupational distribution

England, 24; competition from, 7–8, 23, 35; imports from, 23, 27

Entrepreneurs: in textile industry, 8, 10, 11–2, 19, 22; and poor relief, 13–4

Epidemics, *see* cholera

Factory production: in harbour towns, 26, 194–5 n. 42; percentage of national population in, 168

Families, supported: size of, 118–9; types of, 116–7

Family, importance of, 150–1, 153–4, 158

Famine, *see* dearth

Female labour, *see* women

Food consumption: bread/grain, 88–9, 91–2, 94; butter, 90, 95; cheese, 90; fish, 87–8, 91; meat, 87–8, 90–1, 99–100; potatoes, 91–2, 94–5; sugar, 93; *see also* calories; diet, vitamins

Food-processing industries, numbers engaged in, 57, 171, 179–80

Food tickets, distribution of, 98, 131, 132–3, 137–8

Fortifications, 42, 65

Foster, John, 166

Foundling Hospital, 145; diet in, 89

Foundlings, number of, 144–6

France: competition from, 7–8, 20; exports to, 23, 25; migration from, 28, 42

Frères de la Charité, 154, 158

Friends, contacts with, 158–9

Galloons, weaving of, 7

Geel, 25

Germany: exports to, 25, 35; migrants from, 28, 80–1, 91; transit trade to, 29, 30

Gezondstraat, 72

Ghent, 7, 25, cotton industry in, 18, 19, 22, 23–4; food consumption in, 99, 100; housing conditions in, 78; level of employment in, 32; migration to, 42; population of, 197 n. 5; poverty in, 113; rents in, 202 n. 27

Ghettos, location of, 70, 71–2

Gin: adulteration of, 93; consumption of, 89, 92–3

Grote Kauwenberg, 72

Guilds, decline of, 11

Hainaut, consumption of meat in, 100

Hamburg, poverty in, 168

Hannes, Jules, 31, 56

Harbour towns, and industry, 26, 194–5 n. 42

Harrington, Michael, 2

Heathcoat, John, 25

Heist-op-den-Berg, 49, 50

d'Herbouville, Charles, 19–20, 21